DIGNITY AND DYING

A Christian Appraisal

A *Horizons in Bioethics Series* Book from

THE CENTER FOR
BIETHICS
AND HUMAN DIGNITY

The *Horizons in Bioethics Series* brings together an array of insightful
writers to address important bioethical issues from a forward-looking
Christian perspective. The introductory volume, *Bioethics and the
Future of Medicine*, covers a broad range of topics and foundational
matters. Subsequent volumes focus on a particular set of issues,
beginning with the end-of-life theme of *Dignity and Dying*.

The series is a project of The Center for Bioethics and Human
Dignity, an international center located just north of Chicago, Illinois
in the United States of America. The Center endeavors to bring
Christian perspectives to bear on today's many pressing bioethical
challenges. It pursues this task by developing two books series, three
audio tape series, three video tape series, numerous conferences in
different parts of the world, and a variety of other printed and
computer based resources. Through its membership program, The
Center networks and provides resources for people interested in
bioethical matters all over the world. Members receive The Center's
international journal, *Ethics and Medicine*, The Center's newsletter,
Dignity, The Center's Update Letters, and discounts on most bioethics
resources in print.

For more information on membership in The Center or its various
resources, including present or future books in the *Horizons in Bioethics
Series*, contact The Center at:

The Center for Bioethics and Human Dignity
2065 Half Day Road
Bannockburn, IL 60015 USA
Phone: (847) 317–8180
Fax: (847) 317–8141

Information and ordering is also available through The Center's World
Wide Web site on the Internet: http://www.bioethix.org

THE CENTER FOR
BIOETHICS
AND HUMAN DIGNITY

presents

DIGNITY
AND DYING

A Christian Appraisal

Edited by
John F Kilner,
Arlene B Miller
and Edmund D Pellegrino

paternoster press

WILLIAM B EERDMANS PUBLISHING COMPANY
GRAND RAPIDS, MICHIGAN

© The Editors and Contributors 1996

First published 1996 jointly
in the U.K. by Paternoster Press,
P.O. Box 300, Carlisle, Cumbria CA3 0QS
and in the U.S.A. by Wm. B. Eerdmans Publishing Co.,
225 Jefferson Ave. S.E., Grand Rapids, Michigan 49503

02 01 00 99 98 97 96   7 6 5 4 3 2 1

British Library Cataloging-in-Publication Data

A catalogue record for this book is available from the British Library

ISBN 0-85364-756-9

Library of Congress Cataloging-in-Publication Data
Dignity and dying.
The Center for Bioethics and Human Dignity presents Dignity
and dying : a Christian appraisal / edited by John F. Kilner,
Arlene B. Miller, and Edmund D. Pellegrino.
p.   cm. — (Horizons in bioethics series)
Includes bibliographical references.
ISBN 0-8028-4232-1 (pbk. : alk. paper)
1. Death — Religious aspects — Christianity.   2. Terminal care —
Religious aspects — Christianity.   3. Church work with the terminally
ill.   I. Kilner, John Frederic.   II. Miller, Arlene B., 1935-.   III.
Pellegrino, Edmund D., 1920-   .   IV. Center for Bioethics
and Human Dignity.   V. Title.   VI. Series.
BT825.D54   1996
241'.697 — dc20   96-2784
                                                          CIP

Typeset by Photoprint, Torquay, Devon, UK
Printed in the United States of America

Contents

Preface

As never before, people today are experiencing the pressure to change their values and beliefs. Health care delivery systems are increasingly driven by economic considerations. The value of autonomy reigns supreme and suffering is viewed as both unnecessary and an embarrassment. Popular and scholarly books on death and dying abound. But as to what happens after one dies, little is written or else it is couched in romantic language such as the 'final stage of development'. In this climate of change and uncertainty, some are accepting the request for death as rational and a right, even an economic necessity. A Christian perspective on dignity and dying has much to offer in such a climate.

Currently, the field of discourse is dominated by a secular, autonomy-driven, privacy-oriented approach. This outlook is not confined to scholarly discussion in learned journals. It is promulgated in talk shows, in the popular press, in legislative chambers, and in societies and associations devoted to 'dignified death', 'assistance in dying', or some other euphemism for terminating human life in the name of compassion. The countervailing positions based in a belief in God's sovereignty over life typically do not receive the kind of celebration accorded the advocates of euthanasia. Compassion, dignity, and freedom are also in biblical teachings, but there they are different in spirit and content from the secular construal of those sentiments.

Matters are complicated by the almost automatic intellectual disenfranchisement of believers in the public arena. The climate and rules of discourse are set so that any argument based on faith is inadmissible simply by virtue of its being religious. Yet a majority of people, at least in some countries such as the United States, still find the ultimate source of morality in religious belief. In too many cases, Christians are yielding to the appeals of euthanasia enthusiasts because Christians, too, wish to be in favour of compassion, dignity, and freedom. Without hearing biblical voices and witnesses, even Christians may fail to perceive what fidelity to Christian belief requires of them. Others also need to hear an alternative view authentically and unequivocally articulated. They need to know how Christian belief can prepare humans to confront the realities of suffering and dying with true compassion and a God-given dignity without killing the sufferer.

The difficulties of the engagement of Christians with others on human life issues must not be underestimated. Christian scholars and teachers, in conscience, cannot abandon the field simply because secularists say that Christian beliefs are incommensurable with their own. Christians must engage and counter the arguments with both faith and reason. Any fair-minded person who may be attracted by the pleas for compassion, mercy, self-determination, and dignity set out by the proponents of euthanasia and assisted suicide is compelled in justice to learn what Christians believe is the more profound, Christian meaning contained in these words and sentiments.

The authors of the present volume engage matters of dignity and dying from a variety of perspectives. The three authors of the Introduction, David Schiedermayer, Arlene Miller, and Gregory Waybright, root the book in the experience of dying itself. In Part I, authors Nigel Cameron, John Dunlop, Marsha Fowler, and Allen Verhey give careful attention to topics that provide guiding vision for approaches to dignity and dying: autonomy, death, suffering, and faithfulness. Four of the most pressing end-of-life challenges — forgoing treatment, medical futility, definition of death, and assisted-suicide/euthanasia — are then examined in some detail by authors John Kilner, Christopher Hook, Holly Vautier, and Edmund Pellegrino. Part III is devoted to Ben Mitchell's, Jerome Wernow's, Arthur Dyck's, and Henk Jochemsen's investigations of key settings where people have wrestled with these challenges: i.e., Nazi Germany, Oregon (USA), North American legal systems, and The Netherlands. The book concludes, then, with discussions of five potentially constructive alternatives to the premature ending of life: hospice care (by Martha Twaddle), long-term care (by James Thobaben), wise advocacy (by James Reitman), parish nursing (by Norma Small), and congregational ministry (by Dennis Hollinger).

It is no exaggeration to acknowledge the growth of a culture of death and to posit the need for meeting its challenges via the gospel of life. The present volume attempts to trace out the implications of this 'good news of life' for the issue today that challenges it most directly: dignity and dying.

John F Kilner
Arlene B Miller
Edmund D Pellegrino

[INTRODUCTION:]

The Experience of Dying

A Physician's Experience

David L Schiedermayer, MD

My neighbour, a pharmacist, is running frantically across my front yard. 'There's a man who collapsed down at the stop sign,' she says. 'He's convulsing!' I follow her as she runs back down the street. My family runs along behind me, other neighbours join in, and from 100 feet away I can tell that the man who is lying on the street is unconscious or dead from the way his arms and legs are flat and motionless on the ground.

As I get closer I see several people begin to do CPR. 'I know CPR' I say, and in a few seconds I find myself trying to blow air into his mouth and his airway. The taste is salty — either sweat or blood. He has a half day growth of whiskers, about right for this time of the day. But the air comes back at me. I reposition his jaw and head, and sweep his tongue back. A bit of air comes back — maybe there is some hope. I try pursing my lips and exhale harder. Someone is doing chest compressions. Emergency help has been called, and I hear the sirens.

I see that the man's skin is gray, his eyes are blank and rolled back in his head, his pupils are dilated. I wonder how long it will be before he vomits.

This is sudden death. Derek fell off his bike, at peak exercise, age 45. Although he is technically dead, we are trying to revive him. As far as I can tell, he is not conscious of any of this, unless he is having an out-of-body experience. He had an arrhythmia, maybe due to coronary disease, which I later learn is common in his family, and he fell limply off his bike. The man who is doing CPR beside me witnessed it and said he saw him fall and hit the ground hard.

Sudden deaths have an amnestic quality — they have built-in anaesthesia. As I do CPR I sense the surreal nature of sudden catastrophe — the sky is a beautiful light blue, the temperature is a perfect 22°C, a light breeze blows, and I hear a steam train in the background which gives tours at the zoo.

Paramedics arrive, they put an endotracheal tube in, and I assume my favourite position at a code: I move to the man's feet and look at the heart monitor while feeling for a pulse. Ventricular

3

fib — we shock him, twice, and his body jolts on the pavement. The spectators gathered by the curb wince at seeing this technical trauma. But it works. A slow rhythm returns — and I feel a thready pulse. He begins to breathe on his own.

I walk home, pushing Derek's bike while he is carried off in the ambulance to the ICU. When I call over to the hospital a half an hour later he is still in the trauma room — a bad sign, perhaps they are coding him again.

Some people die slowly. Mrs Anna Velosian, my patient who survived the Armenian holocaust, died in her 80s of thyroid cancer she had had since she was 60. Mr Albert Tsosie, a Navajo man, died of end-stage renal disease and the complications of diabetes. These are slow deaths. Intensive care unit deaths are also often slow.

I remember my friend who died of AIDS:

I came to visit you, my friend,
and I saw that you were on the vent.
Your lungs were whited out.
Hadn't you called me, just days earlier,
telling me how short of breath you were?
And hadn't you seemed short of wind
when we last had lunch together,
after we spoke on the dangers of AIDS
to the high school students
the man with AIDS and the doctor
vying for the honor of scaring them the most
(I think you won — seeing the size of the pills
you waved was more worrisome than my graphs)

So here you are, and we will never talk again.
You are sedated to the max.
I should have pushed them to take you off sooner,
but all your friends were visiting,
your family was trying to come to grips
and your Durable Power of Attorney was waiting
just a bit.

Day 18.
We thought this would be the day
when we should stop the vent.
I could not bear to stay.
It was too much of a scene.
At least you were not alone.

I remember meeting you for breakfast,
was it every month for that many years
and seeing your AIDS progress,
from a dropping CD4 count to Kaposis'

and now this pneumocystis pneumonia
which is taking you.

It ended up
they didn't stop the vent, just turned down
the oxygen level a bit
and you let go of the spoon.
For a guy with AIDS
you sure knew how to keep your weight up
I miss you and I still owe you an ice cream cone.

Other deaths are even slower. We fear three things about very slow death: not being able to breathe, being in terrible pain, and being alone. An extensive literature exists on very slow deaths, which require good pain control, supportive or palliative treatment, and spiritual counsel. In one study of 687 physicians and 759 nurses, 70 percent of all house officers acknowledged that they had violated their conscience when caring for terminally ill patients. By a ratio of 4 to 1, this violation involved giving overly aggressive treatment rather than undertreatment.[1] Sometimes, however, patients' pain is not managed properly. Physicians and nurses undertreat with narcotics, although this is less common than it was before the hospice model found acceptance.[2]

In a recent article, Quill and Brody outline the case of a patient near death with barbiturate sedation and terminal voluntary dehydration. They point out that even methods short of physician-assisted suicide, including palliative treatment and pain control, require scrutiny and safeguards.[3] Most deaths, they argue, can be made tolerable if not comfortable, but some diseases are so unpredictable and variable that they result in harsh deaths. For my part I try not to promise patients good deaths — these are the sorts of promises one cannot keep. Instead, I promise that I will stay with them in the process and not let them suffer alone.

Some patients are conscious at the time of death, but the burden of disease, the dementia or cancer, has caused them to be less aware and more dependent. Mrs Iona Christenson was being cared for by her husband at home, where I visited her for several years. She had diabetes and a seizure disorder. One day she suffered permanent brain damage from a severe seizure. She could sit up and eat, but could not talk, and she lacked bowel control.

Dying like this requires some family members to assume heavy duties:

Mrs Christenson, your husband is obsessed
with taking care of you,
how he waits on you.

I do not think he abused you in the past.
If he owes you, it is certainly not this much.
This is not guilt.
I know it is duty. He was a military man.
Perhaps, after all, you are like his country now.

I want you to know even though you are unable to speak
he talks to you and brushes your hair
He feeds you from a spoon
Washes and turns you.

When it came time for you to die
I came over and put an IV just under the skin of your thigh
to keep you alive a few days longer.
Both he and I knew it was an endgame.
But we needed the time:
he to begin to think of something else to do,
me to make sure there was nothing else to do.
It was like the reverse of Pitocin
(a medicine which speeds up labor):
I was giving you medicine to slow death
until we were both ready.

But death came fast anyway,
when it did,
and I cried just like he did:
and didn't we look down on you together
and think of all you had meant.

At the funeral — the priest waved incense
around the coffin
and a relative asked me if I was a Catholic
no I said,
but I liked the incense.

Jesus was familiar with such deaths. We are told in John 11 — that when Lazarus died . . . Jesus wept. The experience of dying and death is usually a shared experience, and may actually affect many people. Consider the death of a pastor who was my patient:

Pastor, your high blood pressure was easy to treat
You took your pills well
the gout was quiet
But when I felt your pulse:
irregularly irregular.
The atrial fibrillation was the first sign of trouble.
I sent you to the cardiologist
he did an echo
which showed the enlarged heart
of an otherwise well
80 year-old African-American preacher
who was part of the civil rights movement in Texas,

who used his VISA card to bail out protesters
who grew up amid segregation
working for something better.

The power remained.
Even in your older age
You kept the youth group in line
fought church politics
kept the ranks happy
and started a new building project.

When your brother died, you insisted on driving
to the funeral instead of flying like usual.
You were driving tired.
After pulling back on the road,
you probably had a stroke or an MI —
your wife saw you dead at the wheel,
with your eyes in an open stare as you leaned on it
and you went off the road over the high ditch
where whatever life may have been left
was extinguished by the crash itself.
Your wife lived.

But it was just as you said
at one of your last services
your work was finished
your time was at hand
others should carry on.
One does not say these things for melodrama.
Sometimes we know we will die.

The inner city turned out for the funeral
the mayor came, the dignitaries were there
I did help to carry you down the stairs
your coffin was heavy, as befits royalty
I could feel the muscles tense and pull in my low back.

When I saw your wife at home,
she had a seat belt bruise and several broken ribs.
Also: the new minister means well
but has a tough act to follow.
You had the voice of James Earl Jones
the history of the civil rights movement
and 240 pounds on six foot two.
I would carry you again
but only if we could put the whole thing in reverse,
wind it up and start it all over
like the golden alarm clock
you traveled with and your wife gave me
in remembrance of you.

Part of the experience of dying is also the physician's own struggle
against death. In this era of discussion of physician-assisted
suicide, by far still the dominant paradigm is that physicians are to

struggle against death. Death is always beating us, always frustrating us, and we cannot gain victory over death in the human sphere. Only Christ has conquered death — we physicians cannot slash and suture our way to eternal life. We personalize death, we dream about death. This may account for much of the ambivalence we have about treating the terminally ill — we struggle against death rather than aim for a good death.

> I have seen death
> he is a gray Toyota
> on a cold gray winter day
> coming out of my blind spot
> I stare at the bumper
> five feet away
> I was going to mail
> a letter.
> He is a professor
> always asking me questions
> I can't answer
> and just when I say
> I don't know
> he turns to the next student
> he is on the cancer ward
> when the chest x-ray
> shows this big goomba
> this honker
> and the chemo has a
> 20 percent response rate
> or in the ICU
> when the belly is swollen
> with ascites
> he is trying to catch me
> off-guard.
> Easy enough.

As those who are close to the dying, as those who keep them company as they go through the valley of the shadow, we physicians are affected also. Sherwin Nuland offers a moving account of the death of his grandmother, focusing not only on her physiological death from ischemia but also on her personality and his relationship with her.[4] Unfortunately, for Nuland there is nothing beyond death. But he is right to say that death deprives us of the company of others. Life is a blessing, a benison. The sick are looking for a blessing.

> Are you depressed,
> I asked on the phone.
> Of course, was the answer.
> Who wouldn't be, after all,
> with the cancer

and the chemo
with the setbacks
the trips back
to the hospital.
Who wouldn't be,
after losing control
of the colon cancer
after changes in the
schedule,
but most of all
the loss of the quiet hope
all cancer patients have
that things will go
somehow smoothly.
Cancer is not known
for being a smooth disease.

'Terrors overwhelm me;
my dignity is driven away
as by the wind.
Night pierces my bones
my gnawing pains never rest,'
said Job
when he had
this feeling of dying.
I shrink from platitudes
remembering what Job's friends learned,
that it is unwise to judge
the reasons for curses or blessings
for early dying.
But allow me, since we ask God's blessing
on those who sneeze
even in our modern society
where a sneeze is considered just an irritation
instead of a harbinger of death
allow me to at least ask for a benison
for you a stranger in a strange land
of tumor margins, grading and staging,
for you who sits in the cancer clinic
with those who know better than the rest of us
that something terrible has gone wrong.
Here is the ancient benediction,
the benison for sojourners:
'The Lord bless you and keep you;
the Lord make His face shine upon you,
and be gracious unto you,
the Lord lift up His countenance upon you,
and give you His peace.'

James Andrew Miller, reflecting on his experience with colon cancer, describes feeling a 'glittering kind of pain shooting across the lower stretches of my abdomen.' He was working on a theology paper, and planning to go to Severance Hall, but there were other plans. He was to die of colon cancer. He believes in the One who conquered death, and he notes that all of us are 'somewhere on an unfolding continuum between life and death. Terminal. Between countries. Emigres.'[5]

Sometimes we escape for a time. I go back the day after Derek's cardiac arrest and find him waking up, moving all fours. His pupils are reactive. He will live. He drinks two six packs of beer a day, smokes a pack of cigarettes as well. In speaking with him I soon realize that he would not be my first choice of a person to save. But that is my problem. For God sends the rain on the just and the unjust. I look at my white coat as I speak to Derek, and feel more shielded than I did during the code on the street. I have my costume on.

But my own white coat is a flimsy costume,[6] a set of dress whites. Underneath I see a human body, intricate but prone to disease, adaptable but ageing. The physician's humanity cannot be covered for long by name tags, instruments, pocket texts, and white cloth. My personal fragility links me to you, and you to me. All of our costumes are flimsy and temporary, for there comes a time, sooner or later, when they will all hang empty in hall closets. When our beliefs will be tested. When we will determine if there is a resurrection of the body and a life everlasting.

Each of us will have a turn. My turn, my experience of dying, will remind you, and yours will remind me, of what we always and finally have in common.

NOTES

1. Solomon M Z, O'Donnell L, Jennings B., 'Decisions near the end of life'. *Am J Public Health* (1993), 83:14–23.

2. Seale C F., 'What happens in hospices? A review of research evidence.' *Soc Sci Med* (1989), 28:551–559.

3. Quill T E, Brody R V., 'You promised me I wouldn't die like this: A bad death as a medical emergency.' *Arch Int Med* (1995), 155:1250–1254.

4. Nuland S B., *How we die: Reflections on life's final chapter.* (New York, NY: Alfred A. Knopf Inc; 1994).

5. Miller J A., *First Things.* (March 1993), pp. 26–33.

6. Schiedermayer D L., *Putting the soul back in medicine: Reflections on compassion and ethics.* (Baker Books, 1995, Grand Rapids Michigan), p. 183.

A Nurse's Experience

Arlene B Miller, RN, PhD

Academic ethical discussions about dying are one thing. Real life ethical decisions are another. Families struggling with day-to-day care of one of their own are often exhausted, perplexed, and guilt-ridden. Basics of life taken for granted by the healthy such as eating, drinking, toileting, dressing, bathing, and oral hygiene all require vast expenditures of energy. Adding a complicated medical regimen may make physical care overwhelming. When it becomes impossible to follow the schedules for medications and treatments because either the patient or caregiver cannot carry them out, worry adds to the burden. Caregivers often become so enmeshed with the psyche of the dying person that they function as extensions, the arms and legs, of the individual who cannot feed, move, chase a fly, get a drink, lower the volume on the radio, and hundreds of other actions. The caregiver, often unsuccessfully, tries to suppress anger and resentment as her or his identity becomes progressively submerged. The following story from my own experience illustrates this picture.[1]

I and a senior nursing student, Ms Sen were making a visit to Mrs Lawson. She was an elderly woman recently discharged from the hospital with end-stage congestive heart failure. Mrs Lawson had been taken from her own home a few blocks away to the home of her son, himself disabled. It was a modest frame building located in a town dominated by a large, but dying, steel factory. This African-American family had moved from the South to find employment during the Second World War, an experience typical of many others living there.

I and Ms Sen met Mrs Lawson in a very crowded living room with a hospital bed and other equipment essential for the woman's care. Most of the living room furniture had been moved into the adjoining dining room. Mrs Lawson's daughter-in-law expressed her displeasure at having yet another set of nurses with whom to deal. While we might be quite competent she did not know us and what is more important, we did not know her situation.[2] And her situation was distressing. She had been trying to tell someone,

11

anyone who would take her seriously, that her mother-in-law was not swallowing. Mrs Lawson's son, joining in the conversation from the dining room, agreed with his wife, that even in the hospital his mother was not swallowing. She had been discharged with oral medications they had been trying in vain to administer. They were advised to 'try harder'.

Our attempts to have Mrs Lawson drink some orange juice proved futile. Whether she would not or could not swallow was not clear to me, but I suspected the latter. She was quiet during our visit and made no attempts to speak. It was easy to see that instead of retaining excess body fluid, the expected pattern of her condition, Mrs Lawson was becoming dehydrated, lacking in body fluids. When Mrs Lawson's physician was contacted by telephone he ordered all medications stopped since he thought the problem was medication-related. I doubted that this was the case, but his order really did not change the situation since Mrs Lawson had not been swallowing medications anyway.

Things were not going smoothly in this household. The daughter-in-law, who bore the main burden of care both for her husband and her mother-in-law, was frustrated. Her son was worried because his mother was not eating or drinking. Wasn't there something we could do? While we were dealing with these questions Mrs Lawson's grandson came to the home inquiring about her condition. Now there were six people in two small crowded rooms, the patient, her son and daughter-in-law, her grandson, and two nurses. During the next hour the pastor would also come to give communion to Mrs Lawson and then to her son who decided that he wanted to be included. What was to be a 'routine' assessment had become a complex situation.

I acknowledged the family's concern about Mrs Lawson's not swallowing and explained the possible ways to give her nutrition and fluids: directly into the veins, through a tube passed through the nose into the stomach, or through a tube implanted into the stomach through a small surgical incision. Mrs Lawson would probably need to have her hands restrained if any of these were used since she had removed all tubes while in the hospital. Her son remembered having been restrained himself during his own hospitalization and objected to the idea for his mother.

The daughter-in-law listened quietly to these explanations. She said that she did not get up at night with Mrs Lawson, but that she did hear her every move in bed. My comment that she must be very tired brought tears to her eyes. She was caught between the worry of her husband (her own as well) about his mother and her inability to supply the basic needs of Mrs Lawson. Clearly this woman was near the limits of what she could give. The potential for abuse lurked around the edges of this situation.

I suggested that we needed to consider how Mrs Lawson could be made most comfortable during her last days of life. I do not know if anyone had opened the subject of death before but her daughter-in-law seemed relieved to hear this. I sensed that her son, however, was becoming anxious. He now entered the discussion — at one point abruptly asking the pastor to give him communion.

I and Ms Sen tried to assure this family that their concerns were taken seriously. After returning to the agency we arranged to have Mrs Lawson transferred to the hospice team. This would make more home-care and other resources available. We did not see this family again and I thought no more about them. It was several weeks later when the hospice nurse told us how much the Lawson family had appreciated our visit. It was because we had taken time to listen, had acknowledged the concern about not swallowing, and had given them explanations about the options open to them. They had not forgotten us.

There are several things we can learn about dying from this story: Dying is hard work, patients and caregivers involved with dying need practical assistance, and ethical choices made in such situations flow out of the character and values of those involved. Dying, even for Christians, is a fearsome thing, taking its toll on every part of our being and exhausting us physically, emotionally, socially, spiritually. Because it is still the enemy, albeit a conquered enemy for Christians, we resist death's encroachment upon our bodily integrity, our mental functioning, our social ties. Such resistance is hard work. We should resist until that moment when we acknowledge that death will have its way for the time being.

Because dying is work, those struggling with it — the dying and those caring for them — need practical assistance and support. Someone needs to clear the way for them in the complex health care system, helping them to get the assistance they need. Patients and families need clear explanations of the options within their reach, of what is happening to all of them, of the resources available to them. They need spiritual guidance and support as they struggle with questions of faith, guilt, anger, resentment, and frustration. Health care givers, pressured for time though they are, must listen to and acknowledge concerns even if there is not much to be done. Knowing that one is heard is a tremendous comfort and affirmation of dignity. Much of what the dying and their families need can be given by non-professionals, caring friends, and churches. Meals, notes, funny stories, quiet presence, respite care: all are ways to say, 'We care.'

Finally, ethical decisions made in such 'crowded living rooms' flow out of the values and character of those involved. For this

African-American family, nurtured in the Baptist church, caring for this dying woman was a freely accepted responsibility. They were willing to move the furniture to make room for Mrs Lawson's bed. The idea of 'tying her down' was repugnant to her son, an assault on the dignity of his mother. The moral guidance of the church was woven into their very beings. For professional caregivers this means that theologically informed reflection on issues surrounding dying is often essential. The helping professions are casting about for acceptable ethical guides, exploring world views that are antithetical to sustaining care, fighting the good fight to sustain life. Pressures on caregivers to act on other than biblical values will only increase.

For all of us this means that churches have a vital role to play in educating members — patients and caregivers — about these matters. Excellent materials for use in church schools are available for this purpose. It is crucial that churches assume this responsibility, for we will all face the 'conquered enemy' sometime. How we respond will in large part be determined by how well we have (been) prepared.

NOTES

1. This example is from the author's own experience of teaching home health nursing to senior nursing students.

2. Continuity of care in which the same nurse sees a patient, building a relationship with her or him, has given way under the influence of work restructuring and economic pressures to assigning anyone who can perform the required tasks. Robert Bellah sounds a warning about 'market totalitarianism' which threatens genuine practices of caring, including health care, as the concern for profit comes to the fore. Robert N Bellah, (1994). 'Understanding caring in contemporary America.' In: *The Crisis of Care: affirming and restoring caring practices in the helping professions*. Susan S Phillips and Patricia Benner eds. (Washington, DC: Georgetown University Press), pp. 21–35.

A Pastor's Experience

Gregory L Waybright, MDiv, PhD

Nobel prize recipient George Wald wrote, 'Just realize, I am 69 and have never seen a person die. Imagine it; the most dramatic event of human life has been taken out of my experience.'[1]

Wald's testimony is not unique. I imagine that most people in our society have never seen a person die. I find that most of us, in our success-oriented world, try to ignore it. It is often difficult even to utter the word 'death', with many opting for euphemisms like 'passed away' or 'no longer with us.' It used to be that people experienced birth and death in the same house, even in the same bed. Personal experiences of birth and death happened in the normal course of family life. But, no more. Now, death is often confined to the terminal wards. It has been called 'the universal human repression of our day.'

One of the painful privileges of having been a pastor for 18 years is that I have come into contact with death so often:

- Five funerals in my first week as a 26-year-old pastor;
- Meeting with grieving people, both Christian and agnostic, religious and irreligious; and
- Providing pastoral care at the deaths of those 2 or 18 or 100-years-old, even for parents wanting a belated service for an aborted child.

And, yes, I have seen people die, including my second daughter. I was holding her in my arms on a Sunday evening 11 years ago when death came. I can, therefore, no longer deal with death simply as a 'professional matter for which I am trained'. No, I understand what C S Lewis felt when he wrote in *A Grief Observed*, 'No one ever told me that grief felt so like fear. I am not afraid, but the sensation is like being afraid. The same fluttering in the stomach, the same restlessness, the same yawning. I keep on swallowing . . .'[2]

One problem with death is that is feels so final. I have been trained to deal with dying people wrestling with that finality. I have learned what stages of grief to look for, what phrases to express and which ones to avoid. But I have found that the

15

essential problem with death is that its finality confronts us in such a personal way. Death is a certainty, unless Christ returns soon. Death will come to me . . . to **me**. We can theorize about death when we are in the profession saying, 'Well, it is sad that she is dead. Let us care for the loved ones as we've been accustomed.' All the while, we can hold on to the fact that we are not dead ourselves. 'Life goes on,' we say. 'We must keep our focus on that. We pastors and professionals must help the family cope.' Those thoughts might sustain me in my pastoral role and keep me from being so intimately involved.

But, I have found that I cannot easily maintain that emotional distance for I have seen death and I know it is coming to me. Therefore, when I speak about a perspective on death, I must first come to grips with the fact that someday I will die. I have conducted many funerals, but someday someone will conduct mine. Someday I will no longer be the counsellor, but the dying one. What then? Where will I be after I die? If death is the end of everything, then life is a crazy, futile, unjust charade. Death as ultimate ending would be a blank wall against which all of our aspirations and hopes are mercilessly shattered. Our most tender memories, our greatest achievements, all our deepest relationships — what would be the point of such things if we are simply to be annihilated and erased from existence? People may do a great deal in our generation with medicine, technology and science. We may find ourselves defeating many enemies of society. Nevertheless, if that last enemy, death, is a final termination, then human beings will always remain slaves to an unstoppable fate that casts its shadow over every aspect of life.

With all that in mind, I want to say clearly that this is one of the very reasons that I have been thankful for the privilege of being a minister of the good news of Jesus Christ. The Christian message says that this mysterious enemy called death no longer has to remain something about which we know little. We no longer have to speculate about what happens after death. Something tremendous happened in our world that has taken life after death out of the realm of guesswork or superstition and moved it into the realm of fact. Jesus Christ died and was raised from the dead. For the early church, this was no myth. It was an event in history witnessed by hundreds of eyewitnesses. More than that, Jesus promised that all who trust in him are guaranteed their own resurrection from death to go to a place better by far. Belief in that made people like the apostle Paul view death as something no more troublesome than swatting a mosquito from the brow. He said that, in the light of what we Christians believe about Jesus, 'Where, O death, is your sting? Where, O grave, is your victory?'

(1 Cor. 15:55). This is the essence of the good news to a dying world. Eternal life has become accessible.

Having said that, I must also say that applying the good news of hope to particular situations has not always been easy for me as a pastor. Hear me clearly: I proclaim without wavering that personal faith in the One who defeated death by his resurrection changes everything about the experience of dying. Being a Christian makes a difference. However, I am compelled to make a few clarifying statements concerning that affirmation:

1) **I find that Christians and non-Christians alike experience sorrow and pain in the face of death**. This sorrow is what Lewis described so graphically in *A Grief Observed*, which was actually his diary kept in the months following the death of his wife. It is that same sorrow and pain and anger I felt when well-meaning people would say to me after my daughter's death, 'Aren't you rejoicing that your little one is now in the hands of God?' No, I wasn't. I wanted to hear her, see her, touch her.

   The difference is that the Christian's sorrow is a sorrow that is not devoid of hope. We miss the one who has died. We long to be with that person we love, but we are confident that the separation is only temporary. I appreciate how Paul wrote about it to the Thessalonians in 1 Thess. 4:13. At times of death, we do not 'grieve like the rest of men, who have no hope'. We still grieve, but it is a grief that is hope-filled.

2) **I find that Christians and non-Christians alike have no sufficient answer to many of the 'why' questions**. When people come to talk with me as they are dealing with untimely deaths, I often say, 'If you are expecting soothing pat answers to "Why did this happen?", you have come to the wrong person.' I still ask that question myself, though some of my parishioners tell me I should not. I find the biblical writers asking it. It is a part of my ongoing relationship to God. I am convinced that, if it is the question on my mind, I must ask it candidly if my relationship to God is to be one of openness and integrity.

   So I ask, 'Why did that young godly high school boy drown at church camp trying to save a struggling camper?' 'Why did my 43-year-old brother die instead of the drunk driver who hit him?' 'Why did that father of three young children die of cancer?' 'Why did my daughter die before her life had hardly begun?'

   I have never found adequate answers to those questions, but I wrestle with them. My ability to cope in the face of such things comes from a simple word . . . trust. As a child, I had to learn to trust my parents when they forced me to go to school or made me go through painful treatments for respiratory problems. With my PhD in Theology, it has been quite humbling when, in the face of pain, I have been reduced to asking simply, 'Do I trust God? Is he good? Is he in control? Is he doing something I cannot see?'

We become Christians through childlike faith. We must live as Christians by childlike faith too. Is this not precisely what Jesus said to his disciples when they could not understand that he must soon die? He said, 'Do not let your hearts be troubled. You trust in God. Trust me.' That is basic Christianity — Christianity 101. We give our lives to Christ. We believe he knows what he is doing. We wait for him to do it. My testimony is that I have discovered he is worthy of that trust.

3) **I find that Christians and non-Christians do not experience much consolation in the face of death when their focus is 'this-worldly'.** This is especially true of narcissistic church-goers obsessed with personal success, health and prosperity. There seem to be so many who feel that, if we go to church, live right, pray right and believe hard enough, then things like sickness and death will never come. How can those who follow a Lord who went to a horrid death on a cross ever think that? But many do. Many have never grasped that the purpose of a Christian's existence is neither just to live or to die, but to honour God in whatever happens. Paul knew it and could say, 'For me to live is Christ and to die is far better for it takes me to a place better by far' (Philp. 1:21, 23 paraphrase).

Frankly speaking, I run across so many religious people who, by their obsession with healing and wonders, lose the ability to honour God in the way they die. Instead of trusting their Heavenly Father and accepting death triumphantly as simply one more step in the purpose of God for his people, I find a hysterical search for miracle healing as if it would be impossible for a Christian to die. The result is that, instead of a courageous testimony, there is an attitude that, to the world, looks little different from cowardice.

But, for the one who believes the message of Easter and who trusts God even when his purpose is not clear, there is confidence in the face of death. Paul said that in 2 Cor. 5:6–8. Speaking of death, he said twice that we Christians are confident. We are confident as we 'live by faith, not by sight'.

The word confidence is one I have never been able to use at a non-Christian's funeral. At those services and wakes, I have found people wanting to talk about the casket that has been chosen, the beauty of the flowers that have been sent, how well the mortician has done his work, 'Doesn't he look natural?'

'Wasn't she beautiful?' The focus is on anything but the one crucial issue. 'Where is the deceased? Death has come. Where is he or she?'

Christianity has often been called a crutch for the weak by its critics. But, as a pastor who comes face to face with death so often, I know how wrong that criticism is. I have learned that, faced with the reality of the grave, it is the genuine Christian alone who does not have to run away. We can look death in the face because we trust in a Lord risen from the dead.

Earlier this year I met with Andrew Furuyama, a major church leader in Japan. He was in his hospital bed suffering from pancreatic cancer. A few days later he would die. But, on that evening, this particular dying man was very much alive. He, in fact, was encouraging me as he assured me, 'Brother Greg, this is the message we have learned so well cognitively, but I am telling you it is true and practical. I am not afraid because Jesus said, "I am the resurrection and life. He who believes in me will live even though he die" ' (Jn. 11:25).

I thought how different that was from a documentary I saw in Great Britain while I was doing my doctoral studies. It was a BBC production called *Sea of Faith*. In it, theologian Don Cupitt was telling of the time when he, as a young priest, was assigned to visit a dying man at a hospital. Though a theologian and priest, Cupitt was and is an agnostic.

Cupitt said that, as he went to the hospital room, the man was obviously in his last hours. As a priest, he took his book and read the appropriate words and prayed the prescribed prayers. Before Cupitt left, the man died.

As he was going home, Cupitt reported, 'I didn't suppose that my words had magically altered the eternal destiny of the man and yet, I felt it had been worthwhile turning out. And I hoped that, when my time came, someone would do the same for me. I learned that day that religion is a way of affirming human dignity in the face of an indifferent universe.'

Though eloquent, his words left me empty. Is that all we pastors have to offer to a dying world? Will that message offer our world the kind of hope to see us into the twenty-first century and the terrors that are surely there?

Which of these two pastors would you want to visit you at your deathbed — Furuyama or Cupitt? It is a simple and clear cut decision for me. Jesus does not offer us merely an affirmation of human dignity. He offers personal access to eternal life with God. That is the message I proclaim as pastor. And, when I die, I do not need a clergyman affirming my dignity, but a Pastor Furuyama simply reminding me of the message of Jesus, 'He who believes in me will live even though he dies, for I am the resurrection and the life.'

NOTES

1. Wald, George, 'George Wald: The Man, the Speech', *New York Times Magazine*, (Aug. 17, 1969), p. 89.
2. Lewis, C S, *A Grief Observed* (Toronto and New York: Bantom Books, 1963), chapter 1, page 1.

[PART I]

Guiding Vision

[1]

Autonomy and the 'Right to Die'[1]

Nigel M de S Cameron, BDiv, PhD

The rhetoric of the right to die makes a fascinating study, for in the human rights vernacular of the late twentieth century, it asserts a principle which would set the combined morals and jurisprudence of this millennium and the last upon its head.

The right–to–die/suicide syllogism seems impenetrable:

I am my own;
The time and means of my dying lie at the heart of my private life;
I therefore retain the 'right to die', and no-one may take it from me.

THE VALIDITY OF THE SYLLOGISM

We need to note as we begin that the phrase 'the right to die' is itself a considerable curiosity.[2] For one thing, it seems to assert as a 'right' something which is an inevitable feature of human experience, since death is universal. The Bible's reiterated refrain 'And he died' continues to punctuate the passage of the generations, as every 'he' and every 'she' lays final claim to obsequies in the community and obituary in the press. There are some parallels between the rhetorical role of the 'right to die' and that of another ambiguous right, the 'right to work' (which has played a not insignificant role in the propaganda of socialism). The parallel is incomplete, of course, because it is perfectly possible to go from the cradle all the way to an experience of the final human right, the right to die, without actually experiencing the dignity and indignity of human labour. Yet the claimed 'right to work' does not imply a state-mandated policy of full employment. It implies an opportunity, *ceteris paribus*, to take up employment if one has opportunity, without public policy declaring 'thou shalt not'. By the same token, the 'right to die' is, if we wish to couch it as a human right, one with universal exercise. As George Bernard Shaw had it, it is 'the ultimate statistic that one out of one dies'. No one has taken a stand with King Canute and declared 'thou shalt not die', except the serpent in the garden. This debate is about something else.

23

At the same time, as well we know, the claim put forward in the syllogism is one from which those who promote it immediately seek to draw back. The argument proves altogether too much, and this takes us to the heart of the practical debate about the 'right to die' and public policy. The radicals for whom this is a battle cry are actually much less radical than they seem. In deploying the logic of a radical libertarianism to support their demand for some form of voluntary euthanasia, they discover that they have let the suicide genie out of the bottle, and many immediately try to push him back in. The libertarian syllogism says nothing about criteria: six months to live, intolerable suffering, the good-faith judgement of two physicians — let alone some calculus of social cost, or life membership in the Hemlock Society, or whatever other bureaucratic controls are favoured by those who claim to be the 'responsible' proponents of a euthanasia regime. The charm of the suicide syllogism is its supposed simplicity. But that simplicity, with its correlated social-control requirements which would recruit physicians or others to aid or effect the process, has little bearing on the convoluted proposals for public policy that are somehow held to flow from its conclusion.

Part of the problem with the proposal of a voluntary euthanasia regime lies precisely in this contradiction. While it is plain that strict social controls would greatly mitigate the effects of what, otherwise, would be a suicide charter, they also bureaucratize the application of the 'right to die' based on principles which enshrine the very opposite of the libertarianism of the syllogism. That is to say, the practical case for euthanasia changes its clothes midway through the discussion. It is initially libertarian, in setting out its assault on the tradition. Then, having undermined the taboo on self-killing, we find a reversal of principle: the bureaucratic mindset takes over. It is for the state to determine whether people have grounds on which to exercise their 'right to die'. Whatever grounds the state may elect, whether in the convoluted pronouncements of the Dutch courts, or the criteria of statutes recently enacted in Oregon and the Australian Northern territory, the 'right to die' is delivered into the hands of the social controllers. The practical implication, which is of course so deeply disturbing, is that the state now sets the criteria for death.

The candidate for death now must both wish to exercise the right, and have his or her application approved; there must be socially valid reasons for death. Since there is almost no interest in a mere charter for suicide, this second-guessing by the community lies at the heart of contemporary euthanasia proposals. In policy terms, it is their Achilles' heel, for it moves from the individual to the state the responsibility for death. It grants the state powers which, in our culture, it has never before been able legitimately to claim: to authorize innocent death. In moving from the libertarian/suicide axis to one of life-not-worth-living/death-seems-a-good-idea, it demonstrates the innate connection between voluntary and involuntary euthanasia. The state is then confronted with the question of the incompetent patient who displays those symptoms which are on the approved list for euthanasia applications; and, next, the competent patient, with those same symptoms, who has not elected to apply. It is important to note that this argument is not simply about the potential for abuse in the bureaucratization of decisions for the killing of innocent persons. It is an argument about the logic of the justification for euthanasia. The suicide syllogism which would claim the 'right to die' as a human right does not provide any justification for the social euthanasia regimes which are currently being initiated. It offers a clear-cut rationale for a right of suicide, and, by extension, a basis for a possible right to be killed, all deriving from an individual's judgement about how she or he chooses to dispose of her or his life. While it is used as an argument in favour of social euthanasia, for which it represents the chief argument, the social euthanasia regimes must seek legitimacy altogether elsewhere. They must look to that place where their operating principles lie, in a claimed right of the state to approve individual acts of authorized 'suicide'. More fundamentally, since suicide can never be an adequate term for a publicly authorized act, and because where a medical attendant or relative is involved we have euthanasia (by definition the killing of another), the public policy regulation of suicide-euthanasia depends on a claimed right of the state to authorize the killing of the innocent, i.e., to sponsor homicide. How little connection that has with the 'right to die' syllogism and its libertarian claims is not hard to determine![3]

But let us return to that original claim, so redolent of the emerging social assumptions of our culture as it seeks to reinvent itself in anticipation of the collapse of the Judeo-Christian tradition. The 'right to die' assumes the liberty of the individual to control his or her own self, above all in this final choice. Its revolutionary character in policy and morals is evident in the fact that the settled assumption of western culture has explicitly denied that very claim. The public policy proscription of suicide in the West has been universal, and vigorous. In its secular form it long took the view that citizens were subjects of the monarch and had no liberty to dispose of themselves. Behind this, of course, lay the theological characterization of suicide as sin, and the final authorization for such a view of the relationship of monarch and subject in the assertion that 'the LORD gives', and 'the LORD takes away'. This outlook is echoed in the pivotal phrase of the apostle, which

could not have been better designed as the antidote to radical
libertarianism and its high notion of human autonomy: 'You are
not your own'. Whether one belongs to God (in redemption, as of
course the apostle specifically intends, or simply in creation),
whether one belongs to the monarch as one's feudal Lord, or
whether, in the parlance of contemporary jurisprudence, the state
has an interest in the life of the citizen, the principle is one. And
the question, if we may so put it, which lies back of all this
argument, is whether we are indeed 'our own'. Are we ours, to
dispose as we see fit, or are we, as well as ours, also another's?

There are many levels on which the argument can be pursued.
Yet to counter the radical autonomy case, which is the core of the
contemporary right-to-die claim, we do not need to claim the
distinctives of Judeo-Christian theism. All that is necessary is to
demonstrate that suicide is not finally a private act; that whoever
we are, we are not finally our own. And that is well demonstrated
by the paternalism inherent in current public policy regimes and
proposals. They all alike deny the privacy of suicidal choices as
they erect a superstructure of public controls designed to limit its
exercise to cases which are socially approved.

The movement for the right to die may also be seen as a demand
not so much to be able to die, which as we have noted is a
universal experience, but rather to be able to avoid dying. In fact,
the demand extends to that controlling analogy of dying which we
find in the experience of chronic disease. That is to say, we
generally use the word 'die' in two distinct senses. One relates
chiefly to the fact that the one who dies ends up dead. So it applies
equally to someone killed instantly by a bullet as to someone
whose passing is extended through years of incremental deterioration through disease. In the second sense, the connotation would
cover the second case but not the first. Plainly, both subjects 'have
died'. But what we have termed the controlling analogy of dying,
which directs our attention to the process of physical and perhaps
psychological degradation, covers only the second. And the claim
of the 'right to die' may be construed as an ironic claim to the right
to avoid having to die; to move straight from a state of health to
that state of being dead, without, as it were, having to 'die' at all.

It should be noted that this is not a mere debating point. The
autonomy claim is rooted in a deep-seated unease with the
passivity of the dying process — with the helplessness of the
patient. That the contemporary patient, at least in the West, has at
his or her disposal a vastly enhanced arsenal of drugs to control
and relieve pain is accorded little significance.

It may be noted that, alongside an appeal to autonomy, there is
a second major argument deployed in favour of suicide-
euthanasia, though typically in a supporting role. That is the

argument from compassion — from sympathy with the suffering of the sufferer. It is helpful to distinguish this very different case for suicide-euthanasia from the case we have been examining. In fact, considered on its own, the compassion argument suggests something near to the converse of the autonomy argument. The compassion argument entails a judgement made not by the self but by another in respect of the suffering of one who may or may not have an opinion as to the continued worthwhileness of life and/or the appropriateness of action to bring about death. While the root meaning of the complex term compassion suggests a shared suffering, it is freighted with the connotation of a commitment to bring the suffering to an end. Freed from the ethic of the sanctity of life, this emotional response to suffering is now an increasingly invoked basis for the killing of the sufferer. It is often linked to autonomy, as if compassion for someone who is autonomous and makes a choice for death offers a double argument. While it could reasonably be suggested that a sense of compassion might encourage a careful listening to the wishes of one who suffers, compassion in and of itself is mute in the face of the question of whether human life may legitimately be taken. It is hard to believe that those who cared for the sick in past ages were less compassionate than those who care for them today. Yet if their degree of compassion has not changed, their conception of the sanctity of life has undergone a sea change. The ending of suffering has now come to include also the ending of the life of the sufferer. We return to the question of suffering and its significance below.

By contrast with the incoherence of linking these two arguments, the compassion justification for suicide-euthanasia offers an altogether better fit with the conception of suicide-euthanasia in public policy which we have addressed. The contradiction between the libertarian starting-point and statist conclusion is avoided. Since compassion, in the nature of the case, is not experienced by the sufferer but by another, it is legitimately open to others to assess, compassionately, the basis for public policy in the titration of innocent death. To put it in those terms is of course to cast the case in a favourable light. But a series of problems then must be addressed. How is compassion to be defined — or, how accurate is a view of suffering which declares a life to be unlivable or unworthy to be lived? What of the unconscious 'sufferer'? And what of 'suffering' experienced by someone other than the candidate for suicide-euthanasia? What of the 'suffering' of a family? A community? A budget?

The point is that the compassion argument fixes the criteria for death decisions squarely and candidly where every suicide-euthanasia public policy proposal has perforce to recognize them to lie: in hands other than those of the person who suffers. The compassion case is not about autonomy and the right to die, but heteronomy and the right to kill.

Yet in public policy discussion the two become one, and public policy euthanasia is revealed as in fact the nemesis of human autonomy. By contrast, the sanctity of life presumption of the western tradition safeguards a limited but clearly determined area of autonomous action on the part of the individual by precluding any heteronomous decision-making which could lead to the taking of innocent life.

QUESTIONS BEHIND THE DEBATE

If the logic of the autonomy justification for suicide-euthanasia is so seriously flawed, whence its mounting support in public and, increasingly, professional opinion? The answer lies not in, but behind, the debate. It lies in the changing assumptions which have come increasingly to dominate our thinking about sickness and death in the context of the cultural collapse in which the debate is taking place. In particular, we can note three such shifts.

I. THE MEANING OF DEATH AND DYING

If the move toward euthanasia can legitimately be understood as a flight from the experience of 'dying' as opposed to becoming dead, addressing the issue of euthanasia requires a wholly fresh assessment of the meaning, or lack of meaning, of the passage from life to what lies beyond. There is here no naive welcome for what Christians have always seen as 'the last enemy', even though they have believed that they have victory over that enemy. A deep-rooted ambivalence about death has been grounded in contrasting theological principles which at one and the same time depict death as the 'wages of sin' and as a move to something 'far better' than mere earthly life. When it has been at its most robust, Christian theology and piety have not shrunk from following both with vigour, since at the tomb of his soon to be raised friend Lazarus, 'Jesus wept'.

Such a theological account of death as a passage from this life to another has of course focused experience of the process of dying as a time of retrospection and preparation. The loss of any theological or, for that matter, other explanation of the human experience and its culmination in death has left the culture bereft of a hermeneutic of the ending, and therefore the very mortality, of human experience. This is, on reflection, curious, since it has left behind a Christian tradition in which the belief in the life to come set a context for candid acknowledgment of mortality. The culture which denies the life to come is, in the manner in which it addresses the character of human experience, in equal denial of mortality. The practical denial of death, one of the most widely-noted features of contemporary western society, offers the immediate backcloth to dying and death. The new view of dying portrays it as something to be cut out, and death itself, insofar as it must indeed be faced, is seen as an experience to be 'mastered' rather than endured. Humanity, as 'the master of things', must finally gain the right to control the final end of human experience, unacknowledged though it is in the general course of the experience which thereby loses its grip on its own nature. The fragility, and finally the mortality, of all human life is dismissed from its controlling place in the actual experience of the race. The stately theme of a work from an earlier century, such as Thomas Gray's *Elegy*, suggests to the modern mind that it was written on another planet:

> The boast of heraldry, the pomp of power,
> And all that beauty, all that wealth e're gave,
> Awaits alike the inevitable hour:
> The paths of glory lead but to the grave.[4]

The abdication of conscious acknowledgment of mortality has greatly diminished the capacity of the West to address any real question concerning human identity, especially at its fragile margins. The ambiguities of unborn human life remain unresolved; and the uncertainties of the processes of degeneration and, finally, dying itself continue unabated.[5]

2.   THE MEANING OF SUFFERING

It is hard to raise a serious question as to the meaning of suffering in polite contemporary conversation. The reason is not that people do not suffer. In fact, an argument could be made that in the death-throes of Judeo-Christian civilization the sufferings of humankind — drug therapies and central heating notwithstanding — have never been greater. The emotional anguish of family life lived under the torment of contractual marriage, together with the pretence of immortality in a world stalked by fear, spool an experience which those who lived shorter and harder lives under the impress of Christendom never had to know. Much depends on how these facets of human life are weighted. This is beyond doubt a culture suffering in ways all its own.

So what about meaning? The know-how books offer little help, despite the anguish of their readers; and, of course, there is good reason. How can there be meaning in suffering, if there is not meaning to be found in the wider vision? What can it mean when life goes wrong, if it meant nothing when it went well?

And so the assumption is widely held that any talk of meaning in suffering is not simply deluded, it is utterly lacking in that quintessential modern emotion-turned-virtue, compassion. How can we feel sorry for someone who is suffering if at the same time we adhere even to the possibility that their suffering is something other than absurd? To put it another way, politically correct compassion denies the possibility of serious redemption in serious suffering. This is not to suggest a naive notion of desert, or an *ex opere operato* conception of redeeming benefit. It is simply to allow the possibility that serious suffering may bring serious benefit to the human experience along with, and not in any sense cancelling out, its disbenefit. The failure to allow both sides of the equation to stand lies at the heart of the contemporary problem of suffering. An essayist of the nineteenth century, for example, could reflect on the significance of the death of children very differently from what would commonly be the case today. He could suggest that the frequent deaths of small children left every child valued in a fresh fashion by his or her family, since childhood could not be viewed as simply a stage in the process of maturation; it had perforce to be seen as an end in itself.[6] This striking outlook, whether or not we find it to have merit, reads at the end of the twentieth century as sheer anachronism. It leaves the equation intact: tragedy does not stand alone, and yet tragedy is left free to stand.[7]

3. THE MEANING OF HUMAN BEING

The harrowing trial of human identity lies at the heart of the crisis of western culture. How shall we know how to die if we do not know how to live? How shall we know how to live if we do not know who we are? The lingering dependence of the remnants of Judeo-Christian civilization on the deep-rooted biblical theology of human beings made in the *imago Dei* and ever standing *coram Deo* has left our generation in fundamental confusion. It will be many generations, even if the process of secularization and revisionism in our cultural identity continues to go forward apace, before we finally lose touch with the immensity of the dignity which Holy Scripture affords to human persons.

The story of contemporary public policy is single: that of growing incoherence between the biblical vision that lies at the heart of the culture, and the fragmentation which growing but still piecemeal repudiations of that tradition has brought to our common life. The issues of bioethics, with their central location in theological anthropology — the nature of human being — offer the clearest but by no means the only windows on this process. As significant at another level, and with many inter-relations, is the concept of human rights which has become the currency of international law and the wider international public policy process associated with the United Nations. Human rights questions were sharply raised by the atrocities which formed part of the public policy of certain nations during World War II. More broadly, the human rights agenda has come down from the Enlightenment of the eighteenth century as a secularized transcription of the Judeo-Christian conception of the dignity of humankind which flows from the bearing of the divine image. The tragic irony of the 1995 Beijing conference on the rights of women, with its deep-seated and commendable affirmation of their full human dignity side by side with widespread advocacy of 'reproductive rights' (i.e., the killing by abortion of human children), will prove emblematic of the further stages in the human rights story. The dilemma in which this complex process places the Christian community will only grow sharper, since the eclecticism which has begun to drive the tradition is the only modus operandi of a culture in collapse.

Our forgetfulness as to who we are leaves us prey to any and every justification for the control of our living and our dying. It should prove no surprise that such justifications will show themselves increasingly sophisticated and tailored to the tastes of the age.

CONCLUSION

Are we our own? And, if we are, can such a presumption translate into public policy? The autonomy argument, thus projected, proves profoundly self-destructive. Yet, if we are not our own, if we were created in the *imago Dei*, and if we were bought with a price, the right to die like the right to live is retained by the God who made and who redeemed. If we recall who we are, and the logic which alone can unravel the notions of rights themselves, the major premise of the suicidal syllogism is shown to be as false as its promise.

NOTES

1. The original version of this essay was presented, with unintended though not unnoticed irony, on Bastille Day, 1995 (July 14).

2. The literature on the language of rights is very extensive. At least two essays in the preceding volume of this series addressed it in the context of Christian perspectives on bioethics: Allen D Verhey, 'Luther's "Freedom of a Christian" and a Patient's Autonomy', and J Daryl Charles, 'The "Right to Die" in the Light of Contemporary Rights-Rhetoric', *Bioethics and the Future of Medicine*, ed. John F Kilner, Nigel M de S Cameron, and David Schiedermayer, (Carlisle, U.K.: Paternoster, and Grand Rapids, Mich., USA: Eerdmans, 1995).

3. Two writers who have lately addressed this theme in an illuminating manner are Leon Kass, 'Is there a Right to Die?', in *Hastings Center Report* 23

(1993) and Yale Kamisar, ' "Right to Die" — Good Slogan, Fuzzy Thinking', in *First Things* 38 (1993).

4. Gray's *Elegy Written in a Country Churchyard* is one of the staples of English poetry, and offers a sustained examination of human glory in the light of mortality. Available in many collections, notably F T Palgrave's *Golden Treasury of English Verse*.

5. This writer is increasingly convinced that the key to the euthanasia debate, and the radical shift in public and professional attitudes in recent years, lies in changed assumptions about the meaning of death. That is part of the explanation for the general lack of intelligent engagement between the two positions. As we say, their proponents talk past each other, a phenomenon which typically indicates the presence of deep and unresolved disagreements beneath the surface of discussion. If in fact there are widely diverse understandings of the connotation of 'death', it may appear as no surprise that some consider a 'right to die' self-evident while others (with the moral tradition of a civilization behind them) consider it unwarranted.

Yet there is little interest in the meaning of death, or in the cultural history which lies behind its changed and changing significance. One major discussion is that of Philippe Ariès, *The Hour of our Death* (New York: Knopf, 1981, ET of the interestingly titled French original, *L'Homme devant la mort*). Two particular features render this fascinating and lengthy discussion less helpful than one might wish: little interest in the euthanasia/suicide question, and (perhaps relatedly) much less focus on the identity of the Judeo-Christian tradition and the significance of the Christian culture of the medieval millennium for the subject. Ariès chronicles, nonetheless, the remarkable shift which in early medieval times brought burial grounds into the cities, and vaults often into the churches themselves. This differs markedly from earlier pagan (and early Christian) aversion to cohabitation between the living and the dead and the current tendency to renew the separation. It is in the impact of modernity on western ideas of death, long-delayed in its full implications like so much else in the agenda of the Enlightenment, that we find the cradle of the modern euthanasia movement. Ariès strikingly characterizes the tradition evident even around the turn of our own century: 'In the early twentieth century, before World War I, throughout the Western world of Latin culture, be it Catholic or Protestant, the death of a man still solemnly altered the space and time of a social group that could be extended to include the entire community. The shutters were closed in the bedroom of the dying man, candles were lit, holy water was sprinkled; the house filled with grave and whispering neighbors, relatives, and friends. . . .' He continues: 'Not only did everyone die in public like Louis XIV, but the death of each person was a public event that moved, literally and figuratively, society as a whole. It was not only an individual who was disappearing, but society itself that had been wounded and that had to be healed. All the changes that have modified attitudes toward death in the past thousand years have not altered this fundamental image, this permanent relationship between death and society.' But we have now urbanized death, anonymous, private, and little mourned, and, as Ariès notes, this is probably just the first stage of the development of a new conception of dying. 'Today, a complete reversal of customs seems to have occurred in one generation.' (559f)

6. Leigh Hunt's essay, 'Deaths of Little Children', reprinted in W Peacocke, *Selected English Essays* (London: Oxford University Press, 1903).

7. Surprisingly scarce are reflections on the significance of suffering in the bioethical literature which is so powerfully driven by this basic human experience. On the fringes of bioethics, Stanley Hauerwas' *Suffering Presence: Theological Reflections on Medicine, the Mentally Handicapped, and the Church* (Notre Dame, Ind.: Notre Dame University Press, 1986) offers a noteworthy exception. As in

the case of death, the assumptions on which bioethics itself operates are little recognized but largely determinative of its discussions. It is in the development of the hospice movement, especially in its original pattern under Dame Cicely Saunders, that we find the deepest challenge to utilitarian, autonomy-based reductions of human experience. Yet what is most salient in that movement has not been the refining of palliative medicine but the commitment to an under- standing of human being in which the suffering and the dying are not cut off from the human community and the medical enterprise. Rather, they are placed at their centre. The 'answer' of the hospice movement to the demand for euthanasia is not that good pain control makes it unnecessary, although that may be the case. The answer is that human dying has to be placed in an appropriately human context, in which medicine is placed at the service of the patient who ineluctably confronts his or her own death and for whom candour and care in the face of death confront the community with a like challenge.

[2]

Death and Dying

John T Dunlop MD

A strong stand for life is biblical, based squarely on the fact that all human life bears the image of God and receives God's protection.

> Whoever sheds the blood of a human, by a human shall that person's blood be shed; for in the image of God has God made humanity (Gen. 9:6).

In the medical world of the 1990s this biblical truth obligates believers to confront the forces of abortion and euthanasia. Although there is some looseness in the contemporary use of the term euthanasia, I refer specifically here to 'active euthanasia' — acting to cause a person's death with or without the victim's consent.[1] Christians have well articulated a theology of life and critiqued euthanasia on biblical, sociological, historical and philosophical grounds.[2]

Our present medical advances give us a wide range of potential interventions that can often reverse or significantly delay the dying process. Still we recognize that in spite of this technological ability, death is inevitable. In some ways we are smarter than we are wise. Our knowledge of how to prolong life has surpassed our wisdom to know when to apply that knowledge. Consequently, there exists the danger that we can use medical technologies to resist God. Resisting God's call at death can be as wrong as resisting God's gift of life through abortion. While we should indeed oppose euthanasia, we must also present a thoroughly biblical and ethical approach to death. Otherwise, a 'pro-life' orientation will mistakenly become 'anti-death'. We must complement our theology of life with a clearly articulated theology of death.

This discussion will first review key elements of a biblical theology of death and will then sketch a Christian perspective on living in the face of death. Finally, this perspective will be amplified by examining the decision many of us will eventually face ourselves or on behalf of our loved ones: a decision to accept death without resistance and no longer to seek aggressive medical treatment.

ELEMENTS OF A BIBLICAL THEOLOGY OF DEATH

Death is a central theme of Scripture. Death was not a feature of the original creation, it came only as a result of the fall of Adam. Genesis 2:17 records the possibility of death, and later its institution is confirmed in Genesis 3:19 after Adam's sin. Paul shows in Romans 5 how death then passed to all people:

> Therefore, just as sin entered the world through one person, and death through sin, and in this way death came to all, because all sinned . . . (Rom. 5:12).

Indeed, death has become the enemy of life.

> The last enemy to be destroyed is death (1 Cor. 15:26).

Yet Christians praise God for the beautiful truth that although death is an enemy, it is a defeated enemy through the death of the Lord Jesus. Paul writes:

> When the perishable has been clothed with the imperishable, and the mortal with immortality, then the saying that is written will come true: 'Death has been swallowed up in victory.' 'Where, O death, is your victory? Where, O death, is your sting?' The sting of death is sin, and the power of sin is the law. But thanks be to God! He gives us the victory through our Lord Jesus Christ (1 Cor. 15:54–57).

God exercises a magnificent ability to use defeats in life to accomplish greater ends. Death itself is the case in point par excellence. God has so defeated death that God can now use it for higher purposes. The Psalmist declares:

> Precious in the sight of the LORD is the death of his saints (Ps. 116:15).

These biblical truths provide great encouragement when a Christian dies. The death of believers is still precious in the sight of the Lord. It is the time of their completion — their ultimate salvation. At death believers stand face to face with their Lord. God will have completed their redemption and restored them to their full potential as those created in the image of God. The work of Christ on the Cross has transformed death from a defeated end to a glorious beginning. Death for children of God is the time of their being taken up as the fruit of God's harvest. Eliphaz spoke of this to Job and in anticipation said:

> You will come to the grave in full vigour, like sheaves gathered in season (Job 5:26).

A believer's death is never a tragedy from the eternal perspective. It is carefully timed and controlled by the loving hands of a sovereign God. David could say:

> All the days ordained for me
> were written in your book
> before one of them came to be (Ps. 139:16).

The Book of Job echoes a similar thought:

> People's days are determined;
> you have decreed the number of their months
> and have set limits they cannot exceed (Job 14:5).

Death for the believer is an enemy, but through Christ it is a defeated enemy. It is in the control of a loving, almighty God. In death people can still trust God's essential goodness and see that goodness in action.

In spite of their intellectual commitment to the defeat of death in Christ, many believers do not live in light of these great truths. What Scripture says of unbelievers 'who all their lives were held in slavery by their fear of death' (Heb. 2:15) — is all too often true of believers. Rather than living in a freedom derived from knowing that death is defeated, people submit to the bondage of the fear of death. It is essential that all believers allow the Holy Spirit to transform their attitudes to death and dying. It is imperative for the church of Jesus Christ to lead people to a proper understanding of death as a part of their process of spiritual maturity.

I am convinced that God wants believers to, in the words of Steve Brown,[3] 'Die Slowly'. Believers are not to cling to the values and material trappings of this life till the very end. Rather they slowly lose their grip on this world as their affections are gradually transferred to the next. 'Dying slowly' must start early in our Christian lives as we learn to accept our own mortality. In his psalm Moses wrote:

> Teach us to number our days aright, that we may gain a heart of wisdom (Ps. 90:12).

None of us embarks on wise living till we deeply experience the fact that we will die. Our lives are limited, our days are numbered. We lack the proper perspective on life until we have come to grips with our own mortality and considered death in this way.

Jesus is our teacher and example regarding a proper perspective on death:

> All who would come after me must deny themselves and take up their crosses daily and follow me (Lk. 9:23).

We must live each day with the perspective of the individual facing crucifixion, with its attendant suffering and shame. Each day will be lived as if it were our last. Picture the criminal who is carrying his cross enroute to execution. He does not admire the fancy houses and sports cars he passes along the way. No, his values transcend these material things. The dying process has already begun. When we live acknowledging our inevitable death, our values will also fall into proper perspective.

Christian baptism testifies to the fact that the dying process has begun. This is death to ourselves and to the things and values of this world:

> Or don't you know that all of us who were baptized into Christ Jesus were baptized into his death? We were therefore buried with him through baptism into death in order that, just as Christ was raised from the dead through the glory of the Father, we too may live a new life (Rom. 6:3–4).

LIVING IN THE FACE OF DEATH

Adopting this biblical view of death will have two natural consequences. One result is that we will be acutely aware that our time on this earth is limited. The second implication is that our anticipation of Heaven will motivate us to intensive service here on earth. As Paul reflects:

> For to me, to live is Christ and to die is gain. If I am to go on living in the body, this will mean fruitful labour for me. Yet what shall I choose? I do not know! I am torn between the two: I desire to depart and be with Christ, which is better by far; but it is more necessary for you that I remain in the body. Convinced of this, I know that I will remain, and I will continue with all of you for your progress and joy in the faith (Philp. 1:20–26).

Paul's focus on dying and being with Christ made him more keenly aware that his days were numbered. It motivated him to fill his days with work for the kingdom of God.

Simultaneously we must consciously seek not only to release our grip on this life but to be progressively taken up with the next. The present generation has lost an emphasis on heaven that was maintained in earlier times. Richard Baxter, the great Puritan pastor, testified that he committed himself to thirty minutes a day meditating on heaven. This focus on heaven, accompanies the longing for God and godliness that is the driving force of our lives as believers.[4]

We need to adapt the mentality of the pioneers of the faith typified by Abraham, and his family of whom it was said:

> Instead, they were longing for a better country — a heavenly one (Heb. 11:16).

It is imperative that maturing Christians begin early the process of dying. They no longer fear death; they see it as a defeated enemy. They begin to relinquish the material values of this life and focus increasingly on the life of eternity that God has prepared for them. Such perspectives prepare them to face the latter days of their lives.

Death for believers has been defeated in Christ. As they grow in their Christian lives, maturing believers become less attached to this world and long more for God and heaven. Within this context of biblical truth it is imperative to arrive at the decision not to pursue life aggressively but to accept the inevitability of death without major resistance. Two basic approaches to end of life decisions are possible: A widely-reprinted cartoon well illustrates the first approach. It pictures an old codger arriving at the pearly gates with several tubes hanging out of him and the caption 'Sorry I am late but they kept me on life supports for the past two weeks.'

The second approach was well exemplified in one of my most memorable experiences of dealing with the dying. Howard was a beloved Christian who had walked with the Lord for many years. I had cared for him for a number of years and came to respect the depth of his Christian maturity and love for the Lord. He had diabetes and had been very compliant with his diet. Following a series of heart attacks, he was bothered by a recurrent rhythm disturbance for which I had asked him to restrict his caffeine. One Sunday afternoon he was admitted to the intensive care unit of our local hospital with another heart attack. By Monday afternoon it was clear that this one was much more serious. After reviewing his course, I felt I had to share with him the situation and its prognosis. In prior discussions he had made it clear that he did not want life supports or aggressive care just to delay the inevitability of his death.

That evening I told him that his heart was failing rapidly. Although we were doing all that was appropriate for him, he was dying and likely would not live out the night. He was fully alert and coherent. His response was unforgettable. He took my hand and said, 'John, thank you for being so candid. I would like to ask for three things. First the visiting policy in this intensive care unit is unfair. My wife and daughters are in the waiting room and I would like them to come back here with me. Second, as you know I have been a diabetic for many years and I have not been able to have my favourite food. Could you get me a piece of chocolate cake with chocolate icing? Third, I have not been able to have a cup of "real coffee" for some time and wonder if you would let me have that.' With tears in my eyes, I agreed to all of his requests. His family came to be with him. We were able to get him a piece of chocolate cake with chocolate icing and a cup of 'real coffee'. He enjoyed these fully and shortly after finishing them laid his head back in his bed and died. I know that he was looking forward to going to be with the Lord in Heaven, but he was not certain that there would be chocolate cake and coffee waiting there for him.

Howard was ready to die. When the time came he did not resist dying and made the necessary decisions so that he could approach death with equanimity and a sense of fulfilment.

There are many examples in Scripture where God's saints, like Howard, no longer resist but quietly resign themselves to death. For instance:

> When Jacob had finished giving instructions to his sons, he drew his feet up into the bed, breathed his last and was gathered to his people (Gen. 49:33).

> Then Paul answered, 'Why are you weeping and breaking my heart? I am ready not only to be bound, but also to die in Jerusalem for the name of the Lord Jesus' (Acts 21:13).

Jesus purposely and deliberately approached his death knowing it was a crucial part of his Father's plan. He endured the agony of his choice in the garden of Gethsemane but then when death came he was submissive to it.

Life, as precious as it is, must ultimately end. The example of Scripture is to accept death rather than exhaust all resources trying to resist it. Such a perspective has important implications for medical decision-making near the end of life.

ACCEPTING DEATH WITHOUT RESISTANCE

When is it appropriate not to pursue aggressive medical care? Three basic considerations are primary: the medical context, spiritual factors, and emotional issues.

THE MEDICAL CONTEXT

First, what medical considerations should one examine when deciding whether or not to pursue aggressive life sustaining medical care? Foremost here is the medical condition encountered and the therapeutic options available. There are several questions that one should try to answer.

What is the exact diagnosis?
A series of tests may be necessary before answering this question. It is usually valuable to obtain a specific diagnosis even if the individual prefers not to seek treatment in order to help make an informed decision possible. A response I often hear is, 'Don't do the tests just let me go.' This course of action is appropriate only if

a careful interview and examination can convincingly establish a diagnosis.

What is the natural prognosis of the condition without treatment?
It is helpful to define what the life expectancy is as well as what quality of life is expected. At times the natural progression of the disease without treatment is not a bad option.

What treatment is available?
The concern here is to determine how potential treatments can be expected to alter the prognosis. Is treatment simply a means to prolong life or does it also preserve or restore function?

What is the chance of success?
One should have some feel for the relative likelihood of success. It is also useful in this regard to consider the 'best case' and 'worse case' scenarios of each type of potential outcome.

What are the potential complications of the treatment under consideration?
So often unexpected problems arise when we try to intervene agressively in end of life situations. So often not just single organ but multi-organ failure is involved, and the probability of therapeutically induced complications increases exponentially.
Notably absent from this series of questions is the issue of pain and suffering. At times, pursuing treatment to minimize pain is reasonable. At times, however, it is God's will for us to undergo suffering. An essential part of our humanity is the possibility of profiting from suffering. This view contradicts the sentiment that labels any human suffering as inhumane. It may be inhumane to allow an animal to suffer but not so for a person who has the potential to develop through the suffering. This ability to profit from suffering is part of what distinguishes human beings from other members of the animal kingdom.
Scripture underscores the value of some suffering:

> Therefore we do not lose heart. Though outwardly we are wasting away, yet inwardly we are being renewed day by day. For our light and momentary troubles are achieving for us an eternal glory that far outweighs them all. So we fix our eyes not on what is seen, but on what is unseen. For what is seen is temporary, but what is unseen is eternal (2 Cor. 4:16–18).

We do not make end of life decisions simply to avoid pain or suffering. These trials must be seen in the total context of God's sovereignty. Even in the midst of pain or suffering we must learn to trust God's loving care.

SPIRITUAL FACTORS

After considering the medical picture, we must consider the patient's spiritual readiness for dying. Patients need encouragement to examine their own thoughts toward death and dying. If they are unable to be involved in treatment decisions, those making the decisions on their behalf must answer relevant questions as they believe the incapacitated patient would. That is why it is imperative to have discussions about these issues with aging loved ones while they are still mentally competent. In these discussions we learn how they would currently make these decisions and how they would alter them if they deteriorate mentally and physically.

Relevant questions to discuss include:

• Can the patient have a significant spiritual ministry in her present state of health?
• Does the patient feel that his life is complete? Can he freely say, 'Yes, I am ready to go home to glory'?
• Is the patient living a quality of life that allows him/her to have fellowship with God?

EMOTIONAL ISSUES

Finally, we must consider the emotions that help shape patients' attitudes toward life. In later years individuals often arrive at a conviction that their life's work is complete. The older patients get, I have observed, the less they are looking forward to future earthly events. At some point they have no plans that tie them to their present life. It is that sense of completion that prepares the believer for the presence of the Lord. Many of my patients eventually weary of this life and long for the Lord to deliver them in death.

Medical, spiritual, and emotional considerations can all be relevant simultaneously. Patients may develops a medical condition that is terminal and renders them less physically or mentally able to pursue aggressive kingdom work. They are weary of this world, longing for Heaven. They sense that their life work is accomplished.

At that point it is time to change the approach to their medical care. Some elderly people will eventually view death with a 'thy will be done' mentality, where previously they felt that it was God's will to overcome illness and vigorously proceed with life. When people have thus entered a dying process and know it, we continue medical care not to prolong life but to preserve the quality of that life. 'Quality of life' is a phrase that has emotional

overtones. Some suggest that for 'quality of life' reasons one
person's life is worth living and another's is not. On the contrary,
all life is sacred; none has more value than another. At the same
time, the quality of that life is also important. While quality of life
considerations do not justify actively terminating a life that we do
not consider worthy, attending to such considerations does foster
an admirable commitment to providing loving support and
comfort for the patient rather than a desperation to squeeze the last
possible moments out of life.

Decisions in the medical world must always be individualized.
Just as a rigid textbook solution is inadequate to diagnose and treat
medical problems, there is not a textbook approach to resolve
ethical dilemmas. John Frame aptly speaks of the biblical, situ-
ational, and existential contexts of all of our medical decisions.[5]
We must be sensitive to the medical context of the patients, their
own feelings, as well as any insight that we derive from Scripture.
This discernment process is often extremely complex. We therefore must approach these decisions with great humility and
dependence on the leading of the Spirit of God and on that
wisdom that comes from God:

> If any of you lack wisdom, they should ask God, who gives
> generously to all without finding fault, and it will be given to them
> (Jam. 1:5).

Once one has the best obtainable medical opinion, it is wise to
meet with family and church leaders.[6] It is extremely beneficial
and comforting to pray and make these decisions with others. It is
then imperative to communicate and implement the decisions.
There must be clear communication within the family and also
with physicians and other significant care givers. When there are
non-Christians involved in these interactions, an excellent opportunity to communicate the practical nature of a faith in Christ —
or perhaps the gospel message itself — arises.

Implementation will take on various forms depending on the
context. It may involve choosing not to pursue a possible medical
treatment, such as surgery, kidney dialysis, or a breathing
machine. It may entail refusing resuscitation if one has a cardiac
arrest while being cared for in a hospital or nursing home.
Enrollment in a hospice programme is another expression of this
change in approach. Executing a living will or creating a limited
power of attorney for medical purposes is also frequently a good
idea.

At the time of death, the patient will require much support.
When death is close at hand there may be no need to resist it.
Telling a patient that it is all right for him to die is appropriate. It is
very helpful for the physician and the family to assure the patient

that they understand that he/she is dying and to tell the patient in very direct terms that this is all right. Repeating this affirmation many times may be necessary. Some patients are afraid to die lest they disappoint someone close to them. At times they need to be told to relax and to stop struggling; then they can rest and commit themselves to the Lord. I found this specially true a number of years ago when dealing with a believer who was dying of chronic lung disease. He was struggling to breathe when I came to see him. I told him that I thought the Lord was calling him home. In prayer we committed him into the loving hands of his Lord. I encouraged him to relax and not to struggle. He did so and within minutes died very peacefully.

As believers we are in a 'win–win' situation. Paul expressed it so beautifully:

For to me, to live is Christ and to die is gain (Philp. 1:21).

Let us pursue life for Christ with all of the wisdom and strength that he allows us. Let us speak out against any forces that would devalue that life. At the same time, when death is inevitable, let us see it as the defeated enemy it is and not seek to resist it. Let us be careful that in our effort to preserve life we do not move into a position where we are resisting the call of God in death. Let us not allow our actions to contradict the fact that in Christ death has been defeated.

NOTES

1. Euthanasia can be categorized as active or passive, as well as voluntary or involuntary. Whereas active euthanasia involves wilfully taking positive steps to terminate life, passive euthanasia entails deciding not to take positive steps to prolong life. Each of these can be either voluntary or involuntary, depending on whether or not the euthanasia is carried out with the informed consent of the individual whose life is in question.

2. See relevant chapters in this book (by Cameron, Fowler, Verhey, Kilner, Pellegrino, Mitchell, Jochemsen, etc.) and sources cited in their notes.

3. Pastor Brown developed this theme rather beautifully several years ago on his nationally syndicated radio programme 'Key Life' while reflecting on the death of his mother.

4. This does not create the individual who is 'so heavenly minded he is of no earthly good.' Such an individual is a logical impossibility. As we truly develop a longing for God and godliness our lives take on a far deeper capacity for strategic and productive life on earth.

5. John Frame, *Medical Ethics Principles, Persons, and Problems*, (Presbyterian and Reformed Publishing Co. 1988), Introduction.

6. No matter what form of church government we adhere to, there should be individuals functioning as elders. These spiritual leaders are intimately acquainted with the members of the congregation. They should be called at a time of illness to attend the sick. James 5 admonishes them to anoint the sick with oil and this is advised in the context of a discussion of prayer. A study of biblical eldership suggests that they should be just as involved in giving counsel in difficult issues like the life and death issues under discussion here.

[3]

Suffering

Marsha D M Fowler, RN, MDiv, PhD

In June of 1993, the *Los Angeles Times* newspaper announced the release of a new film by the highly regarded and internationally respected film director Juzo Itami. His film *Daibyonin* is called 'a comedy about death'. It communicates that science, in the form of hospitals, has won priority over human beings in Japan, which Itami-san sees as a violation of human rights. His concerns are about the medicalization and technologization of the end of life, as well as about how Japanese society views death itself.[1] How clear is the lens through which this Japanese film director looks?

BIOTECHNOLOGICAL ADVANCES: AWESOME POWER AND PERILOUS RESPONSIBILITY

We have come to the point in the United States where what we can do with our medicine and medical technology is what, only a few years ago, we would have regarded as either miraculous or as science fiction. Now, science fiction has come alive. But we have begun more publicly to ask questions of our medical science and of ourselves, no longer limiting such questions to the smaller academic circles of bioethicists, moral theologians, and clinicians. Have we proceeded with our development of medicine and technology, and even bioethics, but failed to ask the deeper questions of that development? I think so: we have begun to suffer the consequences of failing to address the real questions, the hard questions. Where has this failure taken us?

Our medical science is astonishing. This astonishment can often be seen in the general media such as newspaper articles and editorial cartoons. We can splice genes and are working on averting genetic diseases by treatment *in-utero*, concomitantly raising the spectre of genetic tampering. We have 'surrogate mothers' pregnant with another woman's fertilized ovum — and are now, for the first time in history, faced with the difficult question: 'Who is this baby's *mother*?' In a case in San Francisco, a pregnant woman was killed in a car accident. The medical centre sustained the dead woman's body in order to allow the developing

44

fetus to reach a sufficiently safe level of maturity to be delivered. Sixty-three days later by Caesarean section a healthy child was delivered from the dead mother's womb. It is no longer the case that a person has to be alive for us to keep the lungs inflating, the heart beating, the cells metabolizing, the womb nourishing. In another famous case, the young adult Karen Ann Quinlan fell into a persistent vegetative state and was placed on a ventilator. Her parents fought a battle in court to have the ventilator removed and were eventually granted that permission. The news reported that 'Karen Quinlan Dies After 10-Year Coma'. Quinlan lived another 10 years in a persistent vegetative state before she died.[2] Her death raised numerous questions about treatment continuation and cessation. Another newspaper article asks the question: 'Baby Fae is saved — but for what?' and refers to an infant born with left heart hypoplasia who was given a baboon heart before she died.[3] And then, we see articles such as the one that appeared after the Cruzan decision, entitled . . . 'It's no longer human life at a point: it's metabolism.'[4]

Perhaps more poignant and powerful are the editorial cartoons that have appeared. In a series of representative cartoons, collected over a 15 year period, we see a dramatic shift in the characterization of medical technology and its use. In the first cartoon (by Nelson), a man and woman are sitting in a living room. He, reading the *Gazette*, turns to her and says, 'There's been so many medical break-throughs lately, that if you aren't dead already, you probably never will be.' The setting is a comfortable home environment, the most prominent features of the cartoon being the overstuffed chairs, the characters themselves, two lamps and an end table. In the second cartoon (Stayskal) two rather robust male patients are in hospital beds. One turns to the other and says, 'I'm going to take a nap, watch my plugs will you.' The characters themselves, the beds, the overhead lamps and the furniture dominate the cartoon. In the background there is some vaguely outlined equipment, IVs on a standard, an oxygen mask in the bed and a tiny heart monitor. The environment is 'lo-tech' in feel and technology is very much in the less-consequential background.

Then there is a change in the depictions of the cartoons. In the next two-panel cartoon, a family member is ushered by the physician through a door that says 'Technology R Us.' The first panel says, as they progress, 'The good news is your father is still alive . . . ' In the second panel the caption continues '. . . the bad news is that apart from the readouts, you can't tell.' The family member hangs his head. The patient is barely discernable in the dark, nondescript, dripping, and ominous looking 'technology' that covers half of the frame. In the next cartoon (Wright), a policeman is standing over a bedfast patient saying, 'Trying to die, eh, Mr Smith! You could get the [electric] chair for this.' The patient is cachexic, contractured, and diminished by the ominous, if not evil looking, dark technology that now takes up three-quarters of the frame. In the final cartoon (Oliphant) a moribund patient, whose head alone shows above the bed sheets, is surrounded by a morass of life-sustaining technology, dripping wires, and lines. The caption reads, 'Condemned to life'. As the years have progressed, and our medical technology has developed, the cartoon patient changed from being robust to skeletalized. The depiction of medical technology changed from simple to dark and ominous if not evil, and from recessive to dominant.

DOING 'EVERYTHING POSSIBLE'

In the words from a confession from my own faith tradition, we have 'awesome power and perilous responsibility' and have used our power to our own peril.[5] We have moved from overstuffed chairs in the simple living room discussion to the situation of 'condemned to life'. In this move, we have become reluctant ever to acknowledge a patient as 'dying'. In a study by medical anthropologists Muller and Koenig, the researchers looked at the point at which physicians were willing to label a patient as 'dying'. They conclude that

> When physicians are in pursuit of medical interventions, their evaluation of a patient's proximity to death becomes closely linked to their assessment of what is available in the medical and technological armamentarium that could possibly benefit the patient. . . . Dying is defined . . . in terms of the actions — or failed actions — of physicians. In keeping with the predominant technical bias of biomedicine, 'dying' becomes a cultural metaphor which symbolizes treatment failure. The focus of medical work is on doing, and when everything fails then the patient is 'dying.' . . . Acknowledgment of a patient's dying status may not be made until death is imminent or, in some cases, has already occurred.[6]

The writer-poet T S Eliot writes about modern medical care in his play 'The Family Reunion' and gives us additional insight into the 'why' of the medicalization of death. He writes,

> It seems a necessary move
> In an unnecessary action
> Not for the good that it will do
> But that nothing may be left undone
> On the margin of the impossible[7]

How often in clinical practice we hear the words, 'We did everything possible'? Yet when we do everything possible, operating on the margin of the impossible, we violate the very dignity of the person, a dignity that we would otherwise wish to preserve, and engage in nothing short of a vitalistic technological idolatry.

Evidences of this abound. For instance, consider the legal instruments called 'advance directives', including the 'Living Will', the 'Durable Power of Attorney for Health Care', 'Directive to the Physician', and so forth. Such directives have proven to be extraordinarily useful, perhaps indispensable, in the clinical arena. And yet, their very existence stands as sure and certain evidence against the brokenness of our 'health care system'. Most persons complete such directives in order to forestall the unwanted and unwarranted use of life-sustaining technology when they are at the end of life, to direct that when they are irretrievably dying (or in a persistent vegetative state), there should be no further treatment. If we properly understood the place of death in life we would not need such documents to compel the cessation of treatment.

As the field of bioethics attempted, initially, to come to grips with decision-making at the end of life, it focused on the utilization of ethical principles (e.g., justice, respect for autonomy, nonmaleficence, and beneficence) in the process of case analysis and decision making.[8] Yet, this approach to ethics, by itself, has proved to be inadequate to the task of addressing the issue that underlies all clinical ethical dilemmas. Though others have discussed the defining philosophical characteristics of an ethical dilemma, the defining clinical characteristic is that of tragedy or suffering. It is here that we have failed, both in clinical practice and in bioethics.

THE FAILURE OF BIOETHICS AND ITS PRAXIS

Indications of our failure abound in the general media. In a difficult interview with Bruno Bettelheim, the famous child psychologist who committed suicide, journalist Celeste Fremon writes:

> Finally frustrated by his disinterest, I asked him abruptly: 'are you afraid of dying?' Suddenly I had his attention.
> 'No,' he said. 'I fear suffering. The older one gets, the greater the likelihood that one will be kept alive without purpose.'[9]

This is an individual expression of the concern raised in Tolchin's news article 'When Long Life is Too Much: Suicide Rises among the Elderly'.[10] In his discussion of a 25% rise in elder-suicide, he writes that 'some experts speculate that the technological advances extending the lives of the elderly sometimes bring a quality of life that they cannot accept.'

Other evidences claim our attention, for some of us at the ballot box, where we have been asked to vote *yea* or *nay* to physician-

assisted suicide. Arguments for physician-assisted suicide fall
largely into two categories, that of a right to control one's own life
(even to the point of taking it), and that of the avoidance of
suffering (especially in the face of the perceived and real clinical
neglect of suffering).

As another specific example, in an issue of *TV Guide*, actress
Mary Tyler Moore is interviewed about the series of tragedies in
her life. Moore's picture graces the cover with the caption 'Mary
opens up: "I'm not so fearful anymore. I've already seen the
darkness." ' Inside the issue, she speaks about the death of her
sister, the death of her son, the break-up of her 17 year marriage,
and the chronic pain and illness she suffers as a consequence of
being diabetic. On the cover, the darkness of her life — her
suffering — is juxtaposed against another cover caption that asks
'What's cookin' now with Tom and Roseanne?'[11] Mary has seen
the darkness.

In his discussion of the 'psalms of darkness' in *The Message of the
Psalms*, Reformed theologian and Old Testament scholar Walter
Brueggemann writes that these psalms

> . . . lead us into a dangerous acknowledgment of how life really is.
> . . . Perhaps worst, they lead us away from the comfortable religious
> claims of 'modernity' in which everything is managed and controlled.
> In our modern experience, but probably also in every successful and
> affluent culture, it is believed that enough power and knowledge can
> tame the terror and eliminate the darkness. . . . But our honest
> experience, both personal and public, attests to the resilience of the
> darkness in spite of us. The remarkable thing about Israel is that it did
> not banish or deny the darkness from its religious enterprise. It
> embraces the darkness as the very stuff of new life.[12]

What we in America have done is to attempt to use our medical
knowledge and medical power to 'tame the terror and eliminate
the darkness' — which is suffering — from our lives. We have
asked medicine to do something that is not its fundamental
purpose. In its care of the body, medicine and its technology can
dull the sword of disease or pain or even death, but it cannot,
itself, either tell us where to 'draw the line,' or come to grips with
the issue of suffering. No more able is an exclusively obligation-
based bioethics, one that focuses on principles that specify 'duty,'
or what it is right and wrong *to do*. Theologian H R Niebuhr
writes that:

> Because suffering is the exhibition of the presence in our existence of
> that which is not under our control, or of the intrusion into our self-
> legislating existence of an activity operating under another law than
> ours, it cannot be brought adequately within spheres of teleological or
> deontological [obligation based] ethics. Yet it is in response to

suffering that many and perhaps all [persons] . . . define themselves, take on character, develop their ethos.[13]

We do define ourselves in suffering both as individuals and as participants in the shared human condition. It is in suffering that we experience our utter *creatureliness* which Schillebeeckx defines as an experience of ourselves, others, and the world in which we feel as a norm something which transcends at least our arbitrary control of ourselves.[14] It is in suffering that we experience an embodied self-understanding. Miles notes that the consanguinity of human beings depends upon mutual recognition of the common bond of a sentient body, whose most vivid experiences create consciousness.[15] It is in suffering that we sense profoundly that our afflictedness at once is both intensely private and isolative, and yet held in common with all humanity. Our creatureliness, our lack of control, our consanguinity, our individuality and our co-humanity confront us in suffering. Suffering is the central question of medicine, of practical theology, and of our lives. All life stops with suffering, whether it be suffering of our own making, suffering that befalls us, or suffering that we as the social system induce. It strikes at the very marrow of the soul and flays and scourges it. It strikes where it will. Suffering is not ours to control in the sense of its random intrusion into our lives. It is ours to control in terms of how we respond to it individually and collectively.

THE NEGLECT OF SUFFERING

In general, we have neglected suffering through the avoidance techniques of medicalization, isolation, flawed symptom control, platitudes and evasion, or theologization. We medicalize suffering as the cartoon 'condemned to life' so forcefully asserts. We isolate it by placing it in the room farthest from the nursing station, or in our declining visits to those in our church life who are afflicted with protracted suffering or who do not 'suffer gracefully'. We neglect it by failing to provide adequate symptom control.[16] We neglect it by platitudes and evasion. In writing of her critical injuries in a motor vehicle collision, Madeline L'Engle speaks of her darkness, pain, and of a clergyman's evasion of her suffering.

> The next two weeks were as dark as any I have known. My body had taken a terrible battering . . . I lay in the Intensive Care Unit wrapped in pain and thought, Lord, if I'm going to die, that's all right. But please let me die. If I'm going to live, help me.
> Deborah, who was to have been my [host] for the week of lectures that I was missing, came to see me in ICU and reported later that I was so plugged into all kinds of tubes that I was barely visible. I said

to her, 'I've been lying here asking what the meaning of all this can
be.'

Deborah said, 'When you're well enough to leave the hospital, of
course you'll come to me.' And with that great kindness she left.

I had one other visitor in ICU, a clergyman who was a friend of a
friend of mine in New York. He came in, big and rather loud, wearing
a clerical collar. He beamed at me and said, 'Now if there's anything I
can do for you, anything at all, just call me.' And left. No prayer. No
assurance that he was with me, or that God was with me. 'Just call
me.' How on earth was I going to be able to call anybody?

I was far from home, far from friends. At that point I was so ill that
all I could do when I was awake was to keep on breathing. And
breathing hurt . . .[17]

We also neglect suffering by ready theologizing, as in the case of
Job's friends. Their theology was really rather exquisite, yet most
certainly wrong for their friend Job.

It is, of course, understandable that we neglect and avoid
suffering. Hauerwas has written that

> it is useful to reflect on our reaction to someone suffering: suffering
> makes the other a stranger and our first reaction is to be repelled.
> Suffering makes people's otherness stand out in strong relief. . . .[18]

Instead of coming to terms with who we are and the meaning of
suffering, we have allowed it to repel us. We try safely to remove
suffering from our awareness, not infrequently by removing the
sufferer from our awareness. Yet, as Hauerwas again writes,

> It is a burden for those who care for the suffering to know how to
> teach the suffering that they are not thereby excluded from the human
> community. In this sense medicine's primary role is to bind the
> suffering and the nonsuffering into the same community.[19]

The task before us, then, is to 'bind the suffering and the
nonsuffering into the same community'. In the light of all this, if
we have not adequately addressed suffering in clinical practice or
through bioethics, how then ought we to face suffering?

BINDING OURSELVES TO THOSE WHO SUFFER

The answer resides not in the ethics or practice of doing, but in an
ethics and practice of *being*, specifically in being present to, with and
for the one who suffers. The answer is not in the mastery of
suffering, as we have attempted with our medicine and its technology. The answer is not in avoidance of suffering, as we have
attempted with our bioethics. The answer is not in solving the
problem of suffering, as we have attempted in our theology. Rather,
the answer is in facing the experience of suffering. Here, we return to

Job. In one sudden calamitous period of time, Job is afflicted with boils from the soles of his feet to the top of his head; has his crops, cattle and flocks destroyed; sees his seven sons and three daughters killed; and is left with a nagging wife. In response, he says,

> . . . I am allotted months of emptiness, and nights of misery are apportioned to me. . . . My flesh is clothed with worms and dirt; My skin hardens, then breaks out again. My days are swifter than a weaver's shuttle, and come to end without hope. . . . Therefore I will not restrain my mouth; I will speak in the anguish of my spirit; I will complain in the bitterness of my soul.[20]

He does not restrain his mouth; he speaks in the anguish of his spirit; he complains in the bitterness of his soul. He does the very things that cause most of us to be repelled and to flee the sufferer. Initially, however, before Job's friends begin to 'do theology,' they respond to his suffering more immediately.

> Now when Job's three friends heard of all these troubles that had come upon him, each one of them set out from his home. . . . They met together to go and console and comfort him. When they saw him from a distance, they did not recognize him, and they raised their voices and wept aloud; they tore their robes and threw dust in the air upon their heads. They sat down with him on the ground seven days and seven nights, and no one spoke a word to him, for they saw that his suffering was very great.[21]

Job's friends came to *be with* Job, not to *do* to or for Job. Before they devolved into theologizing, they addressed Job's experience of suffering by being, being present to Job in a healing stillness.

How then, more specifically, are we to *be* in the presence of suffering? There are at least three aspects to truly facing suffering. They are to be present to, with and for the sufferer, that is, (a) to reclaim the tragic vision of life, (b) to respond in intimacy, and (c) to become communities of *shalom*.

To reclaim the tragic vision of life is to reclaim our understanding that suffering and death are intrinsic to life and are ultimately inescapable. Despite the cartoon 'condemned to life', eternal life exists on the *other* side of life, not here. While we must cherish life — preserve, nurture and fight for it — suffering is not ours to master and death is not a clinical failure or personal insult. To think otherwise is to confuse ourselves with God. As Brunner has written: 'there must certainly be something distinctive in man [sic] in the fact that, without being absolutely mad, he can confuse himself with God.'[22] As long as suffering is an issue of mastery and death remains an insult, suffering will continue to be neglected in clinical practice as it will remain a biting reminder of our lack of mastery and control, hence of our 'failure'. To reclaim the tragic vision of life is to come to grips with our false images of

ourselves as omnipotent, and to come to grips with the real nature
of creation and the true nature of God.

To reclaim the tragic vision of life is actually to meet those who
are suffering and, rather than fleeing, to walk into their suffering,
to help them name their own suffering, and to name my own as
well. To name the darkness is the first task of addressing suffering.
This involves naming the suffering of my life, that darkness so
unspeakable that all around me would have me remain silent, a
darkness so unspeakable that perhaps I will not even utter it to
myself. To name that darkness leads to the piercing cry of
affliction of the soul, to do that which is frighteningly unwelcome, to do what Job did when he did not restrain his mouth,
when he spoke in the anguish of his spirit and when he complained
in the bitterness of his soul. The cry of affliction is a cry of distress
that looks forward, that looks to deliverance. In his masterful
work *Praise and Lament in the Psalms*, Westermann writes that
'lamentation has no meaning in and of itself. . . . It functions as an
appeal. . . . What the lament is concerned with is not a description
of one's own sufferings or with self-pity, but with the removal of
the suffering itself. The lament appeals to the one who can remove
suffering.'[23] In the Psalms, lament is directed solely toward God
the deliverer. In our encounter with suffering, we encounter cries
directed as hope-against-hope, toward God and toward us. Hope
emerges from the cry that is given voice. When we silence
suffering and do not permit its expression we wrest from each
other both the cry and the yearning hope of deliverance. To walk
into the suffering of another, to name the darkness, to help to give
voice to the cry and its hope, and to share in the lament of another
is to be present to the one who suffers. It is the first step in facing
suffering.

The second is to mitigate the dreadful power of suffering, to
dull its edges, by being present with the person. The horror of
suffering resides its sense of abandonment or forsakenness. In all
the world, there is no more anguished cry than that of '*Eli, Eli,
lema sabachthani?*. . . My God, my God, why have you forsaken
me?' (Mt. 27:46). It is not the thorns, the whip, the nails, the
humiliation, the asphyxiation, that gives suffering its potency. It is
the abandonment. The only real response to suffering, the only
answer to the experience of suffering, is found not in doing, but in
being — in *intimacy*. Suffering calls for presence in intimacy with
God and with others, a 'solution' that flies in the face of a culture
that rewards doing, that builds quick, easy and false intimacies,
that embraces a radical individualism. Yet, it is in intimacy that we
discover that 'Even though I walk through the darkest valley, I
fear no evil; for you are with me' (Ps. 23:4a). In the dark valley,
there is no escape, no detour; the way out is *through* it, *with another*.

The third response to suffering must be that of *community*, more specifically a community of *shalom*. The World Health Organization definition of health, 'a state of complete physical, mental, and social well-being, not just the absence of disease or infirmity,' is not adequate to address the issue of suffering which is, ultimately, a spiritual concern.[24] Ultimately, health is better understood as *shalom*. Shalom is

> one of the most significant theological terms in Scripture, [having] a wide semantic range stressing various nuances of its basic meaning: totality or completeness. These nuances include fulfillment, completion, maturity, soundness, wholeness (both individual and communal), community, harmony, tranquility, security, well-being, welfare, friendship, agreement, success, and prosperity.'[25]

Shalom embraces the community *and* the individual as person-within-community, going beyond simple disease or infirmity, beyond complete biopsychosocial well-being, to totality or completeness (that may even exist in the presence of disease, infirmity, terminality, or lack of biopsychosocial well-being). Communities of *shalom* are communities of comfort, character, caring, conviction, refuge and welcome — communities in which one may be frail, or express suffering, or decline — and yet still find a place. It is to be present for the one who suffers, the ones who suffer.

GETTING THE PICTURE

Juzo Itami, the Japanese film director is harsh in his criticism of biomedicine and its technology. His is a criticism that speaks not only to the Japanese context, but to modern medicine more generally. In the interview he states that

> The priority of science has won over human beings in Japan. . . . The hospital is the place to cure people, but what happens when a person who has no hope of a cure goes into a hospital? . . . [Although] there is no hope of recovery [he will receive] treatments to extend life — by even one minute, by even one second. . . . When he enters the hospital — his character, his life, his friends — all are taken away. His existence as a human being is ignored, he goes to his death. . . . [But] facing death, you can raise the level of character by one step — as the last chance. That's the message I want to offer.[26]

There is another way to face suffering and death. Rather than a dehumanizing and undignified second-by-second prolongation of a life moving ineluctably toward death, neglecting the suffering that exists among those involved, another picture is available. There is a cross in a museum in Salzburg. Christ is nailed to the cross. Beneath his feet, the dove of the Holy Spirit flutters upright, as if to support the Lord. Behind the cross, God as the

Father reaches beneath the cross-beam, holding it, as if to support both the cross and Christ. The crux of the cross is surrounded by a Celtic-like circle, as if wrapping God and Christ together in our Lord's suffering. It is a picture of presence and intimacy in suffering. It is a picture of love within the community of the Trinity. It is a picture for us.

The Christian stake in dignity and dying is not to wrest the field of bioethics from secular theoreticians, but rather humbly to confess before God and to one another that we have failed to claim bioethics as both theology *and* ministry. We have felt safer in discussing principle-based decision making, or in posing answers to the problem of suffering, rather than in being present to and with one another in the experience of suffering. My own tradition, again in the *Confession of 1967*, says that 'life is a gift to be received with gratitude and a task to be pursued with courage'.[27] With the aid of the Holy Spirit, insofar as we walk into the suffering of another and share in the lament of the darkness, insofar as we are present to one another in intimacy, and insofar as we become communities of *shalom* — of comfort, welcome and refuge — then will we enter into the kingdom even here. Even so, come Lord Jesus.

NOTES

1. 1 Jameson, Sam, 'A Master at Mixing Comedy, Commentary,' *Los Angeles Times*, (31 May, 1993), Calendar section.

2. 'Karen Quinlan Dies After 10-Year Coma,' *Los Angeles Times*, (12 June, 1985).

3. Jonsen, Albert, 'Baby Fae Is Saved — but for What?' *Los Angeles Times*, (1 November, 1984).

4. 'It's No Longer Human Life at a Point: It's Metabolism,' *Los Angeles Times*. (11 December 1989).

5. Presbyterian Church (USA) *Confession of 1967, Book of Confessions*. (Louisville, KY: Presbyterian Church (USA), 1995).

6. Muller, Jessica and Koenig, Barbara, 'On the Boundary of Life and Death: the Definition of Dying by Medical Residents,' in M. Lock and D. Gordon (eds.), *Biomedicine Examined*. (Dordrecht: Kluwer Academic Books, 1988), pp. 368–9.

7. 3 Eliot, Thomas S. 'The Family Reunion.' *T S Eliot: The Complete Poems and Plays, 1909–1950*. (New York: Harcourt Brace Jovanovich, 1980), pp. 237–8.

8. The development of clinical bioethics has been heavily influenced by the work of Tom Beauchamp and James Childress published in *Principles in Biomedical Ethics*. (1st. Ed. New York: Oxford University Press, 1979), but also propounded in their ethics institutes, courses, and other scholarly work at Georgetown University. Their book is now in its fourth edition and remains widely used, though no longer as unchallenged as it has been.

9. Fremon, Celeste, *Los Angeles Times*, (Sunday Magazine section, 27 January, 1991).

10. Tolchin, Martin, 'When Long Life is Too Much: Suicide Rises among the Elderly,' *The New York Times*, (19 July, 1989).

11. *TV Guide*, (13–19 March, 1993).

12. Brueggemann, Walter, *The Message of the Psalms*. (Minneapolis: Augsburg, 1984), p. 53.

13. Niebuhr, H R, *The Responsible Self.* (New York: Harper and Row, 1963), p. 60.

14. Schillebeeckx, E, *Christ: The Experience of Jesus as Lord*. (New York: Crossroad, 1983), p. 811.

15. Miles, Margaret, *Carnal Knowing*. (New York: Vintage Books, 1989), p. 9.

16. There is a recent body of literature that specifically addresses the under-medication of patients in pain. The reasons for such under-medication are not exclusively those of clinical incompetence or neglect, though that may exist, but also include much more complex issues. See the recent literature on pain as the metaphor for the disease and its progress.

17. L'Engle, Madeline, *The Rock that is Higher*. (Wheaton: Harold Shaw, 1992), pp. 12–13.

18. Hauerwas, Stanley, *Suffering Presence*. (Notre Dame: University of Notre Dame, 1986), p. 25.

19. Hauerwas, Stanley, *Suffering Presence*. (Notre Dame: University of Notre Dame, 1986), p. 26.

20. National Council of Churches of Christ in the United States of America, *Holy Bible: The New Revised Standard Version*. Job 7:3,5–6, 11. (New York: NCC, 1989).

21. *NRSV*, op cit., Job 2:11–13.

22. Brunner, Emil, *Man in Revolt*. (Louisville, KY: Westminster/John Knox, 1979).

23. Westermann, Claus. *Praise and Lament in the Psalms*. (Atlanta: John Knox, 1965), p. 266.

24. The World Health Organization has defined health as 'a state of complete physical, mental, and social well-being, not just the absence of disease or infirmity'. Geneva: WHO, 1946.

25. The word *shalom* is customarily translated as *peace* in English, a translation that heartily fails to reflect the extraordinary richness and complexity of the concept. Youngblood, R F 'Peace,' in Bromily, G (Ed.) *The International Standard Bible Encyclopedia*. Rev. Ed., Vol. 3. (Grand Rapids: W.B. Eerdmans, 1986), p. 732.

26. *Los Angeles Times*, op cit.

27. Presbyterian Church (USA), op cit.

[4]

Faithfulness in the Face of Death

Allen D Verhey, BD,PhD

Perhaps it is a character flaw in me, an irrational disposition to root for the underdog, a curious devotion to St Jude, that patron saint of hopeless cases and lost causes; but when something I care about becomes popular, I get a little anxious. I care about spirituality, about the human sense of a transcendent power and presence that bears down upon our lives and bears them up as well. But now that spirituality is popular, I am a little worried about it.

There can be no doubt that spirituality is popular again. A recent edition of *Books in Print* lists over twenty pages of book titles about spirituality. Yes, spirituality is popular again; and it is not surprising, for human beings are inalienably religious beings.

There is deep in human experience a sense of the divine, what Calvin called a *sensus divinitatis*, a sense of the presence and power of the One on whom we depend in our strength and in our weakness, in our living and in our dying. Human beings simply *are* religious. Spirituality is as natural to human beings as breathing. (It is perhaps little wonder that in both Hebrew and Greek the word for 'breath,' for that which gives life and animates, is also the word for 'spirit'.) Spirituality is natural to humanity, and I mean to celebrate it, but I am also suspicious of it.

I am suspicious of spirituality because we humans are not only inalienably religious, we are also quite remarkably capable of messing things up — including spirituality. I have four worries about spirituality.

I worry about the ease with which spirituality is corrupted into magic. By magic I do not mean simply sleight of hand; I mean the attempt to manipulate the divine presence and power to serve the cause of the magician. Magic recognizes mystery, but then tries to turn that mystery into a technology to solve a problem, a tool to achieve what we already want, whether a fortune or fourteen more healthy years. Prayer, for example, is sometimes corrupted into a technology of last resort. Then God is reduced to a divine 'scalpel in the sky',[1] a heavenly pharmacopeia, magically manipu-

56

lated to rescue us from dangers beyond the reach of more mundane technologies.

Authentic prayer and authentic spirituality are attentive to God and to the cause of God. They make us instruments of God and of God's cause; they do not make the divine presence and power a tool for us. I mean to celebrate spirituality in the face of death, but I worry that it is frequently and easily corrupted into magic.

My second worry about spirituality is that it is easily confused with dualism. By dualism I mean the theory or the practice that drives a wedge between body and spirit. Dualism divides spirit (or soul or self) from the body, as if we were two things, not one whole, and as if these two things do not require each other to be or to be known. The spirit is not in the body the way a taxi driver is in a cab. The union is much more intimate than that. Dualism so compartmentalizes our lives and our care for the dying that we can treat the body as mere organism while we regard the person as disembodied spirit. It is possible, for example, for caregivers expertly to dress a patient's wound while engaging in a conversation with colleagues about their plans for the holidays. This may be to care for the wound — but not for the patient. And it is possible that, later, when the same caregiver notices that the patient seems withdrawn and anxious, he may make an effort to 'deliver' spiritual care, to 'treat' the 'spiritual' symptoms with a little dose of spirituality. I mean to celebrate spirituality, but I worry about both dualism and magic in cases like that.

My third worry is the temptation in spirituality to elitism. In the church at Corinth there were some extraordinarily spiritual persons, gifted with quite extraordinary spiritual powers. But they were elitists. They boasted about their spiritual gifts and claimed to have no need of others, even of Paul. Paul reminded them (in 1 Corinthians 12–14) that each is gifted, that each is gifted for the common good, and that the greatest spiritual gift is the most mundane and commonplace, namely, love. Spirituality can tempt us to pride, to envy, to elitism, especially when it attends to itself rather than God. But if Paul was right, then authentic spirituality has no place for any of that. Like Paul, we should celebrate spirituality, but worry a little about elitism.

My fourth worry is, to be frank, idolatry. The quite natural sense of a transcendent presence and power is always accompanied by interpretation. In one way or another we name that presence and power on which we depend in our living and in our dying. One can, I think, do worse than to name this power wrongly. One can deny these senses and the presence and power which evokes them, or one can distrust the power that bears down on us and sustains us in living and in dying. However, the interpretation we provide and the name we give to that presence and power makes a difference to the way we interpret our circumstances and the way we act in the world, even as we lie dying or stand caring for the dying.

Human spirituality is, as Calvin said, a veritable factory of idols. The Jewish tradition did not invent human spirituality; it celebrated it, but it also chastened it by a radical monotheism, 'Hear, O Israel, the Lord our God is One' (Deut. 6:4). Everywhere a good exists, human spirituality can attach to it an ultimate loyalty and extravagant expectations. The radical monotheism of the Jewish and Christian tradition chastens us with the reminder that this, too, is not God and with the admonition to relate to this not as God but as something from God.

Life, for example, is a good gift from God, but survival can become an idol for health care. Health is a good gift, but it can be a very demanding god. The relief of pain is a good gift, but in the midst of pain it is nearly impossible to resist the temptation to make it an ultimate concern, to curse God or to damn our neighbours, to do or undo anything only for the sake of relieving our pain. And technology is a great gift, but we are easily tempted to expect it to do too much, to be the faithful saviour, to rescue us from our own mortality and from our human vulnerability to suffering, to deliver us to our flourishing.

The problem, as I see it, is not whether to be spiritual. Deciding to be spiritual is, for a human being, like deciding to breathe. We can hardly live our lives — or die our deaths — or care for the dying — without some sense of dependence upon a dimly known but reliable order, without some lively sense of gratitude for the givenness (the gifts) of life and health, without some sad sense of a tragic flaw that runs though our lives and through our care, without some hopeful sense of new possibilities on the horizon, and without a keen sense of responsibility to the inscrutable power who sustains the order, gives the gifts, judges the flaw, and provides the new possibilities.[2]

The problem is how to name that power, how to interpret that presence, how to direct those senses, how to live and die and care in ways attentive to God and faithful to God, how to be spiritual without magic or dualism or elitism or idolatry.

I am a Christian, and I know of no other way to talk faithfully about the presence and power of God than as a Christian. Of course, Christians have not been immune from the dangers inherent in spirituality. We have sometimes treated prayer as a kind of magic and miracle as a technology of last resort. We have sometimes provided dualistic accounts of our lives and of our deaths. The elitists at Corinth were Christians, we should not forget. And we have too often been double-minded, confessing with our lips one God, while living our lives and facing our dying as though something else were God.

Even so, as a Christian, I dare to claim that the One who bears down on us and sustains us is not altogether unknown or unknowable. Of course, it is easy to be presumptuous here, and to claim to know too much. Even so, as a Christian, I dare to claim to know something of the presence and power of God, to know something of the Spirit, and to claim, moreover, that it is good news, also and especially in the face of death. The good news, it should be clear, is not our spirituality. The good news is the presence of the Spirit.

Attention to the Spirit can reform our spirituality and inform our conduct and character in the face of death. It can form us to faithfulness in the face of death, and it calls us to reflect the presence of the Spirit by our own presence to the dying.

It is important to begin by considering the Spirit's presence not only because of some worries about spirituality but also because of a worry about caregivers. Being a caregiver is hard work. I know that; I am married to a nurse. I know that there are days when the work load is too much, when the stress is too great, when too many patients have too many needs. There are times when there is no time, no time to care for a patient in the way nurses or other caregivers could if there were time and in the way they tell themselves they should anyway. I know caregivers sometimes go home and blame themselves for being human, that is to say, for having finite resources of time and energy and compassion. I would not add another burden to the work of those who care for the dying, and I worry that talk of a calling to be a spiritual presence to the sick and dying will be heard as talk of one more task — and a burdensome one, besides. I worry that people will object, 'It is not enough that I have to dispense medication; now I have to start dispensing God.' Well, God doesn't come in little doses; there are no convenient tablets, coated to make God easier to swallow. That is not the way it works.

My hope is that attention to the Spirit will comfort and strengthen those who care for the dying rather than burdening them, that it will encourage and empower them rather than weigh them down with yet another responsibility. It is a confident hope, for the Spirit's presence is good news. Caregivers do not have to dispense God, 'deliver' God, or make God present. The surprising and delightful thing about our lives — and about care for the dying — is that God is *already* there, already present. To focus on the Spirit is not to lessen the significance of the other two persons of the Trinity. Rather, it is to recognize that Jesus Christ himself emphasized the importance of the Spirit (Jn. 14–16, esp. 16:7), and that relatively little attention has been devoted to the place of the Spirit in bioethics.

Consider, then, the presence of the Spirit.

The Spirit was there at the beginning, of course, present at the creation, brooding on the waters of chaos and bringing to birth a cosmos. The Spirit was there at the beginning, the breath that made the mud a living creature. And then, when sin brought death and the curse in its train, the Spirit was there to renew and to bless. The Spirit was still present in the chaos of sin and death, still brooded on the waters of human tears, pledging that death would not have the last word.

The Spirit was there in the hurt, there when Israel took notice of its pain in Egypt and gave it voice, there when the psalmist took note of his suffering and cried out to God in lament, there when Jesus of Nazareth joined his voice to theirs on the cross, 'My God, my God, why?', and there when, as Paul wrote, the whole creation was groaning in travail (Rom. 8:22 — a groaning that continues). All these cried to God in the hope — against hope — that there was someone there to hear their cry.

The Spirit *was* there, hearing the cry, feeling the hurt, answering the pain with promise. The Spirit was there in the promise then, and when the promise became reality: when Israel was delivered from bondage, when the psalmist was assured he would not be abandoned, when Jesus was raised, and when — but this promise is still outstanding — the whole creation is made new, death shall be no more, neither mourning nor crying nor pain shall be anymore (Rev. 21:4), and 'our bodies' will be redeemed (Rom. 8:23). The Spirit is still present in the hurt and in the promise, and to be attentive to the Spirit still means remembrance and hope and, remembering and hoping, to struggle against the evils that threaten our embodied life and our common life.

So it was with Israel. Memory and hope formed their liturgy, their psalms, their prayers, and spilled over into all of life. In remembrance the weak were protected by law. And in hope the prophets beat against injustice with their words. It was the prophet Isaiah who said, 'The Spirit of the Lord God is upon me, because the Lord has anointed me . . . to bring good news to the oppressed, to bind up the brokenhearted . . . [and] to comfort all who mourn' (Isa. 61:1–2).

Those words were repeated by Jesus of Nazareth and fulfilled in words of blessing to the poor and works of healing to the sick. And when the powers of death and doom had done their damnedest, God raised this Jesus up and poured the Spirit out. The Spirit was there at Pentecost, coming to the disciples like fire and like wind, so that the power in their lives was a new power,

God's power, coming to all so that, unlike the scene at the tower of Babel, people understood each other and cared for each other.

The Spirit is also here today, and there tomorrow, even in the chaos of a dying patient's room, and we can be attentive to it and responsive to it, like Mary, like one humble person ready to let the word be made flesh in her, ready to rejoice in any little role by which God's intention to bless and to heal can take embodied shape. It was good news to Mary, and it is good news to us. It is good news when the humble are exalted, when the humiliated are blessed, when the sick are healed, when the dying and grieving are comforted.

Consider, then, the Spirit's presence in our care for the sick and dying.

Note first, again, that we do not create the Spirit's presence. We do not dispense the Spirit like aspirin. But with wonder and delight we may discover that the Spirit is always already present, and closer than the lashes of our eyes.

But let me add that, like the lashes of our eyes, we never see the Spirit immediately. Our experience of the Spirit, other than when the Spirit works *within* us (e.g. Romans 8:13–16), is always mediated, always reflected. In our experience of the world and of others we see reflected sometimes and experience sometimes the presence and the power of the Spirit.

The Spirit *is* always present, but not as one 'item' among several. It is not as if we could say, 'There's the patient. There's the doctor. There's the nurse. There's the chaplain. There's the chart. There's the monitor. And there, in the corner, is the Spirit.'

The Spirit *is* always present, but mediated. The Spirit is present to us in and through the presence of others, and to others in and through our presence. This is stunning and always finally surprizing — but also usually altogether mundane and ordinary.

It was surely stunning and surprizing to those in the parable (Matt. 25:31–46) who heard the Son of Man say, 'Inasmuch as you have not been kind or considerate or even moderately helpful to one of the least of these, you were not kind or considerate or helpful to me.' And it was no less surprizing to those who heard him say, 'Inasmuch as you did it to one of the least of these you did it unto me.' Absolutely stunning — but also quite mundane and ordinary, for what they did was nothing more (or less) spectacular than to give the thirsty a cup of water, to visit the sick, to care for those pressed down and crushed by hurt and harm — nothing more (or less) extraordinary than a simple act of love.

The parable provides an important reminder that the presence of God is mediated to caregivers through the patient, that each patient, in their very weakness and vulnerability, in their hurt and loneliness, presents a spiritual presence to the caregiver. We stand there sputtering and stuttering, 'Do you mean to say that that was you, Lord? That that fat old fart was you, Lord? That that irritating gomer was you, Lord? She certainly had a rough life, and she was you, even so? Do you really mean to say that that broken body was your spiritual presence, the image of God, the face of Jesus, the presence of the Spirit?' And the answer is always, 'Yes', and the answer calls for a kind of reverence in response, a relating to the patient as the patient is related to God. Why, we might even have eyes to see the dignity of one who sits in the undignified mess of their own incontinence.

Many patients, of course, have no sense of the presence of the Spirit in them, and many have no sense of the presence of the Spirit to them. Some patients feel like hell. And they sometimes think of themselves as being in hell, in that place where God is not. The presence of God has been eclipsed by their fear or by their anger, by their pain or by their loneliness. It would be good news to them, indeed, as they lie dying, if God were present, and it would, indeed, be a ministry to signal somehow the presence of God to such a patient, to reflect somehow the presence of the Spirit when God has been eclipsed.

That the Spirit *is* present is good news to caregivers, too, to those who would minister to the sick and dying, for because the Spirit is there, we can be, too. Caregivers need not anxiously substitute for an absent God. They need not accept the intolerable burden of being messiah, of making everything turn out right for each patient. The same parable of the Son of Man is enough to remind us that we are not the messiah, that if anyone is messiah, the patient is. We need not pretend to be some divine doc, or a messianic nurse, or Rev. Superchaplain. We can ask for help in our helping, help to care for a patient, and help to care for ourselves. Attentive to the presence of the Spirit, we are freed from the anxiety of needing to substitute for an absent God; we are freed for a more carefree care.[3]

The Spirit's presence is a gift, and we may and must respond to that gift with gratitude, gratitude for the patients who in their very vulnerability place one in the presence of Christ, and gratitude for opportunities great and small to reflect God's care for them — sometimes by saving their life, sometimes by easing their pain, sometimes by relieving the loneliness of their tears, sometimes simply by wiping those tears with compassion. The Spirit's presence is a reminder that we are gifted, that each caregiver is gifted — and not only with patients, but with opportunities and powers to reflect the presence of God to patients when God has been eclipsed, to make the presence of the Spirit a little less opaque to patients, to mediate in ways awesome and humble the presence and power of God, to be there with and for patients.

Gratitude is a mark of faithfulness in health care. The ideal of much health care is philanthropy; the virtue is beneficence. This is not to be despised, for it commends to the caregiver a love for humankind that issues in deeds of service. But it divides the human race — and a hospital — into two groups: the relatively self-sufficient benefactors and the needy beneficiaries. Gratitude provides a different picture — and different relations — a world, and a hospital, in which each is a recipient of gifts, in which human giving is put, as William May says, 'in the context of primordial receiving.'[4] Gratitude also commends and forms deeds of love and service, but not as a self-important conceit of philanthropy — rather, as little deeds of kindness which are no less a response to the gift of God's presence than prayers of thanksgiving themselves.

The greatest gift, of course, is the most mundane and ordinary of all, love. It is no accident that Paul told the Corinthian elitists of a 'more excellent way' (1 Cor. 12:31), of a way that signals the presence of the Spirit more elegantly and eloquently than the talk of angels, and that the way is love. It is no accident that love comes first in the list of the Spirit's fruit (Gal. 5:22–23).

The patient, remember, was in hell, was without God, it seemed. Evil was having its way; chaos, its victory; death, its triumph. Where in that hell is God? Sometimes God is in a doctor's care, in a nurse's touch, in a chaplain's word, in a friend's listening that lets a patient notice her hurt and give it voice and that shares the pain with a compassionate cry. Sometimes God is in a simple favour someone takes time to do, in a kind inquiry about a patient's children or grandchildren, but always in love and in such humble works and words of love. Everything else will pass away, but love is already the mark of God's good future (1 Cor. 13:8–13).

It is not yet that good future, of course. The power of death has not yet laid down its arms and admitted defeat. Yet, already, love hopes for that future, and hope for that future loves. The presence of the Spirit does not make liars of us. It is the Spirit of truth, after all. In the light of the cross there can be no denial of the reality of death or the terrible power it can hold over the dying and over our care for the dying. Death is real, and it is a real evil. It threatens to separate people from their own flesh, from their communities, and from God.[5]

Death threatens to separate people from their bodies. The threat is real and terrible, for human beings are embodied selves, not ghosts. They live and move and exist in the world God made as embodied selves. They walk, talk, eat, work, and play in their flesh. In their bodies they exercise control over themselves and over the world. More than that: in their bodies they discover all the wonderful variety of colour, shape, sound, scent, and texture of the creation. And most of all: their bodies are the site of the revelation of one human self to another — in a gesture or a word, in a smile or a tear, in a touch.

And the threat of death makes its power felt when the sick or dying are alienated from their own flesh. It makes its power felt in the weakness that robs the sick of the capacity to exercise responsible control of themselves and of their world. More than that: it makes its power felt when the wonderful variety of God's creation is reduced to something barren and sterile, to something dull, colourless, and tasteless, to something inhospitable and alien. Most of all, it makes its power felt in lonely dumbness, in the inability to communicate our self. Notice this, therefore: ironically, death can and sometimes does make its power felt in a hospital and in the sort of health care that is technically oriented to biological survival.

Death is real, and it is a terrifying evil, but where the Spirit is, it is not the last word. Because Jesus has been raised and the Spirit poured out, hope loves, and love hopes. The presence — and the future — of God makes its power felt, I think, not where the dying cling desperately to life nor where the dying are deliberately killed, but where dying is faced with courage and accompanied by care. Faithfulness in the face of death practises the presence of God and celebrates the first fruits of the Spirit by attention to embodied selves, by relieving pain and nurturing the strength of patients to exercise self-control and responsibility; by attention, yes, to the delights of the flesh, to the music patients like and to the flowers they love, to their environment and to their dining (no less than to their diet); and by the human touch that signals compassion.

Death threatens to separate people from their communities. The threat is real and horrible, for human beings are communal selves, not isolated individuals. Human life is a life lived with others, and death threatens separation and removal, exclusion and abandonment. Death makes its power felt when the sick or dying are removed and separated from those with whom they share a common life. It makes its power felt when their environment is inhospitable to family and friends. It makes its power felt when the disease so monopolizes attention that there is no space for the tasks of reconciliation, forgiveness, and community. It makes its power felt when the fear of being abandoned is not met by the presence of others who care. Notice this, therefore: ironically, death can and sometimes does make its power felt in a hospital and in the sort of health care that neglects a patient's community.

Death is real, and it is a terrifying evil, but where the Spirit is, it is not the last word. The presence — and the future — of God are made known and practised in care for people in their communities. The first fruits of the Spirit are celebrated by simple hospitality not only to patients but to those whom patients love and by whom they are loved, by making those visiting the sick and dying comfortable and welcome, by ministering to those who can only stand and wait. By such hospitality people care for the patient, too, and answer the threat of death with love and hope.

Death threatens people, finally, in their relationship with God. The threat is real and terrifying, for human beings are religious, in spite of the denials of secularism. Death threatens any sense that the One who bears down on us and sustains us is dependable and caring. It threatens abandonment by God and separation from God. It threatens human beings in their identity as cherished children of God. And death makes its power felt whenever the sick and dying are not assured of the presence of a loving God who cares.

Faithfulness in the face of death requires more than simply shouting a prohibition against assisted suicide; it demands something more than preaching that God is present; it calls us to mediate the presence of God, not simply to mention it, even if we can mediate it only in ways mundane and humble. Such faithfulness must not be undertaken as though God were not present to those threatened by death unless someone produces God. On the contrary, it can be and should be undertaken as a sign of a divine love which is already present and always real and as a signal of a hope which is always and already present. Faithfulness in the face of death does not pretend to have God under control. It does not presume to be able to manage and manipulate God. It does not attempt to dispense God in tidy, well-regulated doses. Rather, it recognizes and celebrates the presence of the Spirit. It practises the presence of God by being present to dying patients in ways appropriate to the presence of God to them. It exhibits a humble confidence that neither life nor death shall be able to separate us from the love of God that is revealed in Jesus Christ our Lord.

NOTES

1. William F May, *The Physician's Covenant: Images of the Healer in Medical Ethics* (Philadelphia: Westminster Press, 1983), p. 60.

2. This account of the *sensus divinitatis* is indebted to James M Gustafson, *Ethics from a Theocentric Perspective: Theology and Ethics* (Chicago: University of Chicago Press, 1981), pp. 129–136.

3. William F May, *The Physician' Covenant*, p. 60.

4. William F May, 'Images that Shape the Public Obligations of the Minister,' *Bulletin of the Park Ridge Center* 4:1 (January, 1989), pp. 20–37, p. 28.

5. See William F May, 'The Sacral Power of Death in Contemporary Experience,' in Stephen E Lammers and Allen Verhey (eds.), *On Moral Medicine: Theological Perspectives in Medical Ethics* (Grand Rapids: Eerdmans, 1987), pp. 175–184. The following paragraphs are especially indebted to pp. 181–184.

[PART II]

Pressing Challenges

Forgoing Treatment

John F Kilner, MDiv, PhD

We live in a curious time. Dying patients in the West find themselves in the midst of two dangerous cultural currents pushing in opposite directions. One patient may be subjected to overtreatment — everything possible being done to the bitter end (and it can indeed be bitter). Another patient may have the radically different experience of undertreatment — explicitly or subtly being encouraged to forgo beneficial care. It is important to examine why pressures to overtreat and undertreat are so great today. We can then consider how best to respond to these pressures.

OVERTREATMENT AND UNDERTREATMENT

Dying patients have long expressed the worry that they would be kept alive *too* long. They have read or heard reports of overtreatment and seen this scenario played out in the lives of family members or friends. Such overtreatment is attributable to many factors, including people's fascination with technology. We have it — we've made it — so we must use it. A form of idolatry is at work here.

More hidden yet more powerful is the fear of death that underlies much overtreatment. People are afraid of death because death marks the end of all that is most familiar. For those who do not believe in eternal life, life is limited to the present, material world. Death is extinction; it is annihilation. No wonder people will go to such great lengths to avoid it. But even for those who do believe in eternal life, that belief is so often a matter of doctrine alone — mere 'head knowledge'. 'Heart knowledge' is quite a different matter, for that goes beyond cognitive 'belief' to include a trusting love that casts out fear.[1] People with head knowledge alone are still subject to a fear of death that can so easily prompt desperate overtreatment.

Patients may fear death in this way and demand overtreatment as a result. But fear of death is also a major problem for many physicians and other caregivers. Where this fear is operative, the entire caregiving process can be reduced to a battle with death. This redefinition of the caregiving process may not be conscious, but it can nevertheless subtly influence the caregiver to do anything possible to avoid the defeat of death. Needless to say, if death signifies defeat and failure for the caregiver, then the caregiver is guaranteed to fail sooner or later with every patient. Something is wrong with a concept of caregiving in which it *cannot* consistently be done well. A reconceptualization of caregiving requires nothing less than a better understanding of dying itself.

While overtreatment is a significant problem in some cases, undertreatment is rapidly overtaking it as the primary end-of-life ethical concern. Consider the example of the United States. Stricter limits are being placed on how much health care people can receive. Through a variety of managed care arrangements, programme administrators increasingly restrict the ability of physicians to provide whatever care they believe their patients medically require.

The growing reliance on managed care reflects the economically-related array of problems plaguing health care in the U.S. Two of the most frequently highlighted problems involve insurance and technology.[2] Because so many millions of people are deterred from treatment due to lack of public or private health insurance, the health of a sizable number suffers.[3] Substantially increased expenditures for these people are problematic in light of constant federal deficits and tight economic conditions.

Other economic pressures behind the movement toward managed care are related to the increasing availability and expense of medical technology. To be sure, less expensive technologies sometimes replace those that are more expensive. However, huge cost increases more commonly accompany technological innovations such as organ transplants and CAT scans. They not only generate new costs but they also keep people alive longer to incur more health care costs later.

Against this economic backdrop — which includes many additional factors such as inefficiencies and waste in health care — managed care has arisen. While efforts to eliminate inefficiencies and waste are widely applauded, their limited success and limited effect even when successful have fuelled efforts to find other ways to limit health care expenditures. At a time when assisted suicide is being promoted in various private and public arenas, older, dying patients come readily to mind. 'Managed care' and 'managed death' become closely aligned.[4] Such an environment fosters a proclivity to undertreat those who are least valuable in the eyes of society. In today's utilitarian society, particularly at risk are those whose quality of life or economic productivity or both are low. These are among 'the weak' for whom those of biblical faith are charged to have special concern as a matter of justice.[5]

A CHRISTIAN ALTERNATIVE

What, then, is a suitable Christian response to the current pressures to overtreat and undertreat? There are, among others, two key types of response. First, Christians must work to counter the pressures. Second, Christians must formulate and follow an ethically sound approach to end–of–life treatment decisions — an approach shaped by Scripture rather than by current pressures. The first type of response is illustrated elsewhere in this volume. Christians and others are crafting many effective approaches to health care today in order to counter pressures to overtreat and, increasingly, pressures to undertreat. These include not only various forms of home health care but also hospice programmes,[6] innovative long–term care,[7] parish nursing programmes,[8] and caring church congregations.[9] The second type of response — developing an ethically sound approach to end–of–life treatment decisions — will be the focus of the remainder of this chapter. While forgoing treatment has received extensive attention in clinical,[10] social,[11] and even religious[12] settings, there is a more specific need to consider when it is biblically acceptable to forgo treatment.

Why be concerned about the Bible? If we want to get to the heart of a Christian perspective, we have to look beyond secular and broadly 'religious' discussions, and even beyond the teachings that separate the various Christian traditions and denominations, and look to the ethical source that has nourished and guided the church throughout its existence: the Bible. To be sure, there is a risk here. Many bioethical issues and end–of–life technologies are not explicitly discussed in the Bible. But the Bible is not intended to be an answer book for every dilemma that we may encounter. Life is too rich and varied for any book to contain specific counsel for every possible situation. The Bible offers something much better: a way of thinking. In fact, it is a way of thinking rooted in a way of being. It addresses the big questions of life — how we are to view people, how we are to understand death, etc. It is answers to such basic questions that will help us to formulate a perspective on forgoing treatment.

Before formulating such a perspective, however, it is necessary to clarify some key terms. The categories we adopt shape our thinking. Slipping unknowingly into unbiblical positions is all too easy if we uncritically adopt at the outset the common secular categories that govern most discussions of end–of–life treatment.

For example, ethical surveys of end-of-life treatment may adopt the general heading of 'euthanasia.' Euthanasia is then divided into various types, typically 'voluntary' vs. 'involuntary' and 'passive' vs. 'active.' The ethical task, then, becomes to determine which types of euthanasia are acceptable and which are not.

The problem here is that this approach hides rather than clarifies the important ethical distinctions. It identifies merely descriptive categories, not normative ethical ones. Consider each of the pairs of categories just cited, beginning with the voluntary/involuntary distinction. This distinction addresses only whether or not a patient is conscious, competent, and thus able to participate in decision-making. It is not concerned with whether or not the patient's wishes are being followed — only with whether or not they can be expressed. Accordingly, the distinction misses the relevant ethical issue.

The passive/active distinction is also merely descriptive. It is concerned only with identifying the medical cause of death. If the medical cause of death is the disease itself, passive euthanasia is involved. In such cases, a decision is made not to attempt to forestall death by treating the patient but instead to let the disease take its fatal course. On the other hand, active euthanasia is involved if the medical cause of death is some sort of human intervention, such as a fatal injection of potassium chloride. Many people employ this distinction in order to argue that active euthanasia is abominable and passive euthanasia is allowable. But others rightly point out that people can stand by and let a terrible, avoidable event unfold — such as an unnecessary death — and hardly be ethically excused simply because they did not inflict a fatal blow. The ethics of the situation hinges on something other than the descriptive passive/active distinction.[13]

Accordingly, we must look for categories other than voluntary/involuntary and passive/active to guide ethical decisions to forgo treatment. In fact, we need a different heading altogether under which to examine such questions, for the term euthanasia itself is problematic. On its surface it might seem to be an excellent term, formed from two Greek words meaning 'good death.' However, even without the modifier 'active,' it suggests in the minds of many the intentional causing of a patient's death. As such, it does not serve well as an umbrella term for end-of-life decisions. Moreover, the term is rendered suspect by its historical association with Nazi Germany and the connotations that it still carries for many as a guise for removing 'unworthy lives' or lives too burdensome for society to suppport. Instead of employing the term euthanasia as an umbrella term, we need to specify the issues we intend to address: When is it ethically acceptable to forgo treatment? Is physician-assisted suicide ethical? Etc.

A BIBLICAL OUTLOOK

The first of these questions is our present focus, and the biblical writings do indeed prove extremely helpful in addressing it. As explained previously, though, the biblical writings do not provide an 'answer book' so much as a basic way of approaching life. While the biblical writings are diverse in many ways, there are three characteristics that consistently mark a biblical way of thinking.[14] It is God-centred, reality-bounded, and love-impelled. Each characteristic warrants explanation.

A biblical outlook is, first of all, **God-centred**. Rather than beginning with human reason (with all of its self-serving judgements and intuitions) as the basis of right and wrong, a biblical outlook begins with God. God is the source of all that exists and knows far more than we do about how people can truly flourish. In particular, Christ is the wisdom and power of God — which is distinctly different from the 'wisdom' of the world (i.e., human reasoning divorced from God (1 Cor. 1:20–24). Such a God-centred outlook sees people not merely as the product of time and chance, but in terms of their relationship to God.

The sanctity of human life is rooted, first of all, in the creation of people 'in the image of God' (Gen. 1:26–27; cf. 5:1). That people are images suggests that God is the original after whom people are patterned. It says more about who people are than it does about who are people. There is an unfortunate tendency to try to dissect the concept of the image of God into a set of defining characteristics of people, in order to have a basis for deciding which beings are 'truly human' or are 'persons' deserving the special respect (e.g., health care) reserved for persons. Such an attempt is just one of many efforts to tear apart that which God has put together. As Colossians 3:10–11 elaborates, being created and renewed in the image of God entails a negative and a positive. It involves not only a healthy scepticism of efforts to exclude the unworthy or unlovely (whether Greek, uncircumcised, barbarian, or slave) from the human community, but also the importance of living a holy, God-centred life that reflects favourably on God.[15]

Secondly, a biblical outlook may be characterized as **reality-bounded**. As the Bible reveals, there is much more to reality than meets the contemporary eye. The Bible describes many aspects of reality that have tremendous ethical significance — for example, the divine creation of the world and Christ's incarnation, death, resurrection, and return. The sanctity of human life is rooted firmly in numerous such realities.

However, using terms like sanctity, sacred, and reverence in relation to life's significance can be dangerous. Life can take the place of God and become an idol. Just as neglecting the sanctity of

human life can lead to a premature ending of it, idolizing life can
lead to useless attempts to prolong life when life is unavoidably at
an end — adding to the suffering of dying in the process. The best
way to avoid either pitfall is to understand life's particular place in
the purposes of God in creation.

Another biblical concern rooted in how people are created to be
is freedom. Biblical freedom involves the absence of various
impediments and forms of bondage, but is not merely an end in
itself. Rather, it is a means to a greater end. People are freed for
something and not merely from something. Freedom is a state of
doing as much as it is a state of being (cf. Gal. 5:1–2; Jas. 1:25).
People are freed precisely in order to be able to live a God-centred,
reality-bounded, and love-impelled life wherein lies their fulfilment (cf. 1 Pt. 2:16).

Biblical freedom, then, is radically different from the current
understanding of freedom as autonomy. Autonomy (from two
Greek words meaning 'self law') asserts that the self creates its
own moral law. Whatever the self chooses is right for the self
simply because the self chooses it. Autonomy by definition knows
no law but the self, whereas God intends that even this law be
replaced — and fulfilled — by love of God and neighbour.[16]
People are not forced by God to live a God-directed life. They are
mistaken not to do so, but God gives them the freedom to be
wrong. After all, the relationship that God desires to have with
people requires an obedience freely chosen out of love, not a
forced submission.

The third, **love-impelled** dimension of a biblical outlook is
probably the most familiar and needs the least introduction. Of all
the commandments, Jesus singles out the mandate to love as the
'greatest' (Matt. 22:34–40). Similarly, Paul calls love 'the most
excellent way' (1 Cor. 12:31) — a perspective echoed by John and
other biblical writers. People are called upon throughout the Bible
to strive to enable others to experience as much 'good' as possible.
Yet such 'love of neighbour' is actually the 'second greatest'
commandment, always understood within the context of 'loving
God' (Matt. 22). Anything called 'love of neighbour' is not
authentically so if it contradicts the God-centred, reality-bounded
perspective required by love of God.

Love of neighbour involves seeking mutuality in community.
What this means in practice is self-sacrifice, because people are
constantly prone to think of themselves more highly than is
warranted (Mk. 7:21–22; cf. Rom. 12:3,16). But the goal is
interdependent community. Accordingly, Paul commends Jesus'
self-sacrifice (Phil. 2:6–8), yet interprets its message to believers as:
'Each of you should look not only to your own interests, but also
to the interests of others' (vv. 4–5).

A God-centred, reality-bounded, and love-impelled perspective is particularly instructive with regard to end-of-life treatment decisions. It suggests that two important questions must be asked before a final ethical assessment of treatment options is possible: 'Is the patient willing?' and 'Is death intended?'

THE PATIENT'S WILLINGNESS

The first question — 'Is the patient willing?' — is important because it flows from the previously-explained biblical understanding of freedom. God has given us the freedom to make the decisions that significantly shape our lives. In fact, according to the biblical writings, even our eternal destinies are tied to the choices we make. How much more so are we responsible for decisions that affect our temporal lives. Such personal responsibility is appropriate, since the patient, more than anyone else, will bear the burden of the results of any decisions made. One might think that another person such as a physician could at least assess the quality of a patient's life and the burdensomeness of treatment with reasonable accuracy. However, much evidence suggests that this is not the case, because of the difference between the patient's and the physician's point of view.[17] Accordingly, the law in the U.S. and elsewhere has increasingly protected people's 'right' and 'responsibility' to make end-of-life treatment decisions.[18]

Biblical freedom is not autonomy, however, as explained earlier. Simply because one chooses to forgo treatment, the decision is not necessarily biblically warranted. Other considerations yet to be discussed may be relevant. Yet the willingness of patients is crucial both to ensure that unwanted harm does not come to them and to safeguard their God-given responsibility for their lives. Even an otherwise sound decision will not be completely moral if it is not in accordance with the wishes of the patient, as far as those can be ascertained.

How, then, are patients' wishes to be determined? The answer depends on whether or not patients have the mental capacity (or mental competence, to use the comparable legal term) to express them. When capacity is present, caregivers typically employ the standard of 'informed consent' to identify patients' wishes. However, there are two serious problems with informed consent: the term 'informed' and the term 'consent.'

The standard of informed consent arose as a protection against paternalistic treatment decisions made by caregivers — decisions that took the responsibility away from patients.[19] Giving the responsibility to patients would seem to be in line with biblical notions of freedom. Yet patients do not really have responsibility if they are not encouraged to make whatever decision seems best to them. Because the process is described as caregivers obtaining *consent* from patients, patients are still encouraged (at least subtly) to go along with what their caregivers have proposed. A more neutral term like 'decision-making' is needed in place of 'consent' if true freedom and responsibility are to be ensured.

The term *informed* is also problematic in that it focuses the caregiver's responsibility exclusively on providing information. This focus has led to an 'informed consent process' which encourages caregivers to see their responsibility in terms of obtaining the patient's signature on a small-type, densely-written document that specifies one particular treatment approach.

Information is necessary, but there is much more to the process than that. First, care must be taken to be certain that the patient has the mental *capacity* to make decisions. Such capacity requires that people be able to take in information, consider it in relation to their beliefs and values, and communicate a decision. Second, there must be *voluntariness*. Not only must overt forms of coercion be absent, but subtle forms of coercion — familial, financial, etc. — must also be excluded. Third, the patient does need *information*. However, the information must not just be a statement of what is going to be done but rather a description of the problem (diagnosis), the possible treatment options (including doing nothing), and a projection of likely benefits and harms attached to each option. Even if the patient receives such information, though, something more is necessary: *understanding*. People need not only the data but also an appreciation of its significance. In other words, caregivers must speak in meaningful language, avoiding medical jargon and explaining the risks of medical procedures by analogy to risks in everyday life. They must also give patients time to take in and adjust to threatening information.[20] Those who truly want to know if patients have made an 'ethical decision' (as opposed to merely giving 'informed consent') can ask patients to explain why they have reached the decisions they have and then evaluate their responses in light of the four considerations just noted.

The approach to ethical decision-making just described is fine when patients have the mental capacity to make treatment decisions. If they do not, then we must try to identify their wishes in another way. Advance directives, which are patients' own statements about how they want treatment decisions to be made for them, have the potential to be helpful here.[21] But all advance directives are not created equal.

The most familiar form is the living will — a patient's written statement identifying the circumstances under which she or he does or does not want certain treatments. Many people, including

Christians, have understandably resisted the living will as ethically problematic.[22] Some are concerned that living wills were first developed by organizations as a strategic step toward fulfilling a broad euthanasia agenda. This historical fact alone, though, should not cause one to reject living wills out of hand but rather to examine them on their merits much more carefully. Others do precisely that — scrutinize them critically — and find them to be dangerous. Because people can never anticipate all possible future scenarios, living wills can easily give permission to withhold or withdraw treatment under unique circumstances in which a person would actually want it.

For this reason, a second form of advance directive has gained favour: a durable power of attorney for health care. This document legally enables the present or future patient to indicate which person would be in the best position to make treatment decisions in accordance with the patient's wishes, if the patient ever lacked the mental capacity to do so. It is not a perfect vehicle, but it provides the best means available to ascertain the wishes and values of a patient without mental capacity. Such a person's wishes and values should still be respected because and as long as she or he remains a living human being.

If people want to put some of their wishes and values in a living will (or a living will section of a durable power of attorney for health care document), that information may prove helpful to their surrogate decision-makers. Such information can include not only concerns about avoiding over-treatment — the reason living wills arose — but also, increasingly, concerns about avoiding under-treatment. Employed in this latter way, living will provisions work directly counter to the drift toward 'euthanasia' that those concerned about advance directives fear. Nevertheless, people should explicitly state that any living-will-type information in their advance directive(s) is advisory only, and that judgements of their surrogates are final.[23] People must also communicate the existence of their advance directives to their family members and primary caregivers — an often-neglected final step that commonly renders advance directives ineffective.[24]

INTENDING LIFE

Ensuring that decisions to forgo treatment are in accordance with patients' wishes, then, is one important preliminary concern from a biblical standpoint. Because God has given people such responsibility for their lives, we must ultimately[25] accept people's decisions to forgo treatment even if we do not agree with them. But for the believer there is more to decision-making than one's personal wishes. Simply wanting something does not make it

right, for biblical freedom is not mere autonomy. A second
question must also be raised if decisions are to reflect crucial
biblical concerns: 'Is death intended?'

The relevance of this question is rooted in the biblical understanding of the significance of life discussed earlier. Life is a
precious gift of God, and death is destructive of it. People must
choose what their basic orientation will be: will they choose life or
choose death (e.g., see Deut. 30:15–20; Prov. 8:35–36; Jer. 21:8;
Matt. 7:13–14; Rom. 8:6; 1 John 3:14–15)? From the very
beginning of human history, according to Genesis 2, God has
provided the means for sustaining life (v. 16); and God warned
that death would come if people sought provision outside those
means (v. 17). People did so, and death became a part of human
experience, as described in Genesis 3. There appears to be no
attempt to limit the focus to physical or non-physical life or death,
probably because this distinction is foreign to the holistic perspective of Genesis.

The New Testament perspective is in harmony with that of
Genesis. Paul, for example, also reflects a holistic understanding
of death and its antithesis to life in his letters. As he notes, death
first came to humanity because of human disobedience, and it is an
'enemy' that will ultimately be destroyed by Christ (Rom. 5:12; 1
Cor. 15:20–26, 54–55). As other writers add, death is a tool of the
devil (Heb. 2:14) that can persist only as long as the devil does
(Heb. 2:14; Rev. 20:10–14). In the end, God will again live with
people as originally intended in Genesis 2–3, and so 'there will be
no more death' (Rev. 21:3–4).[26]

Accordingly, since death is destructive of life and an 'enemy,' it
is not to be chosen or facilitated. As in all of life (e.g., see 'The
Sermon on the Mount' in Matthew 5), not only our actions but
also the intentions behind what we do are important here. We are
not to do anything or omit anything in order to bring about death.
This does not mean that we are to fear death or desperately resist
it. To do so would be the idolatrous vitalism rejected earlier.
Rather, it means we do not choose or encourage death.

'But is not death essentially unavoidable and should we not
accept it when it comes?' one may object. 'Can it not even be a
blessing under certain circumstances?' There is a crucial difference
between 'accepting death' and 'intending death.' There are some
evils in this world that we cannot always avoid, death being but
one of them. If one is caught in a situation of poverty, for
example, it is appropriate to try to escape it. However, we are to
learn contentment in all circumstances, so that when we encounter
evils we cannot change, our peace and joy are not dependent on
circumstances being other than they are (cf. Phil. 4:12). We will
not be tempted to do evil ourselves in order to change the

circumstances (cf. Rom. 3:8) but will accept the evil if God does not provide a way to escape it. Paul himself was willing to accept death, knowing that God would bring a greater blessing to him through that evil. But he left the timing of his death in God's hands, knowing that for him intentionally to bring about death sooner than necessary would be inappropriate (Phil. 1:21–26).

In the face of serious illness, it is tempting to see death as something good rather than as an enemy, for death can provide release from suffering. But God can bring good things out of bad (e.g., see Rom. 8:28) without making the bad things themselves good. One might as well object that suffering is a good gift of God that one should sometimes foster — in that it, too, can produce good effects. Even those who recognize the good that can come from suffering, however, are not prone to advocate causing (or intending) it. They typically prefer to see the good effects of suffering as the result of God's redemptive work in the midst of something bad that is not God's fault.[27] A view of death as something bad out of which God can bring good effects is more consistent and truer to the biblical texts. It reflects a God–centred rather than a human-centred outlook. We are to accept death when we can no longer forestall it, rejoicing in the knowledge that God will bring us a greater good through it. But if circumstances give us the opportunity to continue to live, then we are not to choose (i.e., intend) death, whether that entails medically causing one's own death or fostering it by forgoing available treatment.

THE NEED FOR DISCERNMENT

At the same time, we must never focus exclusively on our own needs. The needs of others must constantly be kept in view. In certain circumstances, people can be 'life-intending' by caring more for the lives of others than for their own lives, even to the point of forgoing life-sustaining treatment. As Jesus' own decision not to resist death illustrates, it is ethically commendable to risk one's life to pursue something as important as, or more important than, that life. In a 'fallen' world, we experience conflicts between even the most significant ethical mandates. People must discern any considerations in their circumstances that may outweigh the God-centred, reality-bounded, and love-impelled mandate to sustain their own lives. One such consideration would appear to be the lives of others, though rarely do the lives of others literally depend on someone forgoing life-sustaining treatment.[28]

Wise discernment is crucial in other ways as well.[29] A person may be able to answer the two God-centred, reality-bounded questions appropriately: 'Yes, the patient is willing to forgo treatment' and 'No, death is not intended.' However, such answers do not mean that she or he should necessarily forgo treatment. The third dimension of a biblical outlook, the love-impelled dimension, remains. According to this dimension, as long as no God-given realities are violated in the process, one is to promote people's well-being as much as possible. Doing so entails not only the concern for the lives of others just discussed, but also a sensitivity to others in timing the forgoing of treatment. For example, while forgoing treatment in a particular situation might not conflict with the ethical considerations previously examined, a family member may need the patient to be available a while longer in order to resolve some relational issues or to celebrate a unique occasion. In other situations, patients may themselves prefer to continue treatment because the benefits to them of doing so outweigh the burdens.

Others, though, will reach a point at which they discern that an unavoidable dying process is at hand, and that treatment will only add suffering to the dying process. Forgoing treatment under such circumstances is generally warranted. Two types of discernment are involved here. One concerns whether or not a dying process is genuinely at hand. In one sense, all people are 'terminal cases,' but they are not dying in the sense intended here. Even those with a specific terminal illness who can live for years are not in a dying process as that term is employed here, since there is a substantial period of life remaining — whatever one thinks of the quality of that life. At some point in the deterioration of many patients, however, death becomes 'imminent'. The term is not a precise one, indicating that death is virtually certain to occur in hours, days, weeks, or perhaps even in the next few months.[30] In some cases it is not clear whether or not a patient's death is imminent in this sense. But in many other situations, with the benefit of the best available medical counsel, patients can recognize that their death is at hand. They ethically forgo treatment in such situations not because they intend death — life to a significant degree cannot continue even with treatment — but because treatment will only add suffering to dying.

Discerning whether treatment will be too burdensome is the other form of discernment that is key here. Where possible, treatment such as the use of a ventilator or kidney dialysis machine can be tried temporarily to gain a more accurate understanding of the burden. In such cases, withdrawing treatment already begun is no worse ethically than withholding it in the first place. In fact, withdrawal may even be ethically preferable when temporary treatment enables patients to make better end-of-life treatment decisions. Where a trial of treatment is not possible, patients must rely exclusively on the guidance of the Holy Spirit to direct one's 'heart, soul, mind, and strength,' through such mediums as prayer, Scripture, and the counsel of others.[31] But, then, who better to rely on under any circumstances than God, who knows all that lies ahead and loves us more than we love ourselves?

NOTES

1. See 1 John 4:13–18 for a discussion of the relationship between fear and love.

2. John F Kilner, 'Rationing and Health Care Reform', in John Kilner, Nigel Cameron, and David Schiedermayer (eds.), *Bioethics and the Future of Medicine: A Christian Appraisal* (Grand Rapids, MI: Wm B Eerdmans Publishing Co., 1995), pp. 290–301.

3. See Stephen H Long and M Susan Marquis, published in 'The Uninsured "Access Gap" and the Cost of Universal Coverage', *Health Affairs* 13 (Spring, 1994, no.2), pp. 211–20. According to this study, 21 million people in the U.S. go uninsured for more than one year; on any given day 37 million people are without coverage; at some point during the past year 57 million people have been without health insurance; and another 20 million people are underinsured. The U.S. Office of Technology Assessment documents that the lack of health insurance leads to reduced access to health care and, in turn, impaired health. See their study *Does Health Insurance Make a Difference?* (Washington, DC: U.S. Government Printing Office, 1992).

4. Daniel P Sulmasy, 'Managed Care and Managed Death', *Archives of Internal Medicine* 155 (January 23, 1995), pp. 133–36.

5. Stephen C Mott, 'The Use of the New Testament for Social Ethics', *Journal of Religious Ethics* 15 (Fall, 1987), pp. 244–45.

6. See Martha Twaddle's chapter on 'Hospice Care' in this volume.

7. See James Thobaben's chapter on 'Long-Term Care' in this volume.

8. See Norma Small's chapter on 'Parish Nursing' in this volume.

9. See Dennis Hollinger's chapter on 'Congregational Ministry' in this volume.

10. Examples in the clinical literature include the Cleveland Clinic (James P Orlowski et al., 'Forgoing Life-Supporting or Death-Prolonging Therapy: A Policy Statement,' *Cleveland Clinic Journal of Medicine* 60 [January–February, 1993], pp. 81–85] and the University of Minnesota Hospital (Kathy Faber-Langendoen and Dianne M Bartels, 'Process of Forgoing Life-Sustaining Treatment in a University Hospital: An Empirical Study,' *Critical Care Medicine* 20 [No. 5, 1992], pp. 570–77).

11. For discussions of a developing social consensus, see Lee M Sanders and Thomas A Raffin, 'The Ethics of Withholding and Withdrawing Critical Care,' *Cambridge Quarterly of Healthcare Ethics* 2 (Spring, 1993), pp. 175–184; and John M Stanley (ed.), 'The Appleton International Conference: Developing Guidelines for Decisions to Forgo Life-Prolonging Medical Treatment,' *Journal of Medical Ethics* 18-Suppl. (September, 1992), pp. S3–S22. Compare Robert M Veatch ('Forgoing Life-Sustaining Treatment: Limits to the Consensus,' Kennedy Institute of Ethics Journal 3 [March, 1993], pp. 1–19), who identifies significant areas of persistent disagreement.

12. See Kenneth L Vaux, 'Moral Education about Dying: Reflections on Twenty-Five Years,' Religious Education 85 (Fall, 1990), pp. 571–587; and James J Walter, 'Termination of Medical Treatment: The Setting of Moral Limits from Infancy to Old Age [bibliography],' *Religious Studies Review* 16 (October, 1990), pp. 302–7.

13. For a detailed philosophical analysis of this distinction and much of the key

literature addressing it, see Jeff McMahan, 'Killing, Letting Die, and Withdrawing Aid,' *Ethics* 103 (January, 1993), pp. 250–79.

14. This understanding of biblical ethics is developed at length in John F
Kilner, *Life on the Line: Ethics, Aging, Ending Patients' Lives, and Allocating Vital
Resources* (Grand Rapids, MI: Wm B Eerdmans Publishing Co., 1992), where the
three characteristics are developed inductively from the teachings of Jesus, the
letters of Paul, and a variety of other biblical materials in both testaments.

15. Further development of the 'image of God' and implications for forgoing
treatment may be found in Peter A Emmett, 'The Image of God and the Ending
of Life,' *Asbury Theological Journal* 47 (Spring, 1992), pp. 53–62. See also David
Atkinson, *The Message of Genesis 1–11* (Downers Grove, IL: InterVarsity Press,
1990), pp. 37–41, which argues that the divine image is more about relationship
than capabilities.

16. For more on autonomy, see Nigel Cameron's chapter on 'Autonomy and
the Right to Die' in this volume.

17. J Grimley Evans, 'Age and Equality', *Annals of the New York Academy of
Sciences* 530 (1988), p. 119; U.S. Congress Office of Technology Assessment,
Life-Sustaining Technologies and the Elderly, OTA-BA-306 (Washington, DC:
U.S. Government Printing Office, 1987), pp. 261–262; *National Kidney Dialysis
and Kidney Transplantation Study* (Seattle, WA: Battelle Human Affairs Research
Centers, 1986), chap. 6, pp. 25–27.

18. See Alan Meisel, 'The Legal Consensus About Foregoing Life-Sustaining
Treatment: Its Status and Its Prospects,' *Kennedy Institute of Ethics Journal* 2 (No.
4, 1992), pp. 309–45.

19. For a history of this term, see Ruth R Faden and Tom L Beauchamp, *A
History and Theory of Informed Consent* (New York: Oxford University Press,
1986).

20. See Robert D Orr, 'Awakening: Bad News and Good News,' *Journal of
Clinical Ethics* 3 (Fall, 1992), pp. 204–5.

21. For a more extended biblical justification of advance directives, see Peter L
Jaggard, 'Advance Directives: The Case for Greater Dialogue,' in John Kilner,
Nigel Cameron, and David Schiedermayer (eds.), *Bioethics and the Future of
Medicine: A Christian Appraisal* (Grand Rapids, MI: Wm B Eerdmans Publishing
Company, 1995), pp. 250–262.

22. Common concerns are discussed in Alan S Brett, 'Limitations of Listing
Specific Medical Interventions in Advance Directives,' *Journal of the American
Medical Association* 266 (No. 6, 1991), pp. 825–828.

23. Situations frequently arise that people do not anticipate, in which they
would prefer the judgement of their surrogates over the directions they have
recorded in their living will. See Ashwini Sehgal et al., 'How Strictly Do Dialysis
Patients Want their Advance Directives Followed?' *Journal of the American Medical
Association* 267 (No. 1, 1992), pp. 59–63.

24. Joan Teno et al., 'Do Formal Advance Directives Affect Resuscitation
Decisions and the Use of Resources for Seriously Ill Patients?' *Journal of Clinical
Ethics* 5 (No. 1, 1994), pp. 23–61.

25. 'Ultimate acceptance' means that we will not force treatment on people
against their wishes. It does not mean that we will refrain from trying to persuade
them to change their minds. If people are making bad choices and we care for
them, we should explain to them why we think they should decide otherwise. In
fact, patients' decisions to forgo treatments that probably would have allowed
them to live significantly longer may reflect self-judgements that their lives are
merely a burden to others and not worth living. Too readily going along with
such decisions only confirms people's worst fears. For other reasons why caution
is appropriate when people reject life-sustaining treatment, see David R Patterson
et al., 'When Life Support is Questioned Early in the Care of Patients with

Cervical-Level Quadriplegia,' *New England Journal of Medicine* 328 (February 18, 1993), pp. 506–9.

26. See also John Dunlop's chapter on 'Death and Dying' in this volume.

27. See, for example, Paul D Simmons, *Birth and Death* (Philadelphia: Westminster Press, 1983), pp. 142–144. Cf. Marsha Fowler's chapter on 'Suffering' in this volume.

28. On considering others as a requirement of justice, see Nancy S Jecker, 'Being a Burden on Others,' *Journal of Clinical Ethics* 4 (Spring, 1993), pp. 16–20. From a biblical perspective, however, personal wishes, whether selfish or other-oriented, are not definitive. Other considerations such as the significance of one's own life, as discussed previously, must be considered as well. For further discussion of this matter, see John Kilner, *Life on the Line*, pp. 145–49.

29. For more on the place of wisdom, see James Reitman's chapter on 'Wise Advocacy' in this volume.

30. For sources addressing the clinical and public viability of this term, see John Kilner, *Life on the Line*, pp. 225–26.

31. See Allen Verhey's chapter on 'Faithfulness in the Face of Death' in this volume.

[6]

Medical Futility

C Christopher Hook, MD

Beginning with the *Quinlan* court decision[1] and continuing through *Cruzan*,[2] it has been well-established in the United States that competent patients and/or their surrogates may refuse any and all medical treatments. Does this right of control over the interventions done to one's body translate into a right to demand treatment as well, even if the caregivers believe the treatment is a waste of time or futile? Or do caregivers have the right unilaterally to refuse treatment that is deemed to be futile? This essay will examine this growing debate beginning with its origins. Following that, the difficulties involved in trying to define medical futility will be considered, including the question of who is to define it, and the contribution of Christian faith to the debate.

Two judicial cases serve well as an introduction to the concept of medical futility. The first involved an 86-year-old retired teacher named Helga Wanglie.[3] Mrs Wanglie was admitted to the Hennepin County Medical Center in Minneapolis in December 1989 with a hip fracture. With a history of chronic bronchitis, she developed a postoperative pneumonia that progressed to respiratory failure after the fracture repair. The patient was intubated and placed on a respirator. Because of her underlying lung disease she could not be weaned from the ventilator. The following May Mrs Wanglie experienced a cardiac arrest from which she was resuscitated but never again regained consciousness. Later her physicians declared her to be in a persistent vegetative state. Because she was not able to weaned from the ventilator, and because there seemed to be no hope for her recovery from the vegetative state, her physicians recommended that the ventilator be discontinued. At the very least, they maintained, she should not be resuscitated if she again had a cardiac arrest.

Mr Wanglie, a retired lawyer, was her guardian and had her power of attorney for health care. He stated that the physicians should not play God, and that it was not in Mrs Wanglie's best interest to be dead. He and Mrs Wanglie's children insistently reiterated the fact that Mrs Wanglie had always implored them never to give up on her and to continue to provide ongoing support regardless of her 'quality of life'. They articulated this in the context of their deeply held religious convictions.

In February 1991 the hospital went to court to impeach Mr Wanglie as guardian. Hospital representatives did not appeal to the court for permission to discontinue the ventilator on the basis of 'futility', but rather because they believed the intervention 'not beneficial'. They noted that the benefits of the ventilator were: 1) Healing the underlying pulmonary disease; 2) relieving suffering in terminal illness; and/or 3) enabling disabled persons to enjoy life. In their view, none of these benefits could be achieved for Mrs Wanglie because of her chronic bronchitis and her persistent vegetative state. Therefore, because continued ventilatory support was not beneficial, the hospital argued that they should not be obligated to provide it. However, the court had been asked to rule only on Mr Wanglie's capacity to serve as her surrogate. It ruled in favour of the family and the patient and rejected the hospital's request. The patient died three days later while still on the ventilator.

The second case involved an anencephalic baby girl known as Baby K.[4] Stephanie Keene was born on October 13, 1992. Prenatal testing had led to the diagnosis of anencephaly, that is, an absence of development of the cerebral cortex of the brain. Her mother refused to have the abortion offered her. She instead requested that all care be rendered for her child because she knew that God would heal her baby. Following delivery by Caesarean section, the baby was placed on a ventilator. This was done not only to abide by the mother's requests, but also to confirm the diagnosis and to allow Baby K's mother a full opportunity to understand the meaning of anencephaly.

In subsequent discussions, however, the mother refused the do-not-resuscitate status for her infant and demanded that all necessary care be rendered to keep Baby K alive. The medical staff and the hospital Institutional Ethics Committee stated that continuing to provide care for this child without a cerebral cortex was futile because the child would never experience her surroundings or achieve anything close to a fully functioning life. The infant was eventually weaned from the ventilator and transferred to a nursing home, but she required readmission to the hospital several times for respiratory difficulties. The hospital then sought judicial permission to refuse continued aggressive management for Baby K's recurrent respiratory problems. Federal Judge Claude Hilton ruled on July 1, 1993 that the hospital had a duty to provide full medical care under the Federal Rehabilitation Act of 1973, The Americans With Disabilities Act of 1990 and the Emergency Medical Treatment and Active Labor Act (EMTALA). In

December 1994 the United States Fourth Circuit Court of Appeals affirmed Judge Hilton's decision stating that EMTALA did not make an exception for anencephalic infants or anyone else. The case was appealed to the Supreme Court which denied a Writ of Certiorari, letting stand the Fourth Circuit's decision on October 3, 1994. Baby K died in April of 1995 at the age of two and a half years. Her mother contended throughout that all life was precious and that God, not doctors, and not herself, should determine her daughter's fate.

These cases raise important questions: Can caregivers unilaterally refuse to provide interventions that they believe are futile? In an age when patient autonomy has been established as the main pillar of bioethical discussion and analysis, is there significant support for the concept that caregivers can or should unilaterally deny a patient's request for life-sustaining intervention? If caregivers are not ethically required to provide all care demanded by patients or their surrogates, then what are the criteria for determining what care can be denied? And, more fundamentally, why have these questions become so pressing today? We examine this last question next.

ORIGIN OF THE FUTILITY DEBATE

The futility debate has its origins in five sources: professional integrity, personal integrity, the backlash against autonomy, economics, and diverse value systems.

1) *Professional integrity.* Some concept of futility and the necessity for caregivers to draw limits is part of the historical tradition of medicine. Hippocrates wrote in his piece, *The Art*: 'First I will define what I conceive medicine to be. In general terms, it is to do away with the sufferings of the sick, to lessen the violence of their diseases, and to refuse to treat those who are overmastered by their disease, realizing that in such cases medicine is powerless.'[5] Later he adds, 'Whenever therefore a man suffers from an ill which is too strong for the means at the disposal of medicine, he surely must not even expect that it can be overcome by medicine.' The caregiver has always had the responsibility to determine which interventions have the possibility of benefiting the patient and not offering those that do not. There is something more to being a physician than being a businessman or a technician. Judgement concerning treatment and commitment to doing good while minimizing harm are significant parts of medical ethics. Caregivers should not administer treatments that cause harm disproportionate to foreseeable benefit. Furthermore, caregivers should not fraudulently misrepresent their knowledge or skills, but rather openly and honestly discuss the limitations of treatment.

2) *Personal integrity*. Beyond the issue of professional integrity is that of individual moral integrity. Healthcare providers should not be required or forced to provide interventions that they believe are morally wrong. Many caregivers believe that performing CPR on a patient who has little or no chance of benefiting from the procedure, such as an individual with end-stage malignant disease, is committing battery. Maintaining ventilatory support and other potentially painful interventions may be seen as cruel rather than beneficial. Anyone who interacts with nurses, therapists, and physicians who have been involved in providing aggressive interventions for patients with irreversible end-stage disorders have frequently heard caregivers complain of a sickening feeling of doing violence to some of these patients. Such violence is contrary to the nature and spirit of what motivated them to become healthcare professionals in the first place. Moreover, the personal integrity of caregivers has been recognized and supported by the courts. The Supreme Judicial Court of Massachusetts stated in the Brophy case '[There is nothing in the law] which would justify compelling medical professionals . . . to take active measures which are contrary to their view of their ethical duty toward their patients.'[6] The subjective feeling that in providing the 'therapy' one is actually doing harm or wrong in these cases has been a powerful motivator in the push to define futility.

3) The *backlash against autonomy*. There is no question that some who have written on medical futility are reacting against the ascendancy of patient autonomy. They believe autonomy has run amuck. Giving caregivers the unilateral right to say no is seen as a balance to the abuse of autonomy. It has been well established in the bioethics, medical, and legal communities that patients have the right to refuse any and all interventions. This fact, however, does not grant to them or their surrogates the right to demand any treatment they desire.

4) *Economics*. Even though futility is a concept that reputedly centres only on the outcomes of interventions, the issues of economics and resource allocation inescapably enter into the debate. Lantos has argued that futility was rediscovered with the creation of prospective payment systems in the late 1980s.[7] Before the days of health insurance, the concept of futility entailed that if a treatment did not offer much hope of working, it was withheld or withdrawn. People could not afford to do something that did not work. Now, however, with the 'bottomless' coffers of health insurance, good sense has given way to unrealistic hope and 'do everything' thinking among caregivers and patients. At the same time, there is no question that caregivers are becoming more and more conscious of expenditure of effort, machinery, and monetary resources in medical interventions. Indeed, it should be the

caregiver's responsibility to be a good steward of these resources and not to squander them in fruitless or futile activities. However, we must be careful to distinguish rationing from futility. The fact that a treatment is costly does not necessarily make it futile. Embodied in these various concerns are two recognitions: that in some interventions the cost, understood in terms of money or the patient's well-being, is disproportionate to the amount of benefit derived; and that the process of treatment — not just its end points — must be taken into consideration.

5) *Diverse value systems.* Ultimately, many of the cases of 'futility' involve disagreement at the level of our deepest values. As Haavi Morreim has profoundly observed, 'This dispute about whether physicians ethically can, or ought, unilaterally to refuse to provide life support revolves around fundamentally irresolvable moral conflicts concerning our most deeply held beliefs about the value of life, especially profoundly diminished life.' She goes on to state, 'Thus the "futility debate" is itself largely futile. The fundamentally intractable nature of this dispute, in turn prompts coercion and the threat of coercion: where dispute cannot be resolved by rational argument or persuasion, then believers of one side can only prevail on dissenting others by force.'[8] In the two cases cited earlier in this essay, the patient and/or family maintained deeply held beliefs of the inestimable value of life without any qualifications. These individuals found themselves at odds with caregivers who neither held nor supported their more vitalistic set of values. It is probably safe to say that most caregivers are not vitalists but have rather come to believe that quality is an important value in assessing life. To these non-vitalists, maintaining life at all costs is not a worthwhile goal if the life cannot be restored to some degree of function other than basic physiologic activity.

Many societies are composites of individuals and groups maintaining diverse value systems — a diversity which inherently creates conflicts. This fact undermines all efforts, professional and legal, to empower caregivers to unilaterally discontinue treatment. It also makes it very difficult to create a just definition of futility that extends beyond the most narrow criteria.

THE PROBLEM OF DEFINING FUTILITY

We are thus faced with the question, 'Can we adequately and fairly define medical futility?' A good place to begin a response is the origins of the word futility itself. Futility derives from the Latin word meaning leaky, *futilis*. According to the Oxford English Dictionary, a futile action is 'leaky, hence untrustworthy, vain, failing of the desired end through intrinsic defect'. In Greek mythology the gods condemned the daughters of Danaus to carry water in leaky buckets or sieves. Regardless of their unending labours they could never achieve the commanded goal of conveying water from one place to the other. Therefore, a futile intervention is one that cannot achieve the goals of the intervention, no matter how often it is repeated. Failure may be predicted because of the inherent nature of the intervention proposed.[9]

Now, we ask, can this understanding of that which is futile be applied in the clinical sphere? The American Medical Association has skirted this question, providing limited support for the concept but leaving us with a somewhat discouraging conclusion. The 1994 Code of Medical Ethics states:

> Physicians are not ethically obligated to deliver care that, in their best professional judgment, will not have a reasonable chance of benefiting their patients. Patients should not be given treatments simply because they demand them. Denial of treatment should be justified by reliance on openly stated ethical principles and accepted standards of care, . . . not on the concept of 'futility' which cannot be meaningfully defined.[10]

There are, however, some situations where it seems very clear that a possible intervention is futile and not required. Such situations could help provide parameters for a definition of medical futility. For instance, if the proposed treatment has no pathophysiologic rationale it is, in accordance with the definition of futility, 'leaky, failing of the desired end through intrinsic defect'. For this reason we do not use cytotoxic chemotherapy for treatment of coronary artery disease. Similarly, if maximal therapy is already being employed but is failing, attempting to add other treatments is futile because they will not improve the situation. A third example would be a request to repeat interventions that have already failed. Finally, if the proposed intervention will not achieve the goals of care, then it is not a valuable undertaking.[11] It has to be clearly recognized, however, that who defines the goals of care is very important. If the patient and caregivers share the same goals it would be relatively easy for them to decide jointly when an intervention is futile. In fact, if patients and caregivers always agreed on the goals of therapy, a discussion of whether or not caregivers should be allowed to refuse interventions unilaterally would not be needed.

The above illustrations of futility, however, are limited and do not cover many of the situations in which clinicians would be tempted to use futility criteria. Probably the best known attempt to create a broader, clinical definition of futility has been proposed by Schneiderman, Jecker, and Jonsen.[12] This definition contains two parts. First is a quantitative definition stating: 'When a physician concludes that in the last 100 cases a medical treatment has been ineffective', it is, therefore, futile. Schneiderman, Jecker, and Jonsen admit that this is an arbitrary level, but believe that it is a threshold with which most would be comfortable. Yet it has not been shown that a five percent cutoff or a one in one thousand cutoff might not be more appropriate, and it is doubtful that universal acceptance of any given threshold will be achieved. Even more troubling are the situations where the odds would tell us that there is no reasonable hope, yet the outcome is positive. The basis on which aggressive treatment was continued in such situations is typically a 'gut' feeling that it was the appropriate thing to do. The clinical 'feel' is not quantifiable; and if we develop policies or establish criteria that will not allow for this element, will we not run into problems from institutions and third party payers balking at continuing interventions based upon intuitions and clinical judgements?

The second part of the Schneiderman definition adds a qualitative notion: 'When a treatment merely prolongs permanent unconsciousness or cannot end dependence on intensive medical intervention even if it has some physiologic effect on some part of the body,' the treatment may also be called futile. This is the most troublesome aspect of their definition because it is so value laden. It states that qualitative life is more important than quantitative life. While the majority of caregivers may agree with this position, the Wanglies and Baby K's mother clearly disagree — and they are not alone in their beliefs. Moreover, this definition is too ambiguous. The statement 'cannot end dependence on intensive medical intervention' is nebulous. How intensive must the intervention be? One could accurately define the intensive ventilatory support and care required to sustain the brilliant astrophysicist Stephen Hawking in his struggle with ALS as futile by this statement. We do not define his care as futile because of Dr Hawking's desire to live and continue to contribute to his science. Are we then biased because of his brilliance and his contributions? Have we not now begun to compare the value of individual lives?

There are many problems with the Schneiderman definition and with all definitions of futility. Are our data adequate to determine what is quantitatively futile? Perhaps the individual clinician may not be familiar with the depth of the medical literature or have enough personal experience to gauge appropriately the probability of outcomes. We are also faced with the problem that caregivers all determine prognosis from their own subjective assessments. Uhlmann and Pearlman have shown that caregivers undervalue the quality of life of patients.[13] Because of these subjective assessments, futility policies will be inconsistently applied. There is also a fear that futility will be used as a trump card when the major concern is actually one of resource allocation.

Applying the term futility to situations where all agree that treatment can provide no conceivable benefit to a patient (medical or otherwise) is one thing. However, attaching the term to certain types of outcomes is another. This latter approach inappropriately uses the term to shortcut what should be a more careful and complex treatment decision. The crucial importance of proportionality in making medical judgements is overlooked. One must compare the burden of the intervention with the potential benefit to be achieved. Thomas Prendergast recently gave an interesting example that illustrates this problem.[14] The situation involved a patient with small cell carcinoma of the lung who developed extensive metastases in spite of chemotherapy. Two options seemed open to his caregivers. The first was transfer to a hospice where the medical director insists on administration of a special herbal tea which he claims has therapeutic efficacy in one out of 100 patients. One patient, having followed this regimen, improved enough to leave the hospice and live at home for a year before dying. The second option was aggressive chemotherapy with autologous bone marrow rescue. One of 100 patients treated with this therapy also improved enough to live at home a year before expiring. Since the probabilities of improvement are the same and satisfy Schneiderman's one percent threshold, are both therapies equally appropriate? Most people would have no problem with attempting the herbal tea. However, many would have a great problem applying chemotherapy to this patient because of the extreme amount of discomfort that will likely be inflicted upon the patient with the chemotherapy. In fact, this treatment may even shorten the patient's life. While he is undergoing therapy he will not be able to enroll in a hospice programme where he could receive palliative care and be in homelike comfort. The relevance of financial cost in assessing the burdensomeness of his treatment must also be considered. Prendergast goes on to state that 'Futility in medicine is not exclusively about prognosis. The likelihood of success is critically important, but so is the process of care. Probability without mention to process conveys nothing about futility; it is just a number.'

WHO DEFINES FUTILITY?

One fundamental question remains unanswered in this debate. Who is responsible for defining futility: patients, caregivers, or society? Only the patient can place a value on her or his life and can individually weigh the burdens of treatment versus the potential benefits. Accordingly, some people such as Robert Veatch have argued that only patients or their surrogates can determine what is futile care.[15] This approach remains respectful of the preeminence of patient's values but does little to resolve the dilemmas created for caregivers who are asked to provide treatment that they believe is futile and wrong. An alternative would be to allow the physician or other caregivers to determine what is futile. But as we have already seen, physicians subjectively underestimate patients' quality of life, and differences between caregivers' value systems and those of their patients can work against patients' interests. Moreover, individual physicians or others may arbitrarily and inconsistently apply futility criteria at the bedside. A third approach would be to define futility by societal consensus. To some degree this approach would prevent caregivers from making arbitrary definitions. It would at least provide caregivers with some tools for responding to inappropriate demands from patients and surrogates. The difficulty with this option is that societal consensus will never be achieved. Ultimately, the majority will establish and impose their values upon minorities such as those groups possessing a vitalistic world view. Again, as Haavi Morreim has pointed out, one side is inevitably coerced in these situations.

The great tragedy of the futility issue is the way most who have written about it insist upon analyzing the problem as a division of power: the power of patient autonomy versus the power of medical knowledge and judgement. This approach fundamentally misses the real source of power in medicine. That power is in the relationship, the coming together of the afflicted and the healer, the blending of needs and goals with knowledge and skill, so that they may come to as good an outcome as possible. There can be no true healing without this relationship. The futility versus autonomy dichotomy pits caregiver against patient. Healing and caring is not a game where one side plays a trump card against the other to win. To resort to the futility card is to admit that the healing relationship has died or is at least severely impaired.

I am particularly haunted by the predicament of a 76-year-old white man who had had partial lobectomies in the past for biopsy-proven adenocarcinoma of the lung. As in multiple previous hospitalizations, he was now suffering from malignant pleural effusions and shortness of breath. Chemotherapy had been tried but the disease had progressed throughout the course of treatment. During previous hospitalizations he had been artificially ventilated until his breathing improved. Now he was admitted to the hospital for placement in the intensive care unit, where he was to have a therapeutic thoracentesis. As in the past, the patient requested full resuscitative measures should he experience a cardiopulmonary arrest, and he particularly wished to be reintubated and placed on a ventilator again as necessary. Obviously he had had enough experience to know what that involved. His expressed goal was to stay alive as long as he could. His caregivers, recognizing his very dim prognosis, believed that resuscitating or even reintubating him in the case of respiratory difficulty was futile. He was going to die very soon anyway, they reasoned, so why keep going through this same invasive and painful routine? They therefore unilaterally assigned the patient to DNR (do not resuscitate) status upon dismissal from intensive care to a regular hospital unit — in direct violation of the patient's expressed wishes. The patient was alert and very aware of his situation, and those who related this story indicated that he and his family felt betrayed and abandoned by his caregivers. The next day, the patient had a cardiopulmonary arrest and died. I ask, 'What was the good achieved here?' There is no debate that the chance of his surviving a cardiopulmonary arrest to dismissal was on average zero, most optimistically four percent. But was not performing a fifteen-minute resuscitation attempt more worthwhile than inflicting on the patient a sense of betrayal? The caregivers did not want to commit battery against this man's body, but what of the trauma to his spirit and soul?

In fairness, I can also recount equally wrenching situations of clearly irrational requests from patients that forced caregivers to attend to bodies that had essentially long since died. The caregivers' sense of wrong and outrage was appropriate. Yet, the troublesome question remains: how can we establish a policy, which will admittedly be arbitrary, to prevent circumstances like these without just as frequently, if not more so, creating situations like the one just presented where patients and families feel betrayed?

Does the Christian faith have anything to contribute to this discussion? Scripture does not compel us to value physical life above all other considerations. Such is idolatry. There is a time to be born and a time to die, as Solomon wrote in Ecclesiastes (3:2). Acknowledging that it may be time to die is compatible with respect for the sanctity of life. There is a heavy responsibility on those of us entrusted with the care of precious lives to determine when we should no longer prolong a life that God has created. I fear that we too frequently err on the side of playing God by artificially prolonging death. While we believe in a God who can perform miracles, we must also remember, with Robert Orr that, 'God is not ventilator-dependent.' We should not put God to the test, nor should we expect to coerce him into performing a miracle by our insistence on using artificial interventions (see Deut. 6:16, Matt. 4:7, Lk. 4:12).

It must also be recognized that there are many within the body of Christ who disagree with this assessment. While we may differ, all deserve respect. It is the caregiver's duty and the duty of society to protect these diverse beliefs. The debate over futility threatens to establish that there are groups in our population whose belief systems we will no longer respect and that if they differ from us we will discontinue their care. This cannot be allowed to happen.

CONCLUSION

So what can be done in response? First of all, we can help people understand that many of the demands for therapy are based upon unrealistic expectations about what medicine can achieve. Murphy et al. published a fascinating study illustrating this point.[16] After patients were educated about the realistic outcomes of cardiopulmonary resuscitation, those still wishing this intervention significantly declined in number. Caregivers are obligated to share honestly with their patients the potential outcomes of treatment in a manner that fosters understanding and communication. We must not ask 'Do you want us to bring you back to life if you die?' Or 'In the event your heart stops would you like us to restart it?' No better is the usual scare tactic, 'Do you want us to break your ribs, shock your body, burn your skin, etc.?' Honest communication without offering alternatives that only engender false hope will do much to resolve the conflicts. Because the healing relationship is key, caregivers should do everything in their means to try to come up with a mutually acceptable course of action. At the same time, however, caregivers should not be required to provide treatment that is contrary to their moral beliefs. If, therefore, a conflict cannot be resolved by further discussion or additional consultation, then transfer of the patient to another caregiver is appropriate. When transfer of care is not possible and the requested treatment is outside of accepted medical practice, the caregiver may be justified in withholding or withdrawing the treatment. If the treatment is the standard of care, as for instance cardiopulmonary resuscitation currently remains, then the caregiver should continue to abide by the patient's or surrogate's wishes. In all situations, caregivers should serve as a healing presence of love, care, and compassion. Our personal commitment to patients and their families is never futile.[17]

NOTES

1. In re Quinlan, 70 N.J. 10, 355 A.2d 647 (1976, U.S.)
2. Cruzan v Director, Missouri Department of Health 110 S.C+. 2841 (1990 U.S.)
3. Miles, Steven H. Informed Demand for 'Non-Beneficial' Medical Interventions. NEJM 325: 512–515, 1991.
4. Flannery, Ellen J. 'One Advocat's Viewpoint: Conflicts and Tension in the Baby K Case' *Journal of Law, Medicine, and Ethics*, 23: 7–12, (1995. U.S.)

5. Hippocrates, 'The Art', in *Hippocrates II. The Loeb Classic Library*. (Harvard University Press, Cambridge, Massachusetts, 1992).

6. Brophy v New England Sinai Hospital, Inc. 398 Mass. 417, 497 N.E. 2 626 (1986, U.S.)

7. Lantos, John D. 'Futility Assessments and the Doctor-Patient Relationship' *Journal of the American Geriatrics Society*, 42:868–870, (1994).

8. Morreim, E Haavi, 'Profoundly Diminished Life: The Casualties of Coercion' *Hastings Center Report*, 24:33–42, 1994.

9. Schneiderman, Lawrence J, Jecker, Nancy S, and Jonsen, Albert R. 'Medical Futility: Its Meaning and Ethical Implications' *Annals of Internal Medicine*, 112:949–954, 1990.

10. American Medical Association Council on Ethical and Judicial Affairs *Medical Ethics: Current Opinions with Annotations*, 1994 Edition. Section 2 035. (American Medical Association, 1994).

11. Lo, Bernard, 'Resolving Ethical Dilemmas: A Guide for Clinicians' Chapter 10, *Futile Interventions*. (Williams and Wilkins, Baltimore, 1995).

12. Schneiderman, Lawrence J, Jecker, and Nancy S, Jonsen, Albert R. 'Medical Futility: Its Meaning and Ethical Implications' *Annals of Internal Medicine*, 112:949–954, (1990).

13. Uhlmann, Richard F. and Pearlman, Robert A. 'Perceived Quality of Life and References for Life-Sustaining Treatment in Older Adults' *Archives of Internal Medicine*, 151:495–497, (1991).

14. Prendergast, Thomas J. 'Futility and the Common Cold: How Requests for Antibiotics Can Illuminate Care at the End of Life' *Chest*, 107–836–49, (1995).

15. Veatch, Robert M. 'Why Physicians Cannot Determine if Care is Futile' *Journal of the American Geriatrics Society*, 42:871–874, (1994).

16. Murphy, Donald J, Burrows, David, Santilli, Sara, Kemp, Anne W, Tenner, Scott, Kreling, Barbara, and Teno, Joan. 'The Influence of the Probability of Survival on Patient's Preferences Regarding Cardiopulmonary Resuscitation' *NEJM*, 330:545–549, (1994).

17. The concluding two paragraphs are a paraphrase of part of the Christian Medical and Dental Society's Statement on Medical Futility (1994), to which the author was a major contributor.

[7]

Definition of Death

B Holly Vautier, MDiv

Modern technology has compelled society to re-evaluate classical definitions of death. Now that it is possible mechanically to sustain cardiac and respiratory functions, traditional criteria for determining death no longer retain their previous meaning. New ambiguities have necessitated new definitions.

While the Danish Council of Ethics has opted to retain the classical cardiac activity standard,[1] most contemporary criteria for death involve some form of brain death determination.[2] Two major versions of brain death — whole-brain and higher-brain (neocortical) — have been proposed.

The Uniform Determination of Death Act is representative of the whole-brain definition. Based on the 1981 President's Commission Report, it has now been endorsed legislatively or judicially by forty-five states.[3] The UDDA defines death as follows:

> either (1) irreversible cessation of circulatory and respiratory functions, or (2) irreversible cessation of all functions of the entire brain, including the brain stem, is dead. A determination of death must be made in accordance with accepted medical standards.[4]

In the United Kingdom, on the other hand, official criteria for death leave room for higher-brain interpretations. The current indicators of death — irreversible unconsciousness and irreversible apnoea — are considered controversial and unacceptable by many religious groups and some physicians. Nevertheless, a person who physiologically fits this description can be declared legally dead.[5]

The choice of either the whole-brain or higher-brain definition is significant, since it involves a philosophical position as well as an empirical formulation.[6] While establishing the criterion for death is primarily a medical concern, defining death may be regarded as a philosophical task.[7] When a patient is determined to be 'dead', for example, may depend more on the observer's definition of such terms as 'person', 'human being', and 'alive' than on specific biological indications. Advocates of the whole-brain perspective tend to hold inclusive views of personhood, pointing out that what is essential to being a person varies widely both within individual societies and interculturally.[8] Alexander Capron cites

96

only one requirement for personhood — 'live birth of the product of a human conception'.[9] On the other hand, proponents of the neocortical position restrict personhood to human beings whose cognitive functioning is intact. John Lizza argues that to be a person one must be conscious and sentient.[10] Robert Veatch proposes that an individual's moral standing within the human community should end 'when it is reasonable to deduce that there has been a break-down of the link between bodily integrity and mental and social capacity'.[11] It is evident, then, that one's definition of death involves one's declaration of the meaning of 'personhood'.

ROOTS AND FRUITS

Divergent views of the meaning of personhood are not new. Origins of both the inclusive (whole-brain) and the cognitive (higher-brain) understandings of personhood are apparent in history and philosophy.

At the root of the inclusive declaration of personhood is a tradition which acknowledges the human being as a single entity having both a material body and an immaterial soul. This unified concept is evident in the Torah and the New Testament, as well as in the writings of Aristotle.[12] The Judeo-Christian perspective points to the Genesis account of creation (Gen.2:7) as indicative of this unity. Berkhof describes the twofold complex of personhood as follows:

> Every act of man is seen as an act of the whole man. It is not the soul but man that sins; it is not the body but man that dies; and it is not merely the soul, but man, body and soul, that is redeemed by Christ.[13]

In *De Anima*, Aristotle affirms the unity of body and soul.[14]

On the other hand, the roots of the cognitive declaration of personhood are evident in the writings of Plato and Descartes. Unlike Aristotle, Plato regards the body as evil — merely an impediment to the progress of the soul. Descartes retains a mind/body dualism that reduces the status of the human body to that of a disposable piece of machinery.[15] While the unified concept attributes goodness to the body, this view robs the body of all significance.

These two dissimilar traditions naturally yield fruits in keeping with their roots. The fruit of the unified concept of personhood is the acknowledgment that all human beings are persons. In traditional western society, this assumption of inclusivism has resulted in a linkage of justice and the value of human life. There has been a prevalent conviction that regardless of an individual's condition, characteristics, or merits, every human being ought to be granted equal right to and protection of one's life.[16] On the other hand, the fruit of the fragmented concept of personhood is the acknowledgment that only certain human beings qualify as persons. In current pluralistic society, this assumption of exclusivism has resulted in indifference with regard to the value of some human life. There is confusion about which categories of human beings are morally entitled to rights to and protection of their lives.[17]

THE PAST: PERILS OF NON-PERSONHOOD

In *Ethics at the Edges of Life*, Paul Ramsey warns his readers that a nation's social policy will ultimately be based on its institutional assumption of who has moral standing within the human community. He convincingly demonstrates how legal, medical, and ethical decisions intersect to determine who will (and who will not) receive legal protection and life-saving or life-sustaining medical care. The treatment one receives will be contingent on the moral ethos prevalent within the society.[18]

The prevailing moral ethos includes the value a culture places on individual human life. Where a strong Judeo-Christian ethic is evident, for example, life is regarded as a gift and a trust.[19] It is seen as an intrinsic rather than merely an instrumental good. This is why, according to Bleich, '. . . it is possible to discern a reinforcement of values in the preservation and prolongation of life even if that life appears to be bereft of value in conventional or social terms.'[20] This sense of the sanctity or dignity of all human life has been influential in maintaining traditional western prohibitions against abortion, suicide, euthanasia, and hazardous medical experimentation on human subjects.

When an ethic which endorses life for all persons is replaced by an ethic of selective personhood, people are valued on conditional terms. Those who qualify for personhood (such as healthy, competent adults) retain their valued status in society. But those who fail to qualify for personhood (fetal life, disabled infants, incompetent adults, individuals who have lost their neocortical functions, for example) lose their status as valued members of the society. When loss of personhood is equated with worthlessness, depersonalization can too easily constitute a license to kill.

The 'euthanasia' murders in Germany (1920s–1940s) were a heinous example of the result of depersonalization. This killing of an estimated 275,000 mental patients was deliberately planned and enthusiastically executed by the psychiatric elite — within the context of a technologically advanced, 'humane' medical community.[21]

The scientific rationale for these outrageous acts was the concept of 'life devoid of value'. This idea, published in the writings of

Professor Karl Binding and Doctor Alfred Hoche in 1920, served to justify the destruction of lives 'not worth living'.[22] Binding included social factors (such as the burdens 'worthless persons' place on their families) as reasons for killing.[23] Hoche used economics as a rationale for murder. He categorized 'worthless persons' according to their disabilities in order to demonstrate how much the continued existence of each group would cost society. His calculating fiscal argument included the statement that '. . . it is easy to estimate what incredible capital is withdrawn from the nation's wealth for food, clothing, and heating — for an unproductive purpose.'[24]

THE PRESENT: FAILING THE PERSONHOOD TEST

What, one may ask, do the past perils of non-personhood have to do with current America? Wildes has observed that the once-dominant moral ethos of western society is 'fundamentally broken'. Considerable controversy already exists about who has moral standing within the community.[25]

Abortion is legal. The fiction of non-personhood, as urged by Marks, has reached even beyond Roe v Wade.[26] It has extended into the special care nursery, where Drs Duff and Campbell have provided involuntary euthanasia for disabled newborns. These physicians have publicly justified allowing death as a 'management option' when 'the hope of meaningful personhood' is absent.[27] Fetal life has failed the personhood test. No legal statute has removed the Fourteenth Amendment rights of disabled infants. They have simply failed the personhood test by default.

At the opposite edge of life, Dr Jack Kevorkian has continued to resist the law and persists in 'assisted suicides'. Is he preparing the terminally ill to fail the personhood test?

Writers in American journals are proposing that the designation of 'dead' be applied to persons whose potential for cognitive functioning has ceased.[28] This idea sounds strangely similar to a British statement that a PVS patient 'can not be a person'[29] and the Danish position that loss of cognitive functioning means 'the extinction of the person'.[30] A recent article in the *Annals of Internal Medicine* carries this proposition to its practical conclusion. Halevy and Brody state:

> We feel that medical care, including artificial nutrition and hydration, can be unilaterally withdrawn from vegetative patients. Organs may be harvested from eligible donors when the standard clinical tests are satisfied.

Their rationale is economic — 'the appropriate use of social resources'.[31] PVS patients are beginning to fail the personhood test.

THE FUTURE: INCLUSIVITY OR UTILITY?

As medical technology advances, there will be an increasing temptation to depersonalize individuals and groups under the aegis of social needs. How we resolve the issue of personhood will determine when our social obligations to individuals begin and end. A social policy that reinforces the inclusive view of personhood will strive to deal justly with the distribution of limited resources; it will recognize both the intrinsic value of human life and the right of individuals to live. On the other hand, the classification of human beings as non-persons opens the door to a utilitarian ethics in which medical treatment is granted or denied on the basis of quality of life or economic criteria. Since a non-personhood policy implies that individual life is dispensable, it could also lead to the sanctioning of the procurement of donor organs from dying patients,[32] the legalization of mercy killing, and the eventuality of involuntary euthanasia. St Martin has noted that the designation of certain groups as non-persons can predispose them to death selection.[33]

As noted above, tacit legal, ethical, and medical policies have already converged to predispose Americans to accept non-personhood status for several groups within society. Ramsey has warned that 'talking about a non-personhood policy in a normless context is a way to promote its sooner actualization'.[34] Daniel Callahan, for example, has already strongly stated his intention to change social consensus to adopt 'a new policy that would refuse reimbursement' for comatose patients who are not likely to regain consciousness.[35] In our increasingly normless culture, we cannot afford to ignore the admonition of Arthur Dyck:

> If a society withdraws its defenses of its most defenseless members, the question arises whether it is in the interest of persons to enter into covenant with such a society.[36]

DEATH, PERSONHOOD, AND LIFE

There is a sobering interconnection between definitions of death, the meaning of personhood, and the value of human life. For this reason, it is vital that societies continue to endorse a single, uniform definition of death which retains the status of all human beings as persons. Any designation of non-personhood invites revisions in medical and legal standards which lead to the devaluing of human life.

There is still some uncertainty as to when the moment of death occurs.[37] Hans Jonas has observed that 'since we do not know the exact borderline between life and death, nothing less than the maximal definition of death will do'.[38] And Helmut Thielicke thoughtfully concludes:

> It is conceivable that a person who is dying may stand in a passageway where human communication has long since been left behind, but which nevertheless contains a self-consciousness different from any other which we know.[39]

Criteria for death should be based on the state of the patient and not on the need for transplantable organs or the cost of continued therapy.[40] People must not allow a combination of Cartesian thinking and increasing cost/ratio panic to legitimize society's disposing of human beings in the same way that we dispose of material objects. Barry Bostrom has insightfully stated:

> . . . law, medicine and health care should be designed to err, if at all, on the side of the preservation of life and the establishment of rational principles for the protection of the most vulnerable persons in society — those who are medically dependent and disabled.[41]

Jewish law astutely recognizes that the worth of every human being:

> . . . is the indispensable foundation of a moral society.[42] . . . One seemingly innocuous inroad into the inviolate sanctuary of human life may threaten the entire ethical structure of society.[43]

Aware of the past perils of non-personhood, alliances of German citizens are now protesting against what they see as the potential for future bioethical crimes against humanity.[44] Yet other western nations remain complacent — seemingly indifferent to the moral and ethical danger signals.

The issues of the sanctity of life and the right to live have particular relevance in the field of gerontology. America is ageing. Public policy in such areas as resource allocation, cost containment, organ transplantation, and euthanasia will directly impact the increasing population of 'oldest old' (aged 85+). On the other hand, if they are knowledgeable and motivated, older persons may have the political potential to influence public policy.

Attitudes that are merely theoretical today can become the laws, ethics, and medical practice of tomorrow. Paul Ramsey reminds us:

> Eternal vigilance is the price public conscience must pay for law that sustains and does not further erode the moral fabric of this nation.[45]

For most of America's history the 'moral fabric of this nation' has been fashioned by the Hippocratic tradition and supported by the biblical ethic of covenant. This outlook upholds the value of human life, produces the fruit of compassion, reinforces the related theological concepts of charity, mercy, and agape, and culminates in care based on need. The Mount Sinai covenant, for example, requires the Israelites to accept compassionate responsibility for widows, orphans, strangers, and the poor. In the New Testament, Jesus attributes worth to the most marginalized persons in society and equates righteousness with the provision of their care.[46] Biblical passages such as Psalm 139:14–16 and Matthew 10:29–31 speak eloquently of the uniqueness and dignity of each human being.

Indeed, 'eternal vigilance' is required in order to prevent further erosion of traditional moral foundations. The health plan proposed by U.S. President Clinton is an example of how changing attitudes toward the care of society's most vulnerable members can influence national health policy. At the core of the Health Security Act is a philosophical shift away from the ethic of giving treatment priority to seriously ill individuals and toward a policy of the greatest good for the greatest number. Instead of care based on need and motivated by covenant values and Christian virtues, the new model is care based on social utility (including quality of life criteria) and motivated by the bottom line. 'For too long,' the Act contends, 'public health funds have been sapped to pay for individual care.'[47]

As the Clinton Plan demonstrates, today's theory can all too easily become tomorrow's practice. In the United States, neocortical definitions of death may currently be only theoretical. But if higher-brain declarations become socially acceptable, increasing categories of human beings are likely to fail the personhood test. In a social climate obsessed by cost containment and captivated by utilitarian thinking, it would be tempting to depersonalize those whose care is the most expensive. Higher-brain definitions of death are compatible with exclusive views of personhood. Non-personhood policies open the door to revisions in medical and legal standards which are conducive to the further devaluing of human life.

Arthur Dyck summarizes the pivotal ethical issue as follows:

> All of us in our daily lives are confronted by arguments based on expediency, and appeals to the greatest good for the greatest number, to the most desirable results, to a new ethic, and the like. The limitations of these simple and superficially plausible modes of reasoning need to be recognized and alternatives proposed and understood. A community that fails to do this will fail properly to distinguish good and evil in thought, and also in practice.[48]

The future of medical ethics will be shaped by the way in which public policy defines death. Such definition will in turn depend on how we understand the meaning of personhood and the intrinsic value of human life.

NOTES

1. B A Rix, 'Danish Ethics Council Rejects Brain Death as the Criterion of Death', *Journal of Medical Ethics* 16 (1990), p. 5.

2. Amir Halevy and Baruch Brody, 'Brain Death: Reconciling Definitions, Criteria, and Tests', *Annals of Internal Medicine* 119 (1993) p. 519.

3. John P Lizza, 'Persons and Death: What's Metaphysically Wrong With Our Current Statutory Definition of Death?', *The Journal of Medicine and Philosophy* 18 (1993), p. 352.

4. President's Commission for the Study of Ethical Problems in Medicine and Biomedical and Behavioral Research, *Defining Death: A Report on the Medical, Legal and Ethical Issues in the Determination of Death* (Washington, DC: U.S. Govt. Printing Office, 1981).

5. John F Catherwood, 'Rosencrantz and Guildenstern are "Dead"?', *Journal of Medical Ethics* 18 (1992) p. 34.

6. Alexander M Capron and Leon R Kass 'A Statutory Definition of The Standards For Determining Human Death: An Appraisal And A Proposal', in Dennis J Horan and David Mall (eds.), *Death, Dying, And Euthanasia* (Frederick, MD: University Publications of America, 1980), p. 47.

7. Charles M Culver and Bernard Gert, *Philosophy in Medicine* (New York: Oxford University Press, 1982), p. 180.

8. President's Commission, p. 39.

9. *Ibid.*, p. 8.

10. Lizza, p. 363.

11. Robert M Veatch, *A Theory of Medical Ethics* (New York: Basic, 1981), p. 245.

12. Patrick G Derr, 'The Historical Development of The Various Concepts of Personhood', in Russell E Smith (ed.), *The Twenty-Fifth Anniversary of Vatican II: A Look Back and A Look Ahead* (Braintree, MA: The Pope John Center, 1990), p. 26.

13. Louis Berkhof, *Systematic Theology* (Grand Rapids: Eerdmans, 1939), p. 192.

14. Derr, p. 20.

15. *Ibid.*, p. 23.

16. Arthur J Dyck, *On Human Care: An Introduction to Ethics* (Nashville: Abingdon, 1977), p. 103.

17. Kevin Wildes, 'Moral Authority, Moral Standing, And Moral Controversy', *The Journal of Medicine and Philosophy* 18 (1993), p. 349.

18. Paul Ramsey, *Ethics at the Edges of Life* (New Haven: Yale University Press, 1978), preface.

19. *Ibid.*, p. 146.

20. J David Bleich, 'Life as an Intrinsic Rather Than Instrumental Good: The "Spiritual" Case against Euthanasia', *Issues In Law and Medicine* 9 (1993), p. 149.

21. Fredric Wertham, 'The Geranium In The Window: The Euthanasia Murders', in Horan and Mall (eds.), *Death, Dying, and Euthanasia*, pp. 603–607.

22. Karl Binding and Alfred Hoche, 'VERBATIM: Permitting the Destruction of Unworthy Life: Its Extent and Form', translated by Walter E Wright, *Issues in Law & Medicine* 8 (1992), p. 244.

23. *Ibid.*, p.249.

24. *Ibid.*, pp. 260–261.

25. Wildes, p. 348.

26. Ramsey, pp. 247–249.

27. Raymond S Duff and A G M Campbell, 'Moral and Ethical Dilemmas In The Special-Care Nursery', in Horan and Mall (eds.), *Death, Dying, And Euthanasia*, pp. 96–97.

28. Lizza, p. 351.
29. Raanan Gillon, 'Death', *Journal of Medical Ethics* 16 (1990), p. 4.
30. Rix, p. 6.
31. Halevy and Brody, p. 524.
32. Rix, p. 6.
33. Thomas St Martin, 'Euthanasia: The Three-In-One Issue', in Dennis J Horan and David Mall (eds.), *Death, Dying, And Euthanasia*, p. 600.
34. Ramsey, p. 249.
35. Daniel Callahan, 'Pursuing a Peaceful Death', *Hastings Center Report* 23 (1993), p. 37.
36. Dyck, p. 102.
37. Halevy and Brody, p. 519.
38. Hans Jonas, *Philosophical Essays: From Ancient Creed to Technological Man* (Englewood Cliffs, NJ: Prentice-Hall, 1974) p. 130.
39. Helmut Thielicke, *The Doctor as Judge of Who Shall Live and Who Shall Die* (Philadelphia: Fortress, 1970), p. 18.
40. David Lamb, 'Wanting It Both Ways', *Journal of Medical Ethics* 16 (1990) p. 9.
41. Barry A Bostrom, 'Euthanasia in the Netherlands: A Model for the United States?', *Issues In Law & Medicine* 4 (1989), p. 486.
42. David M Feldman and Fred Rosner (eds.), *Compendium On Medical Ethics: Jewish Moral, Ethical, and Religious Principles in Medical Practice* (New York: Federation of Jewish Philanthropies of New York 1984), p. 13.
43. *Ibid.*, p. 107.
44. Daniel Wikler and Jeremiah Barondes, 'Bioethics and Anti- Bioethics in Light of Nazi Medicine: What Must We Remember?', *Kennedy Institute of Ethics Journal* 3 (1993), p. 53.
45. Ramsey, p. 26.
46. William F May, *The Physician's Covenant* (Philadelphia: Westminster, 1983), p. 124.
47. *The President's Health Security Plan* (New York: Times Books, 1993), p. 78.
48. Dyck, p. 172.

[8]

Euthanasia and Assisted Suicide

Edmund D Pellegrino, MD

Everyone wishes for a good death — a peaceful and expeditious closing to life. Indeed, this is what the word 'euthanasia' means in its etymology. What is at issue today is not the desire for a good death but what form that ideal should take. For an increasing number of people, a good death must include the possibility — even, perhaps, the obligation — of euthanasia and assisted suicide.* For most Christians, and most followers of the monotheistic religions, deliberate and intentional hastening of death for any reason is a distortion of the ideal of a good death. It is an insult to the sovereignty of God and a failure of human stewardship over God's gift of life.

Nothing illustrates more vividly how different are the world-views of Christians and secularists than their diametrically opposed views on how to approach human suffering. For the secularist, extinction of the suffering person is a rational act of compassion. For the Christian believer, suffering is to be relieved to the extent possible within the constraints imposed by biblical teachings and Christian ethics. Between these two construals of a good death, there is a growing and increasingly divisive gap.

While secular and Christian advocates are on opposite sides of this gap, both are typically sincere and conscientious in their desire to be compassionate, beneficent, and respectful of the dignity of suffering persons. Christians must appreciate this sincerity for it imposes upon them the obligation of a response that goes beyond condemnation. That obligation has several sources. For one thing, all Christians have the obligation of evangelization in the best sense of the word, *i.e.*, to give witness in their lives and in their everyday working world to the truth as it is revealed in the Hebrew and Christian traditions. Christian charity requires that believers speak out against euthanasia and assisted suicide, the beneficence of which is illusory for individuals and disastrous for

---

* Throughout this essay, I will use the term 'euthanasia' in its loose contemporary sense as the active, direct, deliberate, and intentional killing of a human being for generally commendable ends such as the relief of pain and suffering. Assisted suicide will mean providing the means whereby a suffering person may kill himself or herself.

public policy. Many advocates of these practices have adopted a stance of tolerance, if not outright acceptance, for want of a morally serious alternative to their presumed benefits. Moreover, there is an increasing number of Christians who unfortunately interpret 'mercy killing' as consistent with Christian belief. Their testimony needs to be balanced by a more authentically Christian perspective. Finally, there is the special daily challenge for all of us, especially health professionals, to help those among us who are confronting the physical, psychological, and spiritual experiences of dying. All desperately need the sustenance of Christian teaching to help make their deaths truly 'good' deaths.

To fulfil these obligations, Christians must be able to respond to the genuine concerns for suffering and dying well that motivate those who sincerely believe that euthanasia and assisted suicide are morally sound solutions. At a minimum, Christians are obliged to respond in four ways: (1) to the persons who hold such views, (2) to the reasons they advance for holding them, (3) to the persons actually confronting the facts of suffering and death, and (4) to the debate about public policy and legalization of euthanasia and assisted suicide.

I shall examine these four responses in turn, but before doing so, at the outset, it is important to make clear the perspective from which I shall conduct my inquiry: First of all, I do not presume to provide 'the' Christian response, even though I believe the one I will espouse to be authentically Christian. I appreciate that other, equally committed Christians may place their emphases else-where. However, I do not believe, as some Christians do, that one can ever reconcile authentic Christian belief with an acceptance of euthanasia and assisted suicide, compassionate though we may wish to be to those who are suffering. I wish to appeal to all who have a Christian faith commitment, but also to those outside that tradition. I speak as someone engaged in the heart-rending and mind-challenging realities of death, dying, and suffering as a Christian physician for the last fifty years.

I will confine my remarks to responses to the challenge of a good death, but I will not attempt to provide a scriptural or theological foundation for the Christian opposition to killing. Others in this volume undertaken that task. My comments will be based on the fulsome scriptural discourse in Sections I, II, and III of Pope John Paul II's encyclical, *Evangelium Vitae*.[1]

RESPONSES TO PERSONS WHO ADVOCATE EUTHANASIA AND ASSISTED SUICIDE

Christians cannot, nor should they, avoid encounters in private and public life with those who sincerely believe that terminating the life of a person who is suffering intolerably is a morally licit, humane act dictated by human decency. But beliefs and arguments are embodied in persons; therefore, those encounters must begin with sensitivity to the persons who hold the views one opposes.

In these encounters Christians must first of all act charitably towards those who disagree with them even on such vital and fundamental issues as euthanasia and assisted suicide. We must separate opinions with which we disagree from persons who hold those opinions. Our discourse must therefore be patient, courteous, and attentive. Inflammatory prose, speech, and condemnations have no useful role. We must reserve judgements of guilt to God, who alone is the Author of justice. We should confine ourselves to the substance of the justifications invoked by the proponents of euthanasia and assisted suicide and attempt by persuasion to show how those justifications can be viewed differently and more humanely from the perspective of Christian teaching.

From a purely pragmatic and pastoral point of view there is little chance that the Christian perspective will be heard, let alone be persuasive, if Christians do not practise charity in their relationships with those who differ from them. If this is true of those who are not themselves dying, it is even more the case with those who are suffering. We must understand how desperate is their desire for relief and how they may feel abandoned by God and by people. It is difficult indeed to deflect the criticism of heartlessness when we indulge our self-righteousness in the presence of human suffering.

Christians, therefore, must stay engaged, no matter how intensive the discourse or the vehemence with which our own position may be attacked or ridiculed. Even when we think we are getting nowhere we must allow for the Holy Spirit to operate. If we stay within the bounds of charity we may well drop the seed that later grows into belief. None of us is wise enough to know how far a kind word may go in opening another person's mind to faith.

All of this becomes much more difficult when confronting the 'Christian' who sincerely believes that God 'would not want' people to suffer and believes that to hasten death by killing or assisting in suicide is an act of Christian mercy. Here, even more than with the secularist or non-believer, authenticity of belief, charitable behaviour, and understanding are paramount. Often Christians who have taken positions in favour of intentionally hastening death have deep and long-standing negative feelings and attitudes about the faith or the church to which they belong. Their attitudes about euthanasia and assisted suicide may not be alterable without an encounter with these deeper sources.

Those who favour euthanasia and assisted suicide do so for a variety of reasons. It is important to understand these reasons and deal with each reason in a manner appropriate to it.

Some are intellectually convinced that arguments against euthanasia and assisted suicide are illogical, incoherent, or inconsistent. With them the difficulties must be dealt with philosophically before the faith questions will be accepted as suitable terrain for discussion. Others will have arrived at their positions because of misunderstanding. For example, some think that euthanasia and assisted suicide are the only ways to retain control over one's dying, or more specifically to prevent overtreatment. For them, knowledge about living wills, durable power of attorney, and 'Do Not Resuscitate' orders are essential. In this category are those who are unaware of the very significant advances made in pain control in recent years. That physicians do not always use pain medication adequately or ignore advance directives is not sufficient reason to resort to the graver dangers of killing or assisting to kill.

Christians are required to respond charitably, understandingly, and courteously to those who favour intentionally hastening death. But they need not and must not, by that fact, dilute or compromise what they understand to be authentic Christian teaching. They need to engage in dialogue to be sure, but they must also realize that they are also engaged in a true dialectic. Not only are they communicating through words (dialogue — *dia* + *logos*) but in a dialectic, a critical examination of opposing viewpoints, weighing their relative merits philosophically and theologically. 'Dialectic' must not be taken here in the Hegelian sense as implying some synthesis of the opposing viewpoints.[2] On such matters as euthanasia and assisted suicide, there is little room for compromise without capitulation. The challenge is to maintain communication while respectfully presenting one's position as a Christian, even to adversaries hostile to any Christian or theological reason for opposing euthanasia and assisted suicide.

In any case, the dialogue and dialectic, if it is not broken off as futile or in pique, will require an understanding of the fundamental differences in the way the Christian perspective interprets the reasons advanced by the advocates of assisted suicide and euthanasia to support their positions. The same language will be used, and the same phenomena will be described, but their meanings and interpretation will be very different.

RESPONSES TO ARGUMENTS OF ADVOCATES OF EUTHANASIA AND ASSISTED SUICIDE

I have argued elsewhere that the logical arguments favouring euthanasia and assisted suicide are refutable on philosophical grounds alone.[3] But these philosophical arguments are largely in the nature of a rebuttal, a negative response to the justifications for euthanasia and assisted suicide. I believe those arguments against intentional killing are logically and experientially sound, but they are insufficient for an understanding of the Christian response to the challenge presented by the suffering patient. Philosophical arguments can clear the way for the fuller, richer, more human and humane response which grows out of a reflection on Christian teaching. But without that teaching, even powerful, logical arguments can be distorted and put at the service of death rather than life, as Pope John Paul II has so cogently shown in his recent encyclical, *Evangelium Vitae*.

Paradoxically, most Christians and sincere advocates of euthanasia and assisted suicide begin with the same justifications and human impulses. Both want sincerely to act from compassion for the sufferer and a desire to relieve that suffering. Both will want to preserve human freedom to choose how to confront human finitude and dying. Both will want to be compassionate, protect human dignity, and relieve pain and suffering. But the meanings and moral imperatives attached to these motives are sharply divergent when viewed in the light of Christian faith and when viewed by protagonists of euthanasia.

FREEDOM AND AUTONOMY AS JUSTIFICATION

In the last twenty-five years, in ethics generally, and medical ethics in particular, autonomy, freedom, and the supremacy of private judgement have become moral absolutes. On this view, human freedom extends to absolute mastery over one's own life, a mastery which extends to being killed or assisted in suicide so long as these are voluntary acts. This is a right, it is argued, that should be protected by law and physicians should be authorized to satisfy such requests.[4]

For the Christian, this is a distorted sense of freedom that denies life as a gift of God over which we have been given stewardship as with other good things. This kind of freedom violates the truth of God's creative act and providential purposes for each individual's life. It also assumes that the only purpose of human life is freedom from all discomfort and pursuit of each individual's notion of 'quality' of life. It denies any idea of solidarity or community in which each person's life has its special meaning regardless of how demeaned it may seem to the beholder. It accords rights only to those who are fully autonomous, putting the demented, the retarded, or the permanently comatose at serious risk.

Most of all, the secularized notion of freedom fosters a radical moral solipsism, a supreme act of pride, that denies that our lives, however difficult, may be instruments in God's hands to shape the lives of those among whom we reside. Much of our freedom resides in the extent to which we give of ourselves freely to others. The way we live and die may be the gift we are asked to give to others in ways we cannot understand. Christian freedom is not absolute. We are free to accept or reject God's purposes but not to define them in our own terms.

The supreme act of freedom is the act of sacrifice of self for another, or to yield up our freedom to God's purposes. Jesus' words, 'Father, into thy hands I commend my spirit' (Lk. 24:48–49), is Jesus' act of abandonment to the will of the Father, a paradigm of the yielding of freedom to fulfil a will larger than one's own. This is freedom firmly attached to the source of freedom and the ultimate act of freedom of which humans are capable.

THE JUSTIFICATION OF COMPASSION

The most appealing justification offered by the advocates of euthanasia and assisted suicide is that these are compassionate acts. Christians must feel a special affinity for justification by compassion. Jesus' whole life was filled with compassionate acts. Jesus' compassion was evident in his every encounter with children, with the poor, the downtrodden, the maimed, and the sick whom he cured so often. Compassion for the sick and dying is inseparable from the message of the Beatitudes, the parable of the Good Samaritan, and the example of dedicated Christian women and men of the church whose solicitude for human suffering in all its forms inspired, and continues to inspire, believers and non-believers alike.

Christians and secular humanists share a concern for the sufferings of people. Both start with what is a universal human experience — feeling and suffering something of the suffering of another person and being impelled, in consequence, to help to relieve it. Christian and secular humanists differ, however, in the moral status they assign to compassion. For the humanists, the emotion of compassion becomes a principle of justification. Simply feeling compassion warrants taking whatever measures will end suffering or satisfy the desires of the sufferer. Not to act from compassion alone is thought to be cruel and even sadistic.

For Christians, compassion has a different meaning. It is a laudable emotion and motivation, but, by itself, it is not a moral principle, a justification for whatever action appeals to a moral agent as compassionate. Compassion should accompany moral acts but it does not justify them. Compassion cannot justify intrinsically immoral acts like usurping God's sovereignty over human life. Like other emotions, compassion must always be expressed within ethical constraint.

Compassion is a virtue only if its end is a good end. We must never forget what atrocities were committed in the name of 'compassion' in Holocaust and pre-Holocaust Germany when the medical profession practiced euthanasia of those whose lives were not 'worth living,' who were 'useless eaters.'[5] It is compassion to which the Dutch medical profession and public turn to sanction euthanasia as social policy. I cite these examples not to suggest that the advocates of euthanasia and assisted suicide are driven by malicious intent, but to point to the consequences of compassion wrested from its moral and spiritual roots. Christian compassion is grounded in God's love for humans, in Christ's passion and compassion for us. Christian compassion finds its legitimate expression only in terms of that supreme example of love. Without that example to guide it, compassion may end in terror.[6]

THE MEANING OF SUFFERING

For the advocates of euthanasia and assisted suicide, suffering is an unmitigated evil without possible meaning. It compromises quality of life so that prolonging it is therefore cruel, sadistic, or masochistic. On this view, a life whose quality is not acceptable to its possessor, for whatever reason, is disposable. One needs but read the loose definitions of 'suffering' in passed and proposed legislation to legalize 'assisted death' to appreciate how all-encompassing the concept of suffering can be.[7] On such views, to escape suffering by death, self-administered or administered by someone else, is both noble and merciful. Without belief in some purpose to human life outside enjoyment of its goods and pleasures, it is difficult to resist the temptation to oblivion as the remedy.

Christianity gives meaning to suffering because it is linked to the sufferings of God Incarnate, who willingly suffered and died for our redemption. In suffering, we humans follow in his ways, the way of the Cross. Through suffering, rightly confronted, we can grow spiritually. We cannot know precisely what suffering means for ourselves or for those who witness our suffering. For the Christian, as for Job, there will be no explicit response from God to our demand to know why *we* are suffering, why *now*, or *why* people we deem more sinful are not suffering.

Suffering is a difficult conundrum even for believers.[8] Indeed, the problem of evil is perhaps more responsible than any other consideration for defections from faith and prevented conversions. There is no sign or assurance that all suffering is redemptive. Even those who feel steadfast in their faith may utter understandable but peculiar judgements when suffering strikes the 'innocent' — such things as, 'The God to whom I pray would not let this happen.' This is to say that God must fit our definition of goodness or we will disavow him. It is also to fashion God in a way to make him acceptable to us, rather than admitting that we can never know *His* ways, which are not *our* ways. God does not act within the confines of our reason, but mysteriously. It is the nature of mystery to surpass our reason.

None of this is to imply that Christians are compelled to suffer, to seek it out, or to prolong it. We have Christ's many examples of healing to show us that suffering can and should be relieved. We must take advantage of the knowledge of optimum pain management. We must also address the more complex task of suffering and its relief. This is a topic to which I shall return in Section III of this essay. Like their secular counterparts, Christians are called upon to relieve pain and suffering. But, because suffering has meaning, even though a mysterious one, Christians can offer something more than extinction to the suffering person.

LOSS OF HUMAN DIGNITY

Prominent among the justifications for tolerating or legalizing euthanasia and assisted suicide is the desire to provide a 'death with dignity'. Who would not want a dignified death for oneself and one's friends and family? The difficulty arises when we fill in the content of the notion of dignity. It is here that the Christian and secular outlooks diverge.

For the advocates of euthanasia and assisted suicide, dignity consists in retaining absolute control over one's own dying process. It means choosing death rather than a life marked by dependence on others, pain, wasting, or loss of physical powers. By choosing when, where, and how to die, a person can forestall the ravages of disease which reduce a person to a semblance of his or her former self. Thus, it is alleged that one acts independently, and even nobly, by refusing to burden others financially, emotionally, or physically by one's continued living.

There is no doubt that the realities of serious illness are humiliating and that, in the eyes of observers and in the suffering person's own eyes, he or she seems to have lost dignity. But this is *imputed*, not *true*, dignity. This kind of loss of dignity exists in the eyes of the beholders of pain, depression, wasting, anxiety, and physical dissolution perceived in a person's appearance and psychic responses. But, on the Christian view of dignity, imputed dignity is not true dignity. The true dignity of a human being resides neither in one's own estimation of oneself nor in the way in which others perceive one.

For Christians, human dignity resides in the fact that a person is a creature of God who has value simply because one is a person, and not because others attribute dignity to him or her. Human dignity, therefore, can never be lost, even when one is diminished in one's own eyes or the eyes of others, even when one is shunned because of one's appearance, incontinence, or pain. A human person is a creature for whom God chose to die. How can such a creature lose his or her God-given dignity? Human dignity, therefore, is not lost by the retarded, the demented, those in permanent vegetative states. The very term 'vegetative,' though it has physiological accuracy of a kind, is, itself, part of the demeaning process. To deny dignity to those whose sensorial states are impaired is to deny the respect owed them as persons. That road leads to the 'merciful' extirpation of all to whom we no longer impute dignity.[9]

On the Christian view, a dignified death is one in which the suffering person takes advantage of all the measures available to relieve pain and ameliorate the things that cause a loss of imputed dignity but also recognizes that his or her innate dignity remains. A dignified and humane death is one in which we participate in the mystery which is at the root of our existence as creatures. In a dignified death, we affirm ourselves as persons by giving ourselves over to God's presence even in our most despairing moments, just as Jesus did in the awful hours of Gethsemane and Golgotha. Paradoxically, the death by crucifixion was, for the Romans who crucified Jesus, the most undignified of deaths. Yet, in the way Jesus confronted crucifixion, it became the most dignified death the world has ever experienced.

To this point, I have outlined a Christian response to the persons who favour euthanasia and assisted suicide and a response to the justifications for their advocacy. I turn now to the obligations of those who reject intentional death and suicide: first, to persons suffering here and now; and, second, to the debate about public policy on those issues.

RESPONSES TO PERSONS SUFFERING HERE AND NOW

What is the affirmative, practical content of Christian teaching with respect to dying in a world in which medical technology has vastly complicated the traditional obligations of Christians to suffering and dying persons? What is required of those of us who claim to be moved by solicitude for those who are dying and reject euthanasia and assisted suicide as morally legitimate answers? How do we respond effectively, genuinely, and compassionately to persons suffering here and now? What, in effect, are the elements of a Christian, comprehensive, palliative approach for those who aim to support the sufferer, his or her family and friends, and the other health professionals attending to the sufferer?[10]

The first component is to acknowledge the genuine human dimensions of the problem of dying today. This means recognizing the power of medical technology to prolong life as well as the resulting fears of loss of control, of overuse of treatment, and of inadequate pain control that can drive even conscientious Christians to the desperate request for extinction as the only release from technology's grasp.

There is nothing in the Christian tradition that binds patients or physicians to pursue futile and excessively burdensome treatment, *i.e.*, treatment whose benefits are disproportionate to the burdens it imposes — physical, emotional, or fiscal. Patients may reach a point, therefore, in the natural history of their illnesses at which further treatment serves no beneficial purpose. The Christian view of autonomy permits refusing such disproportionate treatments directly or through a living will, durable power of attorney, or a 'do not resuscitate' order.

There is also an obligation to refrain from demanding treatment judged futile by competent medical advice. This is to accept mortality as a fact of the human condition. Preparing for death is most consistent with the Christian tradition. Indeed, we have an obligation to be prepared when the summons comes. Of course, care, pain relief, and addressing suffering are always required. Refusal or discontinuance of treatment with little or no effectiveness or benefit, therefore, does not mean abandonment. On the contrary, it enjoins and entails an obligation for more vigorous efforts at palliative care, hospice, or home support.

Comprehensive palliative care involves a carefully integrated plan of pain relief and support for the suffering person. There should be no hesitance to use analgesics and other agents optimally and in sufficient dose, even if a non-intended side-effect is to accelerate dying.[11] As others have pointed out, pain and suffering are related, but separable, phenomena.[12] Pain is a neuro-physiological response to a noxious stimulus arising in a diseased organ system. Suffering is a subjective response to the fact of pain and its meanings. But suffering also has a variety of causes other than pain, *e.g.*, feelings of guilt at being a burden to others, mental depression, alienation from the world of the healthy, fear of the process of dying, spiritual confusion, the dissolution of life plans, as well as the attitudes of care-givers, friends, or family whose fear and distaste for the sight of suffering will be perceived by the suffering person. These perceptions add to the desire to be rid even of life, to escape.

Suffering is a highly individualized and personal phenomenon, each person having a unique configuration of causes and responses. Christians who take seriously the obligation of visiting, ministering, and attending to the sick must deal with these varied and personalized causes of suffering, separate them out, and address each at its base.

Adequate treatment of suffering obviously will require a cooperative and supportive effort involving the patient, the family, and the care-givers as well as psychologists and pastoral counsellors. The details of this kind of care require fuller discussion than is possible here. A few components are selected for comment.

One aspect of particular relevance for a Christian response is need to recognize that any threatening illness, fatal or not, involves a spiritual crisis, an encounter with one's own finitude as a genuine actuality. For believers, the crisis is the crisis of reconciling illness and suffering with a good God. This is the crisis of Job to which I have already alluded. There is also the believer's confusion about what is permitted in his or her own belief system with respect to refusing or accepting treatment in the face of futility, *etc.* I am impressed how often Christians, and believers of other persuasions, are in a quandary on these issues. Non-believers face the crisis of being forced to come to closure on the question of God and salvation, *i.e.,* to take a final stand on the most important questions humans ever face.

Christian caregivers should be particularly alert to spiritual causes of suffering. They should ensure that appropriate pastoral counselling is available. Obviously, the question of spiritual need should be raised with care. But, too often, Christians and even pastoral counsellors become so enmeshed in the emotional turmoil of suffering that they may, innocently enough, neglect indirect or subtle pleas for spiritual help. After all, it is a matter of very great moment for a human being to request that life be shortened. Even those who approve of euthanasia and assisted suicide would be obliged to examine the sources for such desperation before complying. Christians can do no less.

Like all comprehensive palliative care, comprehensive palliative care devised in accordance with Christian teaching and ethics must be competent and take advantage of all extant knowledge and techniques. In addition, it can offer forms of support, and draw on spiritual resources unavailable in a purely secular hospice or other terminal care programme. This added dimension will become of greater importance as the trend toward acceptance of euthanasia and assisted suicide begins to appeal to some in the hospice movement. Although that movement's successes with the care of the terminally ill have traditionally made it resistant to the current trend toward killing, greater enthusiasm for euthanasia and assisted suicide in this sphere of activities will probably not be long in coming.

Finally, Christian physicians and nurses must take special note of the discouraging findings in the recent 'SUPPORT' report.[13,14] This report showed that, all too often, physicians ignore living wills and other advance directives, fail to get or pay attention to DNR orders, and are unaware of their patients' wishes concerning terminal care. These data are sure to be invoked as further evidence that euthanasia and assisted suicide should be made available to assure that patients are not overtreated and that their wishes are respected.

Disturbing as they are, the 'SUPPORT' data do not constitute valid reasons for legalizing euthanasia and assisted suicide. They do indicate the need for vigorous measures to assure that the legitimate and valid wishes of patients be ascertained and respected. A concerted and genuine effort to do so must surely be an obligation of all Christian physicians.

Closing life well, in conformity with Christian teachings and ethics regarding care of the sick and terminally ill, will build, therefore, on the experience already gained by practitioners of comprehensive palliative care. A Christian perspective will also provide an additional dimension of spiritual and charitable concern that should make comprehensive palliative care an even more effective and more humane alternative to current trends in the direction of euthanasia and assisted suicide.

CHRISTIANS IN THE PUBLIC DEBATE

Perhaps no aspect of the public debate about the social and legal status of euthanasia and assisted suicide is more intense or acrimonious than the extent to which Christian perspectives may be legislated. Advocates of euthanasia and assisted suicide, and some libertarian-minded Christians, object to the introduction of any religious beliefs in public or private debate. They invoke the so-called right of privacy, the right of citizens to do what they wish in their private lives provided no one is injured by their choices.

There are three errors in this argument. For one, there is no constitutional right of privacy.[15] For another, euthanasia and assisted suicide are not private acts. And, finally, euthanasia and assisted suicide are maleficent, rather than beneficent, acts.[16] However, there is a constitutional right of liberty of speech, freedom of religious expression, and the right of access to the mechanisms a democratic society affords all its members to share in fashioning the society in which they live.

Christians, therefore, cannot justly be disenfranchised because their positions on public issues may be inspired by their religious faith. They enjoy as much right as any other group of citizens in a democracy to use the democratic process to shape public opinion and policy. For many of us, a good society would not countenance euthanasia or assisted suicide, for example. These are violations of the sanctity of life imposed on the most vulnerable members of our society, those most in need of the greatest protection from the exigencies of economics or other purely utilitarian purposes.

The argument that restricting access to euthanasia and assisted suicide is an imposition of religious values on those who do not accept them is specious. Most legislation limits our freedom in some way in the interest of the common good. Furthermore, it is just as much an imposition on those who oppose liberalized killing of the terminally ill to impose the values of secularism, which is, in many ways, a substitute religion.

There is no substance, either, to the argument that if a large enough number of people want to legalize what Christians consider morally offensive, that is sufficient warrant for legalization. After all, the argument goes, those who do not agree do not have to avail themselves of the privilege. This is a species of plebescite morality. Right and wrong, good and evil, are not decided by votes, unless one subscribes to a theory of morality totally subservient to societal mores. Those who follow this reasoning fail to take account of the actuality of pathological societies — a reality obvious to any newspaper reader. The same concern applies to the simplistic notion that physicians are practising euthanasia and assisted suicide anyway, so why not make it legal and get it regulated? This approach ignores the inevitable fact of the slippery slope, the slide to ever more liberal interpretations as has occurred with the legalization of abortion and euthanasia in The Netherlands. Violence, burglary, and flaunting of traffic laws are widespread and flagrant. If this reasoning were valid, they, too, should be legalized and regulated by law.

The public duty of Christians is to engage in the public debate, observing charity towards those who disagree, persevering in dialogue and discourse from a firm grounding in biblical and traditional sources of Christian ethics, exhibiting charity in their own behaviour and private lives, and taking the ridicule, fulminations, and counterarguments with patience. We must stay within the bounds of public debate, legislative mechanisms, and judicial restraint requisite to preserve democratic society. In short, we must evangelize in the best sense of that term — to teach and be witnesses to the truth as we understand it in the Christian tradition.

If democratic processes and persuasion fail, we must still be faithful to the teaching of the gospel and still try, by legitimate means, to change societal values and attitudes. It has been suggested that we might have to tolerate setting aside a 'special sector of care where they can practice their beliefs.'[17] But I do not think we have reached that point. There is much we can still do within our rights to free speech and the exercise of our first amendment rights to change the attitudes of society. A 'special sector' of any society set aside for gross violations of human life does not appear justifiable except in a most desperate attempt to maintain civil order and peace.

CONCLUSION

Many societies today are moving rapidly toward social acceptance and legal permission in the acceleration of death by euthanasia and assisted suicide. Few things are more antithetical to Christian traditional and biblical teachings about the sovereignty of God over human life. All Christians have a duty of evangelization, of responding in authentic fashion as Christians to the direction in which our society is moving and to the forces driving it in that direction. I have suggested how this response might be addressed to (1) the persons who favour euthanasia and assisted suicide, (2) the justifications upon which they rely, (3) the persons actually facing suffering and dying, and (4) the public discourse concerning legalization.

The Christian 'response' is not just a negative denial of the reality of suffering. Traditional Christian ethics and teachings have something affirmative and invaluable to offer. With the proponents of euthanasia and assisted suicide, we share a common dedication to a good death, to ending life well. We differ in what we believe constitutes a good death. In making clear to the whole of society what Christian teaching offers in an affirmative way, we may be able to slow or reverse our society's current descent into the moral maelstrom that Pope John Paul II has recently called the 'culture of death'.[18]

NOTES

1. John Paul II, 'Evangelium Vitae,' in *Origins* 24, no. 42 (1995): 689–727.
2. Even further from the sense in which I am using the term is the Kantian use to designate that part of the critique that deals with the difficulties of applying the categories of understanding beyond the realm of phenomena. Cf. Immanuel Kant, *Critique of Pure Reason*, trans. William Kemp Smith (New York: St. Martin's Press, 1965), pp. 99–101.
3. E D Pellegrino, 'Doctors Must Not Kill,' *The Journal of Clinical Ethics* 3(2) (Summer 92):95–l02; E. D. Pellegrino, 'Beneficent Killing: The False Promise of

Euthanasia and Assisted Suicide,' forthcoming in a book edited by Linda Emanuel to be published by Harvard University Press in 1996.

4. Derek Humphrey, *Final Exit* (Secaucus, NJ: Hemlock Society, 1991): Jack Kevorkian, *Prescription Medicine: The Goodness of Planned Death* (Buffalo, NY: Prometheus Books, 1991); Timothy E Quill, *Death and Dignity* (New York: W W Norton, 1993).

5. K Binding and A Hoche, 'Permitting the Destruction of Unworthy Life,' trans. W E Uright, P G Derr, and R Salomn, *Issues in Law and Medicine* Fall 1992; 8:231–65.

6. Robert Jay Lifton, *The Nazi Doctors* (New York: Basic Books, 1986); A Caplan, *When Medicine Went Mad* (Totowa, NJ: Humana Press, 1992); Hugh Gallagher, *By Trust Betrayed* (Arlington, Virginia: Vandamere Press, 1995).

7. Cf. *Oregon Death with Dignity Act*, Oregon Ballot Measure 16, passed November 8, 1994.

8. C S Lewis, *A Grief Observed* (New York: Seabury, 1961); C S Lewis, *The Problem of Pain* (New York: MacMillan, 1970); M C D'Arcy, *The Pain of this World and the Providence of God* (London: Longmans Green, 1952); P Wolff, *May I Hate God?* (New York: Paulist Press, 1978).

9. Cf. Binding and Hoche, 'Permitting the Destruction of Unworthy Life,' *op. cit.*; Lifton, *The Nazi Doctors, op. cit.*; Caplan, *When Medicine Went Mad, op. cit.*; Gallagher, *By Trust Betrayed, op. cit.*

10. James F Bresnahan, 'The Catholic Art of Dying,' *America* (November 4, 1995), pp. 2–16.

11. Pope Pius XII, 'Address to an International Group of Physicians III,' February 24, 1957.

12. Eric Cassell, *The Nature of Suffering* (New York: Oxford University Press, 1991).

13. SUPPORT, 'A Controlled Trial to Improve Care of Seriously Ill, Hospitalized Patients: The Study to Understand Prognosis and Preferences to Outcomes and Risks of Treatment (SUPPORT),' *Journal of the American Medical Association* (November 22/29, 1995) 274(20):1591–1598.

14. Bernard Lo, 'Improving Care Near the End of Life, Why is It so Hard?' *Journal of the American Medical Association* (November 22/29, 1995) 274(20):1634–36.

15. Cf. *Furman v. Georgia*, 408, U.S.238, 286 (1972); *Compassion in Dying v. Washington*, 1995 WL 94679 at 4.

16. Pellegrino, 'Beneficent Killing: The False Promise of Euthanasia and Assisted Suicide,' *op. cit.*

17. Bresnahan, 'The Catholic Art of Dying,' *op. cit.*, p. 16.

18. Pope John Paul II, *Evangelium Vitae, op. cit.*

[PART III]

Particular Settings

[9]

Nazi Germany's Euphemisms

Ben Mitchell, MDiv

In his Jack W Provonsha Lectureship at the Loma Linda University School of Medicine, Gerald R Winslow observed:

> We should watch the way we talk. Human society can be described as a long conversation about what matters. In this conversation, the language we use to describe our social practices not only reveals our attitudes and virtues, it shapes them.[1]

Nowhere is the revelatory and shaping function of words more evident than in the contemporary debate about euthanasia. Nearly everyone is aware of the role metaphors play in healthcare. Susan Sontag has written of the punitive uses of 'illness as metaphor' in her book by the same title.[2] A blistering commentary on medical education, Samuel Shem's *The House of God* allows non-physicians to peek behind the veil and see the use of pejorative metaphors used by medical residents.[3] In *The House of God*, a patient 'who has lost — often through age — what goes into being a human being' was labelled a GOMER (Get Out Of My Emergency Room). More recently, Edmund Pellegrino has written on the perils of metaphors in healthcare reform in his essay, 'Words *Can* Hurt You: Some Reflections On the Metaphors of Managed Care'.[4] Indeed, words can hurt you.

Words can also help you. That is, the proper choice of words can ennoble the healthcare profession. Says Winslow, 'To call health care a ministry is to emphasize faithful service, devotion, and compassion.'[5] Words can elevate the patient from 'room 3, CABG procedure' to 'William Jones, husband, father, community leader', or even from '*the* patient' to '*my* patient'.[6].

In addition to metaphor, euphemism shapes the way we think about healthcare, physicians, and patients. According to linguists Keith Allan and Kate Burridge, 'a euphemism is used as an alternative to a disprefered expression, in order to avoid possible loss of face: either one's own face or, through giving offense, that of the audience, or of some third party'.[7] Through the use of euphemism and dysphemism, say Allan and Burridge, language may be used as either a shield or a weapon.

To speak euphemistically is to use language like a shield against the feared, the disliked, the unpleasant; euphemisms are motivated by the desire not to be offensive, and so they have positive connotations; in the least euphemisms seek to avoid too many negative connotations. They are used to upgrade the denotation (as a shield against scorn); they are used deceptively to conceal the unpleasant aspects of the denotation (as a shield against anger); and they are used to display in-group identity (as a shield against the intrusion of the out-groupers).[8]

The use of euphemisms has important implications for the practice of moral medicine. In fact, the erosion of medicine under Hitler was, at least in part, due to the way euphemisms for medicalized murder were so effectively used. The present debate about euthanasia and assisted suicide desperately needs to be informed by this history. The language games played by the Nazi doctors have critical implications for the present debate.

There are those who reject the Nazi analogy as inappropriate in the contemporary euthanasia debate. Ronald Cranford, for instance, asserts 'that it is an insult to thinking people to suggest that there are meaningful analogies between the contemporary euthanasia movement and the Nazi euthanasia program'.[9]

However, there are indeed important similarities which must be explored. To be sure, no one should argue that today's proponents of euthanasia are 'neo-Nazis'. Nevertheless, the manipulation of the language of killing, the economic pressures of scarce medical resources, the growing acceptance of terminating nutrition and hydration, the reality of the human tendency to rationalize one's behaviour all raise what Ruth Macklin has correctly called, 'cautionary alarm about the dangers of the slippery slope'.[10] Whether or not there are *exact* parallels between medicine under Hitler and medicine on the threshold of the Third Millennium, clearly there are lessons to be learned from the past.[11]

This chapter will (1) examine some of the euphemisms used by the Nazi physicians to redefine medicalized killing, (2) compare the Nazi language games with those of contemporary proponents of medicalized killing, and (3) conclude that the consistent application of euphemisms for medicalized killing significantly weakens arguments against assisted killing.

MEDICALIZED MURDER UNDER DICTATORSHIP

Leo Alexander, a physician-consultant on duty with the Chief Counsel for War Crimes, wrote a devastating critique of 'Medical Science Under Dictatorship' in the July 1949 *New England Journal of Medicine*. Alexander asserts that 'Nazi propaganda was highly effective in perverting public opinion and public conscience, in a remarkably short period of time'.[12] Alexander shows how the barrage of propaganda against what he calls 'the traditional nineteenth-century attitudes toward the chronically ill'[13] fuelled the fires of the furnaces at Dachau, Auschwitz, and the other killing centres erected under Hitler. Two silent film documentaries, *Was du erbst* (What You Inherit) and *Erb Krank* (The Hereditarily Ill) depicted images of the severely handicapped and mentally ill.[14] Later, two additional films, *Opfer der Vergangenheit* (Victims of the Past) and *Das Erbe* (The Inheritance) were shown under order of the Führer in all 5,300 German theatres. In 1939, *Dasein ohne Leben* (Existence without Life) was commissioned by those who ran the infamous Operation T-4 euthanasia campaign. This latter film was 'designed to reassure those involved in the euthanasia program that this was an ethical and humane procedure'.[15] While copies of *Dasein ohne Leben* were all destroyed, a copy of the script was recovered after the war.

Commenting on the contents of the script, documentary filmmaker John J Michalczyk observes,

> As the professor clinically describes the masses of 400,000 German patients in mental asylums, images of the helpless wards punctuate his words . . . In a pseudo-humane tone, the lecturer uses religious language of mercy killing to help "liberate" these creatures, while simultaneously denying these individuals their humanity. How cruel it would be to maintain these spiritually dead people as "living corpses." It is a sacred demand of charity that we eliminate the suffering of these helpless individuals, the film advocates. To show how humane this process is, the lecturer concludes by confessing that if he were struck down by a crippling disease, he himself would opt for mercy killing.[16]

From the film:

> Isn't it the duty of those concerned to help the incapable — and that means total idiots and incurable mental patients — to their right?
> Is that not a sacred command of charity?
> Deliver those you cannot heal!
> The Director of a large mental institution asked this question of the parents of all his incurable charges.
> 73 % answered "Yes."
> A mother wrote: "Don't ask, do it!" [this citation literally burning on the screen][17]

Finally, the film with the highest production values was made in 1941. *Ich klage an!* (I Accuse) takes up a familiar story. Hanna Heyt, the heroine of the film, shows signs of physical deterioration due to multiple sclerosis. She makes it clear that she does not wish to spend her last days in a 'vegetative state'. Her husband, Thomas, in consultation with her physician, gives her an overdose which kills her. A dramatic courtroom sequence follows.

. . . Thomas accuses the law of not helping in the case of his wife's suffering. The defence concludes that the law must be changed to allow mercy killing for humanitarian reasons. The film ends by putting the verdict in the hands of the audience.[18]

From the film:

SCHÖNBRUNN Gentlemen, if you ask me, Professor Heyt must be acquitted because he is an example to every doctor. I know I am touching on a sensitive issue, but at the same time it is a very inflexible point in our current moral and social view.
HUMMEL I don't know.. . . if one simply allows this sort of thing — will people still go to see their doctors?
SCHÖNBRUNN 'simply allows?' One must . . .
ROLFS Now look, what if — and I've been drawing an invalidity pension all my life — what if I go off sick one day, then they might simply do away with me?
SCHÖNBRUNN For God's sake! . . . The most important precondition would always be that the patient wished it!
ROLFS Many of them will, for a moment or two.
HUMMEL When one of them is mentally ill, they sometimes want it.
SCHÖNBRUNN Yes: if someone is deranged, or depressed or for one reason or another has no will of his own, then the state must assume responsibility! It must establish a commission consisting of doctors and lawyers, with a proper legal character. One should no longer have to stand by watching thousands of people who in earlier times would have died a gentle death, but who nowadays have to endure the most awful suffering simply because the doctors know how to prolong their poor lives artificially.[19]

The post-war testimony of Nazi doctors confirms the impact of the film in shaping their notions of the morality of euthanasia.[20] For anyone acquainted with the contemporary debate on euthanasia and assisted suicide, these are familiar word pictures and arguments. The film makes use of the euphemisms for euthanasia: 'right to die', 'caring', 'make the poor woman's end less painful', 'I delivered my wife', and others.

As we now know, the euthanasia programme did not stop with the killing of the mentally disabled, the feeble, and the terminally ill. 'In 1941, the SD killing units active in the East reported with barbaric regularity that in addition to "Soviet commissars", Jews, and the mentally ill, they were shooting capital criminals, beggars, and "trouble-makers" '.[21] Patients suffering from specified diseases, persons who were continually institutionalized for at least five years, the criminally insane, and those who were not German citizens or not of Aryan descent were murdered under Hitler's 'Final Solution'.

Interestingly, even the institutions established to evaluate prospective patients for euthanasia were euphemistically named:

'Realm's Work Committee of Institutions for Cure and Care', 'Realm's Committee for Scientific Approach to Severe Illness Due to Heredity and Constitution', 'Charitable Foundation for Institutional Care', and 'Charitable Transport Company for the sick'.[22] According to Alexander, this latter institution 'brought 150–250 brains at a time to a Dr Hallervorden, a neuropathologist for the Third Reich'.[23] Remarked Hallervorden:

> There was wonderful material among those brains, beautiful mental defectives, malformations, and early infantile diseases. I accepted those brains of course. Where they came from and how they came to me was really none of my business.[24]

While examples of the ubiquitous use of euphemisms in Nazi 'medicine' could go on *ad nauseam*, a few examples from Nazi diaries and journals must suffice. Christian Pross has argued persuasively that the best source for understanding the ethos of Nazi medicine is not the post-war interviews with the Nazi doctors found in much of Robert J Lifton's illuminating volume, *The Nazi Doctors: Medical Killing and the Psychology of Genocide*.[25] Rather, says Pross, 'The diaries, letters, and publications of Nazi doctors of the time . . . contain few elements of idealism or the high ethical standards of the "physician-self," and thus scant evidence of doubling.'[26]

Only a few months after the suspension of Operation T-4, legislation was introduced to legalize institutionalized euthanasia. The law prescribed that the Reich Minister of the Interior would appoint a Reich Commissioner whose job it would be to oversee all institutions 'concerned, even in part, with the accommodation and treatment of the mentally ill, feeble-minded, epileptics, and psychopaths'.[27] Euthanasia was justified under the new legislation as part of 'wartime economic measures'. Beds would need to be made available for Nazi soldiers wounded in the war. Thus, something would have to be done with those who were presently occupying the beds and who were exhausting scarce medical resources. According to Götz Aly, by the time the new law became effective the Reich Association of Mental Hospitals had already killed over 70,000 patients. Under the new law the Reich Commissioner for Mental Hospitals was subordinate to the Minister of the Interior and was authorized 'to take necessary measures' to maintain the economic viability of the asylums-turned-army hospitals.[28] Patients were labelled as having lives which were 'usable', 'unusable', 'worthy', and 'unworthy'.[29]

The designation 'Life Unworthy of Living' (*lebensunwertes Leben*) had been an established euphemism for decades before the war. In 1920 Karl Binding and Alfred Hoche wrote the most influential tract on euthanasia, 'Permitting the Destruction of

Unworthy Life'.[30] While Binding and Hoche frequently used the
term 'killing' when referring to euthanasia, they were also fond of
euphemisms. For instance, Binding said of killing a patient who is
experiencing pain, 'This is not "an act of killing in the legal sense"
but is rather the modification of an irrevocably present cause of
death which can no longer be evaded. *In truth it is a purely healing
act.*'[31] Interestingly, this method of referring to medicalized killing
was used by some of the Nazi doctors themselves. One of the
physicians who euthanized children under T-4 said, 'there was no
killing, strictly speaking . . . People felt this is not murder, it is a
putting-to-sleep.'[32]

Murderous medicine was also couched in economic euphemisms. In 1944, for instance, H J Becker, acting head of the Central
Clearinghouse for Mental Hospitals, introduced measures to
govern the so-called 'practical work' of the asylums. This
euphemism was, according to Aly, a reference to 'thousands of
murders' by Nazi physicians.[33] Becker was an indefatigable
number-cruncher. He 'even calculated economic losses due to
friction resulting from "unproductive excitement" over the death
of a "useless person" '.[34]

> As late as February 1945, Hans Joachim Becker issued a form with
> which doctors were to report sick forced laborers who 'would
> probably remain in the institution for more than four weeks,' In the
> final days of the Third Reich, a forced laborer who might not be able
> to work for more than four weeks had lost the right to live. The
> decision was no longer made by a physician but by the Central
> Clearinghouse on the basis of a few lines in a 'report of findings.'[35]

Clearly, euphemisms for murder played a significant role in the
Nazi euthanasia programme. What Lifton calls 'detoxifying language'[36] contributed to an ethos which allowed physicians to turn
from healers to killers. Nazi physicians were convinced that some
patients and, by extension, all Jews were merely 'human ballast'
who had '. . . lives which have so completely lost the attribute of
legal status that their continuation has permanently lost all value,
both for the bearer of that life and for society'.[37] As a result, these
physicians perpetrated undeniable atrocities in human experimentation and euthanasia.

THE CONTEMPORARY CAMPAIGN

Examples of euphemisms are ubiquitous in the contemporary
debate on euthanasia and assisted suicide. Both the popular and
academic presses have inundated the book shelves with euphemistic titles. *Final Exit: The Practicalities of Self-Deliverance and
Assisted Suicide for the Dying,*[38] *The Least Worst Death: Essays in
Bioethics at the End of Life,*[39] and *Prescription: Medicide*[40] are a few

cases in point. Perhaps such titles may be excused by acknowledging the titillating nature of marketing strategies, but a more sobering look at contemporary euphemisms and linguistic strategies is in order.

First, we have our own genre of assisted-dying films from the feature film, *Whose Life is it Anyway?*, to more obscure videos such as, *Please Let Me Die*, to made-for-TV-movies such as *Last Wish*. *Last Wish* is an ABC-TV movie based on Betty Rollin's 1985 book about helping her mother commit suicide. The movie received mixed reactions. David Klinghoffer reviewing the film for the *Washington Times* said the movie was 'a noxious concoction' which ignores 'the entire body of Western moral teaching'.[41] At the same time, movie reviewer Susan Stewart of the *Detroit Free Press* said the film was so 'inspiring' that 'at times, you're actually able to forget you're being proselytized'.[42] In addition, there are the occasional PBS airings of documentaries which bring the Dutch euthanasia experience into our living rooms.

Second, popular culture is suffused with euphemisms for euthanasia. 'Mercy killing', 'merciful death', 'death with dignity', 'painless end to suffering', 'termination of life', 'humane treatment', and even 'comfort care' are part of the public conversation. Most recently, neologisms such as 'managed death'[43] have crept into the glossary of terms for euthanasia (itself an euphemism).

Earlier this year, former member of Congress and professor of law at Georgetown University, Robert F Drinan, published a commentary arguing that 'The debate about the moral and legal issues that arise when a terminally ill patient wants to shorten the period of suffering should not be confused with suicide. Perhaps the more appropriate term is "expedited death".'[44] Though unlikely to catch on, this euphemism, like the others, demonstrates how far some are willing to go to avoid straightforward language.

Third, while Drinan is not himself a proponent of euthanasia, his comments show that he has been sensitized to the power of euphemisms. University of Utah professor and medical ethicist Margaret Pabst Battin takes Drinan one step further. In her challenging volume, *The Least Worst Death: Essays in Bioethics on the End of Life*, Battin argues that American medicine should learn its lessons about euthanasia and assisted suicide not from the Dutch, but from contemporary Germany.

Battin observes that Germans have at least four words for 'suicide'.[45] She laments the obvious poverty of the English language to equal the nuances of colloquial German. The word which possesses the preferred connotation is *Freitod* ('free death'). Says Battin, 'The very concept of *Freitod* — a notion without religious, altruistic overtones and without negative moral or psychological implications, but that celebrates the voluntary choice of death as a personal expression of principled idealism — is, in short, linguistically unfamiliar to English speakers.'[46]

Perceptively, Battin acknowledges that some kind of language game is necessary if American culture is going to accept medicalized killing of any sort.

> Language is crucial in shaping attitudes about end-of-life practices, and because of the very different lexical resources of English and German, it is clear that English speakers cannot straightforwardly understand the very different German conception of these matters. Even in situations of terminal illness, the very concept of voluntary death resonates differently for the German speaker who conceives of it as *Freitod* than it does for the English speaker who conceives of it as *suicide*.[47]

Later in the chapter she admits, '. . . what we see is that we are limited by our own language, and do not have the linguistic resources for understanding the issue in the way members of another culture can.'[48] Clearly, then, for Battin the crux of the matter is the language we use to describe medicalized killing. This brings us full circle. Language matters.

Finally, when euphemisms find their way into public policy, clarity gives way to ambiguity. For instance, Oregon's narrowly passed medicalized killing legislation makes use of at least a couple of critical euphemisms. First, the title of the legislation is, 'The Oregon Death With Dignity Act'. Interestingly, in §1.01, definitions are provided for a host of words found in the legislation, including definitions for 'adult', 'attending physician', 'consulting physician', 'counseling', 'patient', and 'qualified patient', among others. Yet, there is no definition of 'dignity' or even 'death with dignity'. As Paul Ramsey pointed out just over two decades ago, 'death with dignity' may in fact be a gross 'indignity'.[49]

Furthermore, the 'Death With Dignity Act' makes repeated reference to death in 'a humane and dignified manner' without defining or distinguishing between a 'humane act' and an 'inhumane act' Section 4.01.1 on immunities specifies, 'No person shall be subject to civil or criminal liability or professional disciplinary action for participating in good faith with this Act. This includes being present when a qualified patient takes the prescribed medication to end his or her own life in a humane and dignified manner.' Thus, the legislation presupposes that assisted self-murder is, within specified parameters, a 'humane' act. Moreover, the language tends to imply that a physician is 'inhumane' if he or she refuses to comply with the requests of a patient who wants to kill himself or herself. But what makes that the case? Unless 'humane' is appropriately defined, the language of the Act remains ambiguous.

Better designed studies on attitudes toward medicalized killing have sought to rid survey language of the ambiguity of euphemisms. For instance, in a survey of 1355 randomly selected physicians in the state of Washington, Jonathan Cohen et al. used the phrase 'prescription medication [e.g., narcotics or barbiturates] or the counseling of an ill patient so he or she may use an overdose to end his or her own life' instead of 'physician-assisted suicide'.[50] Instead of 'euthanasia' the survey used the phrase, 'deliberate administration of an overdose of medication to an ill patient at his or her request with the primary intent to end his or her life'.[51] One must wonder what the response of voters would have been if the Oregon legislation had been more forthrightly titled, 'The Legalized Self-Murder Act' or 'The Assisted Self-Killing Act'.

THE PROBLEM WITH EUPHEMISMS

Euphemisms are linguistic devices that use a less direct word or phrase for one considered offensive. They are place-holders for notions or practices we would consider abhorrent if we called them what they are. Euphemisms take the sting out of practices we would otherwise disdain.

While it has not been the purpose of this chapter to argue that medicalized killing is wrong, it is the candid presupposition of the entire piece. Whether or not one agrees that medicalized killing is morally reprehensible, arguments can be made from 'both sides of the aisle' that euphemisms do *not* serve the purpose of perspicacious speech or informed decision-making.

It has been argued that the Nazi use of euphemisms aided physicians in the Third Reich to commit horrendous atrocities during the day and yet sleep well at night. Furthermore, we have seen that the omnipresent use of euphemisms in the contemporary debate over medicalized killing contributes to ambiguity and has the effect of salving the consciences of many who embrace its tenets.

If those who oppose medicalized killing are to contribute to informed public debate on the topic, it is important that they are not accomplices in using euphemisms for murder. They must not succumb to such usage under the umbrella of irenic debate. In sum, we need to tell it like it is: euthanasia and assisted suicide are really medicalized murder and complicity to self-murder respectively. The use of euphemisms significantly weakens the argument of those who find medicalized killing morally abhorrent. Such language games permit societies to hide behind the veil of pseudo-mercy and false conceptions of the humane.[52]

If we permit or contribute to the euphemistic speech with respect to medicalized killing, then we will do so, finally, on every front in the current culture war. Adultery, for instance, will become a 'coping mechanism' for a bad marriage or merely an expression of a 'mid-life crisis'. While we are at it, we might as well designate sexual harassment 'gender affirming behaviour'. After all, men, we are told, are merely acknowledging the desirability of the opposite sex and expressing their own evolutionary proclivity toward multiple sexual partnerships as a means of propagating the species.

NOTES

1. Gerald R Winslow, 'Minding Our Language: Metaphors and Biomedical Ethics,' *Update* 10 (December 1994), p. 1.
2. Susan Sontag, *Illness as Metaphor* (New York: Farrar, Straus and Giroux, 1978).
3. Samuel Shem, *The House of God* (New York: Dell Publishing, 1978).
4. Edmund D Pellegrino, 'Words *Can* Hurt You: Some Reflections On the Metaphors Of Managed Care', *JABFP* 7 (Nov-Dec, 1994), pp. 505–510.
5. Winslow, 'Minding Our Language', p. 5.
6. For expositions of the covenantal relationship between physician and patient see, William F May, *The Physician's Covenant: Images of the Healer in Medical Ethics* (Philadelphia: Westminster Press, 1983); Edmund Pellegrino and David C Thomasma, *For The Patient's Good: The Restoration of Beneficence in Health Care* (New York: Oxford University Press, 1988); and Edmund D Pellegrino, *Humanism and the Physician* (Knoxville: The University of Tennessee Press, 1979).
7. Keith Allan and Kate Burridge, *Euphemism and Dysphemism: Language Used as Shield and Weapon* (New York: Oxford University Press, 1991), p. 11.
8. Ibid., pp. 221–222.
9. Ronald Cranford, 'The Contemporary Euthanasia Movement and the Nazi Euthanasia Program', in Arthur L Caplan (ed), *When Medicine Went Mad: Bioethics and the Holocaust* (Totowa, NJ: Humana Press, 1992), p. 209.
10. Ruth Macklin, 'Which Way Down the Slippery Slope?' in Arthur L Caplan (ed), *When Medicine Went Mad: Bioethics and the Holocaust* (Totowa, NJ: Humana Press, 1992), p. 176.
11. This chapter largely assumes that the Nazi experience is an appropriate analogy to apply to the contemporary euthanasia debate. While there is not space to develop an argument to that effect, there is an important literature on this topic. See, for instance, 'Biomedical Ethics and the Shadow of Nazism,' *Hastings Center Report* (Special Supplement) 6 (August 1976) pp. 1–20; Courtney S Campbell, 'Contested Terrain: The Nazi Analogy in Bioethics', *Hastings Center Report* (Aug/Sep 1988), pp. 29–33; and Arthur L Caplan (ed), *When Medicine Went Mad: Bioethics and the Holocaust* (Totowa, NJ: Humana Press, 1992).
12. Leo Alexander, 'Medical Science Under Dictatorship', *The New England Journal of Medicine* 241 (July 14, 1949), p. 40.
13. Ibid.
14. See John Michalczyk, 'Euthanasia in Nazi Propaganda Films: Selling Murder', in John J Michalczyk (ed), *Medicine, Ethics, and the Third Reich: Historical and Contemporary Issues* (Kansas City: Sheed and Ward, 1994), p. 65.
15. Ibid., p. 67.

16. Ibid.

17. Cited in Michael Burleigh, *Death and Deliverance: 'Euthanasia' in Germany 1900–1945* (New York: Cambridge University Press, 1994), p. 199.

18. Ibid., p. 69.

19. Ibid., p. 214.

20. Robert J Lifton, *The Nazi Doctors: Medical Killing and the Psychology of Genocide* (New York: Basic Books, 1995), p. 49.

21. Götz Aly, 'Medicine Against the Useless', in Götz Aly, Peter Chroust, and Christian Pross, *Cleansing the Fatherland: Nazi Medicine and Racial Hygiene* (Baltimore: Johns Hopkins University Press, 1994), p. 59.

22. Leo Alexander, 'Medical Science Under Dictatorship', p. 40–41.

23. Ibid., p. 40.

24. Ibid.

25. Lifton, Op. cit.

26. Christian Pross, 'Introduction', in Aly, Chroust, and Pross, *Cleansing the Fatherland*, p. 13. The notion of 'doubling' to which Pross refers is a notion introduced by Lifton to explain how the Nazi doctors could perform such heinous acts while thinking themselves to be noble, even Hippocratic, physicians. In brief, Lifton argues that the Nazi doctors experienced a psychological 'personality split' in which the 'Auschwitz-Self' and the 'physician-self' existed simultaneously in the same mind.

27. Götz Aly, 'Pure and Tainted Progress', Ibid., p. 165.

28. Ibid.

29. Ibid., p. 172.

30. Fortunately an English translation has been made available by Walter E Wright, Patrick G Derr, and Robert Saloman. See Karl Binding and Alfred Hoche, 'Permitting the Destruction of Unworthy Life', *Issues in Law and Medicine* 8 (Fall 1992), pp. 231–265'.

31. Ibid., p. 240. Emphasis in the translation.

32. Lifton, *The Nazi Doctors*, p. 57.

33. Aly 'Pure and Tainted Progress', in Op. cit., p. 180.

34. Ibid., p. 182.

35. Ibid., p. 182.

36. Lifton, *The Nazi Doctors*, p. 202.

37. Binding and Hoche, 'Permitting the Destruction of Unworthy Life', p. 246.

38. Derek Humphry, *Final Exit: The Practicalities of Self-Deliverance and Assisted Suicide for the Dying* (Eugene, OR: The Hemlock Society, 1991).

39. Margaret Pabst Battin, *The Least Worst Death: Essays in Bioethics on the End of Life* (New York: Oxford University Press, 1994).

40. Jack Kevorkian, *Prescription: Medicide* (New York: Prometheus Books, 1991).

41. David Klinghoffer, *The Washington Times* (12 January 1992).

42. Susan Stewart, *The Detroit Free Press* (10 January 1992).

43. See Daniel P Sulmasy's critique of this euphemism in 'Managed Care and Managed Death', *Archives of Internal Medicine* 155 (January 23, 1995), p. 133–136.

44. Robert F Drinan, 'Commentary: Suicide the wrong term for gravely ill who want to die', *Religion News Service* (25 January 1995).

45. Four German words for 'suicide' are *Selbstmord, Selbsttötung, Suizid*, and *Freitod*.

46. Battin, *The Least Worst Death*, p. 263.

47. Ibid.

48. Ibid., p. 265.

49. Paul Ramsey, 'The Indignity of "Death with Dignity" ', *Hastings Center Studies* 2 (May 1974), pp. 47–62.

50. Jonathan S Cohen, Stephan D Fihn, Edwards J Boyko, Albert R Jonsen, and Robert W Wood, 'Attitudes Toward Assisted Suicide and Euthanasia Among Physicians in Washington State', *New England Journal of Medicine* 331 (July 14, 1994), pp. 89–94.

51. Ibid.

52. See Philip E Devine, *Ethics of Homicide* (Notre Dame: The University of Notre Dame Press, 1978).

10

Oregon's Solution

Jerome R Wernow, PhD, RPh

On November 8, 1994, thirty-nine percent of the registered voters of the state of Oregon in the United States approved an initiative entitled the Oregon 'Death With Dignity Act' (DWDA).[1] It was a solution with which neither the opponents nor the advocates of euthanasia — or less euphemistically put, medicide — were particularly pleased.[2] It was a solution which neither side would permit to be final. This chapter is an attempt to examine the composition of the DWDA, to discuss the moral issues it raises, and to reflect on the public policy dialogue that surrounds it.

The present analysis uses the method of semantico-analytics to clarify the medical and ethical issues associated with the DWDA.[3] The following four elements constitute this method: (1) an analysis of the *material act*, (2) an analysis of the identity of the decision-making *agents*, (3) an analysis of operative *norms, valuations*, and *meta-ethical underpinnings*, and (4) an analysis of the effect of these preceding three elements upon the agent's *will* to act. This chapter also evaluates the rightness or wrongness of the material act and appraises the value or disvalue of the agent's intention behind the act. The overall analysis is both a descriptive and prescriptive endeavour, the latter aspect of which is heavily influenced by tradition-bound Christian perspectives.[4] Such influence has been minimized in the descriptive portions of the analysis.

The analysis will proceed in three sections, addressing the material act, the primary agent, and the operative underpinnings. The first section looks at the action permitted by the DWDA that purports to lead to death. Our findings will demonstrate that the material act necessary and sufficient to produce a so-called death with dignity is left unclear. Agency will then be assessed. This inquiry seeks to uncover the individual(s) who is (are) empowered to execute the material act. It will be shown that patient agency is restricted, rather than radically free as emphasized by referendum proponents. Finally, we will probe the ethical components upon which this measure was built. The inquiry includes uncovering the primary norms, values, and world view which lend warrant to the DWDA. This inquiry reveals naturalistic utilitarianism as the predominant operating world view underpinning the Measure.

THE MATERIAL ACT

A central feature of the Oregon Death with Dignity Act is the voluntary action taken by the patient to 'die when s/he takes the prescribed medication'.[5] The implicit intent here and throughout the Measure is to permit a prescription to be written for an oral medication to be ingested by means of self-administration.[6] The act was supposedly crafted for the express purpose of ending the patient's life.[7] Telephone conversations with Dr Peter Goodwin, public advocate of the Measure, clarified this as the intent. One implication is that the hallmark of this referendum was the writing of a prescription for a lethal dose of an oral medication.

Opponents of this measure question whether the language is so narrow as to restrict the instrument of cause of death to oral medication. For instance, the Coalition for Compassionate Care challenged the supposed limitations of the Measure's language in their campaign materials.

> While much of the language of the Measure presumes prescription to be pills or liquid the patient would swallow, there is nothing in the proposal to prohibit machines like those built by Dr Kevorkian. In fact, both his lethal injection and carbon monoxide mask have the feature that allows the patient to deliver the lethal dose themselves, which is what the proposed measure appears to require.[8]

Was this criticism warranted? A close scrutiny of the document reveals the following details. First, the Measure is clearly a codification of 'prescription for medication' with the intent of using that prescription for producing death.[9] However, a pivotal term of importance, prescription, was neither defined nor restricted to oral administration under the Measure's definitions. The interpretation of the meaning of prescription therefore yields to the existing legal definitions as found in the Oregon Revised Statute 689.005 (29):

> 'Prescription' or 'prescription drug order' means a written or oral direction, given by a practitioner for the preparation and use of a drug. When the context requires, 'prescription' also means the drug prepared under such written or oral directions.[10]

The notion of prescription, then, is inextricably bound to the definition of the term drug. 'Drug' is constituted in the Oregon Statutes as follows:

> 'Drug' means all medicines and preparations for internal and external use of humans, intended to be used for the cure, mitigation or

prevention of diseases or abnormalities, which are recognized in any United States Pharmacopoeia or National Formulary, or otherwise established as a drug.[11]

Since the term 'drug' constitutes prescription and includes injectables, inhalants, naso-gastric solutions, rectal preparations, and percutaneous routes, the possibility of Kevorkian-type administration limited to legend drugs (e.g. self-administration of inhalants and lethal injections) would appear to be permissible. This would not, however, include a carbon monoxide mask as suggested by the Measure's opponents, since this gas is not a prescription item.

The crafters of the Measure reject the opposition's claim regarding the use of lethal injection by contending that Section 3.14 forbids such administration by a secondary agent. The section entitled 'Construction of the Act' states the following:

> Nothing in this Act shall be construed to authorize a physician or any other person to end a patient's life by lethal injection, mercy killing, or active euthanasia. Actions taken in accordance with this Act shall not for any purpose constitute suicide, assisted suicide, mercy killing or homicide, under the law.[12]

These statements seem to militate against both lethal injection and administration of medication by secondary agents.[13] However, neither this statement nor others found in the text clearly precludes the possibility of the patient's self-administration of lethal injection or inhalation. Furthermore, if the patient and physician meet the conditions of the Measure, then they appear to be permitted to utilize all prescription medications within the bounds of the semantical field of the word 'drug' without being implicated in legal remedies attached to suicide, assisted suicide, or mercy killing. It also appears that the language of the Measure permits a broader interpretation allowing those unable to self-administer, quadriplegics for example, to have lethal drugs administered via a secondary agent by all routes except lethal injection, after meeting the conditions of the Measure.[14]

The ambiguities regarding the route of administration necessitated a personal conversation with the crafters of the Act for clarification. After lengthy conversation with Mr Stutsman, personal correspondence was sent outlining concerns regarding the ambiguities of Section 3.14. Clarification of routes of administration, types of medication used, and dosages appropriate for a safe suicide were requested. Stutsman responded in a letter dated September 14, 1994 that he was 'not competent to respond concerning questions of routes of administration and written lists of medications but would bring it up at the next meeting.'[15] This was a most curious response, since he publicly debated with Mr

Derek Humphry on May 21, 1993 at the Unitarian Church in Eugene, Oregon over the very issue of routes of administration prior to my letter. As Thomas Bates, writer for the *Oregonian*, put it,

> From the outset, the big question was whether to go with an oral prescription or a lethal injection bill. Even before the writing started, Stutsman felt it should be the former. When word of his position leaked out, Humphry, who favored a 'two-handed bill' allowing for lethal injection, invited him to Eugene for a debate.[16]

This leaves one to wonder if the route of administration continued to remain ambiguous to Stutsman throughout the campaign.[17]

The ambiguity of the route of administration is further exacerbated by Goodwin's seemingly contradictory statements regarding what actions the Act did and did not permit. In the election brochure endorsed by Goodwin, lethal injection is expressly prohibited.[18] In contrast, during a post election interview with Ted Koppel, Goodwin stated: 'if the patient had a gadget similar to that that Dr Kevorkian used and wanted to do it that way, it's my belief that that would not be excluded as long as the patient had full responsibility.'[19]

The ambiguity and the broader interpretation which includes lethal injection was admittedly avoided during the campaign for purposes of political expediency according to some advocates. The poll taken by ERGO intimated that use of straightforward language about lethal injection in the initiative would probably lead to the Measure's rejection by voters, while the use of euphemisms would lead to its acceptance.[20] As Humphry of ERGO said regarding clear versus ambiguous language; 'The euphemisms won.'[21]

Ambiguity in the route of administration raises questions of professional conscience and beneficent public policy. Is the apparent route of ingestion a safe medical practice to prescribe? The Remmelink Report documented lingering deaths after attempted medicides and assisted suicides.[22] The graph opposite shows the results.*

The difference in the likely frequency of these lingering deaths in Oregon (under the DWDA) and The Netherlands cannot be understated. The Netherlands permits lethal injection as a remedy for lingering deaths. Legal testimony as well as campaign records intimated that the Oregon DWDA was not 'apparently' crafted with the intent to permit a secondary agent to administer a lethal

---

* In the table 5.11 of the report records 7 out of 187 persons lingering between one day to one week and one person lingering for 1–4 weeks after the beginning of medicide until death. Further 28 of the 187 died between one and twenty-four hours after the initiation of medicine.

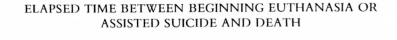

ELAPSED TIME BETWEEN BEGINNING EUTHANASIA OR
ASSISTED SUICIDE AND DEATH

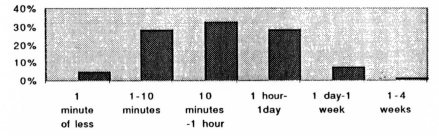

injection for the purpose of mercy killing or euthanasia.[23] However, awareness of the suffering caused by such failures led Humphry to repudiate the current form of the Act he endorsed by saying, 'the Oregon law, which forbids injections, could be disastrous'.[24] Humphry in all likelihood is citing the Admiraal Study, where the author suggested that assisted suicide limited to oral ingestion is an unsafe medical practice.[25] Again focusing on a moral reflection, is it appropriate to sanction and willingly participate in unproven and unsafe medical practices?

All of this is to emphasize that the playing field in public policy remains that of the acceptability of lethal injection. Advocates of the medicide movement are well aware of this. They commissioned a Roper poll to discern what wording the voter would most likely vote for in an election. As previously discussed, the euphemisms prevailed.

Voter preferences indicated that of the 1000 persons asked if they would vote for or against a law that allowed a terminally ill person to choose euthanasia rather than prolonging life there were 55% for and 27% against. When asked whether they would vote for or against a law that allowed a terminally ill person to chose to die with dignity rather than prolong life 65% responded for and 20% against. Lethal injection and physician aided suicide received only 40% for and 39% against.[26]

Humphry and his close colleague Cheryl Smith make it very clear that initiatives crafted in terms of euphemism may lead to questionable public policy but are useful in securing their political objective. Humphry states:

> By using Orwellian 'doublespeak' we might be letting ourselves in for procedures and conclusions which we do not fully comprehend at the time of decision-making. On the other hand, perhaps euphemisms allow people to come to grips with brutal facts which, stated another way, would be repugnant.[27]

Smith's statement resounds with the underlying utilitarian ethics operative in the movement's approach when she says: 'We wanted to know what works.'[28] This outlook is reminiscent of Leo Alexander's characterization of the Third Reich's operative ethic: 'What is useful is good.'[29] The parallel raises numerous questions. Were the crafters cognizant of such parallels? Are they aware of the consequences of embracing this type of teleological ethic? What implications do such tactics have for the trustworthiness of disclosure? If the criteria for informed consent cannot be met at the ballot box, what is our guarantee when patients are confronted with the pine box?

In summary, the material act and hallmark of this legislation is the writing of a lethal prescription. The route of administration or the actual action permitted in this referendum remains unclear. Allusions to oral ingestion are made, but they remain only allusions. There are no clear statements in the initiative limiting administration to the oral route. The lack of clarity leaves some of the crafters interpreting Measure 16 as permitting oral ingestion while others state that the interpretation of the text permits lethal injection. One point is clear. The writing of a lethal prescription is neither a necessary nor a sufficient condition for termination of life. The lack of clarity produces a domino effect upon the entire Act. The route of administration is crucial for determining primary patient agency, and patient agency is crucial for meeting the ethical principle of autonomy, a pillar upon which this initiative is built.

THE PRIMARY AGENT

By primary agent(s) I am referring to the idea derived from the Latin root *agere*, meaning 'to set in motion'.[30] An appropriate lexical meaning in English is 'one who (or that which) acts or exerts power'.[31] In the context of our discussion, the addition of the attributive adjective 'primary' to the noun 'agent' indicates two important points. First, it reveals the recognition of the complexity of relationships leading to the choice and performance of a treatment decision. The adjective does this by intimating that the agent under consideration is principal among other agents affecting the decision's direction. Second, it reveals an existence of priority in this complexity. Priority is emphasized by the continued influence of the etymological root, 'primus,' meaning 'first in rank or station, chief, principal'.[32]

Studies in 'action theory' lend further clarity to the meaning of agency by adding four aspects to the lexical meaning.[33] These include (1) freedom, (2) competence, (3) capacity, and (4) efficient cause. Freedom is recognized when agents think that they are responsible and free in their treatment choices and in expression of those choices, and are in fact correct in this thinking. Competence is recognized when agents comprehend the information in a way that is accurate and can express their judgements in an understandable fashion. Capacity is perceived as existing in agents when they are capable of mobilizing sufficient power to pursue their decisions. In the case of treatment decisions agents must be capable of exercising that power in accordance with purposes and intentions which bring about a subsequent course of events. This ability to bring about a course of events leads us to the fourth recognizable aspect of primary agency, efficient cause. The decision, the administration of a lethal dose of medication, and the subsequent death of the patient can be explained as effects caused by the agent's free choice.

When applying these observations to Measure 16, we find a mitigated primacy of agency. The apparent primary agent, the agent both necessary and sufficient for the performance of the material act of assisted suicide, is the adult patient. His or her primacy is dependent, however, upon the sequestering of power sufficient to mitigate the opposing power operatives of other agents in the causal complex. In other words, the execution of an agent's will to realize medicide is dependent upon the types of power she or he is able to actualize. This observation leads us to a short description of power operatives in medical decision making. According to an article by Kathleen Koch, there are ten power categories in operation in the context of autonomy and medical decision making.[34] The following chart illustrates a selection of nine important categories.

Types of Power

Formal Power (ultimate power)	Expert Power (knowledge power)	Sanction Power (police power)
Referent Power (connections)	Procedural Power (controls decision methods)	Resource Power (resource distribution)
Nuisance Power (threats of public discovery)	Habitual Power (power of *status quo*)	Moral Power (power of widely held values)

An example of the restriction of patient autonomy by these operatives is seen in the patient-physician context. Here physicians serve as secondary and necessary agents in the decision-making complex for assisted suicide. Their function is diagnostic confirmation, rendering of a reasonable prognosis, choosing to participate in medicide, and selecting the appropriate drug(s) at a lethal dose to be obtained by prescription. They exert expert power in these cases as well as procedural power as prescribed by Section 3.01 [1] and 1.01 [12]. The patient's 'right to die' can be denied in these instances if the physician deems the patient to be outside the boundaries of a six month terminal prognosis or to be mentally incompetent to grasp the information disseminated.[35] Furthermore, the physician can exercise primacy as an agent through the use of habitual authority in permitting or denying the practice of medicide as long as society recognizes personal conscience as a value of the *status quo*, as seen in Section 4.01(4).[36]

A concern might be raised regarding expert power and actual patient autonomy in the context of the patient–physician relationship. A number of studies suggest that patient choices in the context of end of life decisions are more illusion than reality.[37] Three findings are of interest. First, physicians inform patients through their own personal value-laden grid. When doing so, the patient, weakened by disease and lacking in expertise, is apt to concur with opinions issuing from the physician's framework. Second, physicians unaware of patient values may inadvertently impose their own will upon them. Finally, in some instances, a physician might judge that the patient is unable to make a meaningful judgement and impose his or her own judgement on the patient.[38] These findings may be of particular significance because of the current shift away from Hippocratic medicine toward one based upon a utilitarian calculus. This new context in concert with the emerging medical industrial complex subjects physicians to the same pressures as employees of many large corporate businesses. Physicians are compelled to honour the corporate culture and thus lose the objectivity and neutrality of a resource gatekeeper. Such is the scenario described by Abrams in which 'caring for the sick becomes an industrial by product'.[39]

What is uncovered in the above discussion is the exercise of power by a third agent in the causal nexus, the institution. Their formal power dictates whether a patient's request will or will not be honoured. They actualize this power through the exercise of resource control or, as intimated by Koch, resource power. An example of this was seen during a recent task force meeting on the implementation of Measure 16. One of the mid-level administrators stated that his large health care complex would not participate in the Measure; nor would it permit its employees to use the corporation's inventory to participate if a patient and physician should agree to medicide.

The pharmacist is also a secondary agent whose participation is a necessary condition in the patient's decision-making complex since the filling of the prescription is the hallmark of the referendum. The pharmacist's power is based upon procedural and resource control. His or her participation as gatekeeper is evident in the context of the use of controlled substances. The United

States Code 21 CFR Ch II (4–1–94 edition) 1306.04 (a) states that the pharmacist assumes corresponding responsibility in the proper prescribing for legitimate medical purpose and dispensing of controlled substances for those purposes. Secondly, ORS 689.015 declares that

> The 'practice of pharmacy' means the interpretation and evaluation of prescription orders; the compounding, dispensing, labeling of drugs . . . ; the participation in drug selection and drug utilization reviews . . . ; the responsibility for advising, where necessary or where regulated, of therapeutic values, content, hazards and use of drugs and devices; the monitoring of therapeutic response or adverse effect to drug therapy; and the conduct, operation, management and control of pharmacy.[40]

These two laws bring the pharmacist into conflict should she or he attempt to follow the federal notion of legitimate use, the state's notion of safe drug selection, and honouring requests for lethal doses of oral controlled substances. In such cases, the pharmacist may with good reason deny the patient's request and thus mitigate that patient's autonomy.

The DWDA also contains a clause which permits secondary agents to choose not to participate in a patient's death wish for whatever reason, professional or private, thus mitigating the patient's desire. The immunities section of the DWDA appears to provide this protection by stating:

> No health care provider shall be under any duty, whether by contract, by status or by any other legal requirement to participate in the provision to a qualified patient of medication to end his or her life in a humane and dignified manner. If a health care provider is unable or unwilling to carry out a patient's request under this Act, and the patient transfers his or her care to a new health care provider, the prior health care provider shall transfer, upon request, a copy of the patient's relevant medical records to the new health care provider.[41]

It is precisely at this point that a major contradiction in the referendum occurs. By providing equal rights to participate or decline, the Act places itself upon the horns of an irresolvable dilemma. When two of these agents collide, one will at least temporarily impose its power upon the other, thereby restricting an agent's autonomy; that is, the other's right to choose. This is exemplified by a policy of one of the two largest retail drug companies in Oregon which admirably tried to uphold the rights of the patient and the employee.[42] Three tenets of the policy, however, jeopardized the rights of a non-participant in the Act. They included the following:

1. The censure of pharmacists by forbidding them to subject a client to 'any kind of lecture'.

2. The forced participation of the pharmacist by mandating that the pharmacist 'make an offer to transfer the prescription'.
3. The censure of a pharmacist's professional discretion by mandating in that 'nothing more be said'.

The horns of the dilemma are clear when comparing this policy with DWDA section 4.01 (2). The Act reads, 'No health care provider may subject a person to censure, discipline, suspension, loss of license, . . . for participating or refusing to participate.' The fundamental source of the difficulty lies not in the emergence of conflicting rights, but rather in an often unspoken collision of world views, as discussed in the next section.

An inability ultimately to empower the patient is evidenced in the preceding discussion. Such an environment exposes the most vulnerable to abuses. The danger of abuse and forced participation in medicide is not a matter of mere speculation or isolated rarities but rather is present in a longer history of similar slippery slopes and concomitant travesties in human history. The difficulty in regulating medicide policies evidenced in our current discussion reflects some similarities with the well documented involuntary medicide experience in The Netherlands now and in the annihilation of vast numbers of vulnerables through the medicide policies of *Aktie Vier*.[43]

Historical parallels with the crafting, campaigning, and implementation of the DWDA arouse concern over the possible repetition of the abuses of medicide. Public non–disclosure during the campaign, an ends–justify–the–means ethics, and the lack of a limit regarding who has the right to die and who does not seem to be harbingers from the past pleading for caution in the present. Considering the shift from Hippocratic care to a health care system driven by economic efficiency and productivity, one may not be far amiss in hearing the question from the past: In an epoch governed by relativistic utilitarianism, will the empowered choose to do less harm to the vulnerable than they are willing to do to themselves?[44] Attempts to answer this question bring us to a discussion of the ethical underpinnings of the Act.

OPERATIVE UNDERPINNINGS

As we have seen, a serious conflict plagues the principle of 'autonomy' upon which the major safeguards of the DWDA are built. This conflict arises when the wills of different agents are in opposition to each other. It seems apparent from our previous discussion that patients are unable to commit suicide under this referendum's conditions unless the physician, institution, and pharmacist *choose* to permit them to acquire the medication to kill themselves. The search for a means to resolve power conflicts and facilitate dialogue toward understanding uncovers an important and often misunderstood level of the discussion, the level of operative underpinnings. We will explore the quintessential issue, the operative norm upon which the DWDA is built, and reflect upon doctrinal conflicts specific to the Act.

Arguably, religion is the essential issue underpinning the differences in norms and policies that surround medicide. Religion may be defined as the verbal and behavioural articulation of a web of belief.[45] Religion in this sense is not restricted to traditional notions of liturgy, preaching, church denominations, and worship, although all of these may be part of a religion. Religion is the tangible expression of beliefs that lie at the core of a person's intuitional, emotional, rational, and, in some contexts, spiritual being.

Much of the religious framework of the DWDA is founded upon stated or unstated beliefs in Darwinian naturalism. The belief in tenets such as Darwin's is as much a religion as is the belief in the tenets of Christianity. Interpretation of reality by both systems requires faith in some basic unprovable axiom.

If this postulation is defensible, then religion becomes a central issue in the entire discussion. In this particular, Derek Humphry is right: 'the euthanasia movement's clash with religion is the heart of the struggle. People lose sight of that. But in a small way, it's altering 2,000 years of Christianity.'[46] The change sought is neither small in the worldview which it calls medicine to abandon nor minute in the magnitude of its potential consequences.

The meta-ethical basis of Humphry, who is often cited as the founding father of the current medicide movement, serves as a good example of a common belief held by many supporting medicide. Humphry describes himself as one fallen away from the Anglican Church of England. O'Keefe remarks after an interview with Humphry that 'after reading Darwin's evolutionary thesis, Humphry concluded that God doesn't exist'.[47] While using Humphry as a representative of the movement might be disputed, the movement's naturalistic tendency is less controversial. Naturalism is found throughout the Anglo-Saxon movement of medicide, beginning with the Unitarian minister and New Humanist Charles Potter who founded the Euthanasia Society of America on January 16, 1938.[48] Naturalism's description of reality rejects suggestions that the metaphysical realm exists or, if it does, that it has much to do with the definition of right and wrong actions or good and bad intentions.

Although the denial of the existence of God is a serious problem, it would seem inappropriate even from a Christian perspective to attempt to impose that which is accepted by faith on those who choose another path. It also would seem inappropriate to impose upon the unbeliever the lifestyle demanded by faith. As Humphry states persuasively; 'there are millions of atheists and agnostics, as well as people of varieties of religions, degrees of spiritual beliefs, and they all have rights, too.'[49] This leads us to the question of moral obligation in the context of moral and religious pluralism.

Humphry's appeal to rights would be compelling except for a questionable important anthropological assumption made by Humphry and the majority of those supporting medicide. They assume that humanity's nature is either basically good or that the morality of humanity's nature is an emotionally imposed non-existent category. In contrast, the Christian tradition does not view human nature in such a positive light. The lack of warrant for Humphry's assumption brings his appeal to private rights into question. As Francis Schaeffer stated in the context of medicide, 'Sinful man becomes the final standard for killing or not killing human life.'[50]

Anthropology, then, becomes the quintessential issue in the public policy debate. It is the real source of dispute. If humanity is basically good, then the Christian has no moral basis or warrant for impeding the practice of medicide. The likelihood of abuse of the vulnerable would be minimal. However, if humanity's nature is indeed radically wounded, as taught in Christian tradition, then the potential of abuse cannot go unconsidered. More specifically, it is incumbent upon those opposing medicide to move beyond the perceived doctrinal rhetoric of the abuses that might take place and to offer historical verifications of these abuses. The preceding discussion referring to the Remmelink Report and *Aktie Vier* provides a beginning. Those objecting to this argument must move beyond their own religious utilitarian rhetoric of euphemisms and *ad hominem* attacks to refute the evidence and demonstrate adequate safeguards for vulnerable populations.

At least three other doctrinal conflicts beside anthropology are evident in the discussion surrounding medicide. We have alluded to one, the denial of the existence of the biblical God of justice. Future reflections should consider the effect which such a denial has had, is having, and may have on just distribution of resources. The Christian doctrine of soteriology exposes a second fundamental conflict involving the positive and negative nature of suffering. Benthamite eudaemonism and its quest for pleasure has all but anathematized suffering. Historical treatises on the place of suffering and its value in society should be revived as part of community and social memory. In its absence, will not the propagation of our hedonistic amnesia bring us to the place of suffering's remembrance in a more destructive manner? Finally, a third doctrinal assumption of those supporting medicide is the rejection of an afterlife. As Humphry puts it:

> If I'm wrong and the pope is right, I'm going straight into Hell and the burning fires, no question I've helped thousands of people to kill themselves. But I'm willing to gamble. My guess is there is no afterlife.[51]

In a pluralistic culture of relativism and hedonism, the Christian expectation of an afterlife seems unacceptable, if not laughable. For the community of believers, however, the prospect of Hell should be quite sobering. It is so rarely preached with biblical content that few take mind of it. Even though few in the public arena of policy formation will grant any consideration to the implications of that which is enacted for eternal existence, a sincere and humble declaration of such considerations may snatch some from the pangs of a far greater death.

CONCLUSION

The opening sentences of this chapter suggested that neither the opponents nor the advocates of medicide were particularly pleased with the Oregon Death with Dignity Act as it is currently crafted. The primary deficiency of the Oregon solution is the likelihood of producing protracted suffering in a significant number of patient participants due to the sub-lethal nature of oral solutions. The spectre of failed attempts at assisted suicide led some opponents to rightly reject this referendum on the basis of the danger such practice poses to those seeking a death with dignity.

The advocates recognized this danger as well. Their final solution was to broaden the scope of the material act sufficiently to include lethal injection. The pre-meditated plan to broaden the Act after the election, however, raises the issue of proper disclosure both on the social level and, by extension, on the individual level. If those promoting the right to an informed choice for a death with dignity neglected disclosure of the necessity for lethal injection in order that the public embrace a less informed Act, is it warranted to assume that they will safeguard voluntary informed choices on the level of private practice? Evidence presented in our treatment brings claims about full disclosure and informed choice into question. Of particular significance are the recent accounts cited earlier, questioning the reality of patient self determination in the United States and a groundbreaking study by the Dutch government intimating that patient autonomy might be somewhat of a social illusion.

This presentation has suggested that one reason behind a questionable patient autonomy is the variability in people's capacity to exercise decision making power. The ability of agents, whether patient, physician, hospital, or society, to actualize their treatment decisions is inextricably bound up with their capacity to exercise power. The primacy of agents is associated with their empowerment. This observation has led us to probe the explanation behind the power struggles of the proponents and opponents engaged in the medicide dispute. At the heart of these struggles is religion: the age old tradition of a Judeo-Christian and Hippocratic medicine versus the resurgence of a naturalistic utilitarianism.

This recognition has brought us to what might well be the quintessential issue of the discussion, that of anthropology. Is the character of humanity such that the practice of medicide will not extend to the abuse of the vulnerables? Can such character and practice be demonstrated historically? Our study suggests that medicide presents a serious threat to a society's safety, welfare, and actualization of justice. Placing this medicide in the context of a rapidly evolving medical industrial complex of efficiency, productivity, and utility exacerbates concerns for the less protected in society. The coalescence of these reflections indicates that Oregon's solution to suffering and patient rights is neither dignified nor final.

To conclude in non-constructive criticism would be unfair to the advocates of the DWDA, unhelpful to those seeking alternatives to medicide, and insensitive to those seeking a death with dignity. I would therefore like to conclude with a call for the development of some of the following ideas in the near future. First is a suggestion to the advocates of medicide. The lack of clarity in the route of administration in policy statements should be resolved. This could easily be accomplished by stating that either self-administration through oral ingestion or lethal injection (or both) will be used for the termination of a person's life. This would be a welcome step toward adequately informing the voter regarding the issues on which they are voting. Second is a suggestion to those seeking the 'right to die' with dignity. Realization of one's autonomy is not a simple matter, as indicated by some of the studies cited in this presentation. Palliative care and control of the sources of one's suffering should be earnestly sought in environments where professionals are trained in full-orbed pain management. Although this path may be more difficult at the outset, it is requisite if anything like autonomous and end-of-life decision-making is to take place.

Finally, for those seeking alternatives to medicide who are still seeking clarification regarding the core issues, Ephesians 6:12ff should be illuminating and engender prayer and direction for engagement. Engagement with those holding different positions is best done through a sincere development of relationships with them. We must strive for more than an agreement to disagree; rather we must honestly consider together all possible alternatives to symptomatically treating the problem of suffering through medicide. The final solution to issues of suffering and dignified death is likely to be located in relationships that transcend self-empowerment, personal utility, and pleasurable states of consciousness. Such transcendent relationships transform the sting of certain death into the breath of everlasting life. Those of Christian tradition might do well to search out the meaning of such relationships in the words of one well acquainted with affliction and death, Paul of Tarsus:

> For none of us lives to himself alone and none of us dies to himself alone. If we live, we live to the Lord; and if we die, we die to the Lord. So, whether we live or die, we belong to the Lord. For this very reason, Christ died and returned to life so that he might be the Lord of both the dead and the living (Rom. 14:7–9).

NOTES

1. Keisling, Phil (Secretary of State) *Official Abstract of Votes General Election* (State Elections Division, Salem, Oregon; November 8, 1994) pp. I, 54. The fact that only thirty-four percent (627,980) of the total number of registered voters (1,832,774) of Oregon voted for the Measure casts a shadow of doubt on the argument that the passing of this initiative was a clear indication of the 'will of the people,' as touted by some Hemlock Society members.

2. The term medicide will be used in place of euthanasia or physician–assisted suicide throughout this presentation. The reason is that the term portrays the medical reality of the practice better than the other terms, particularly the euphemism euthanasia. By medicide I mean 'the application of medicinal practice with the intent and for the purpose of terminating human life'.

3. I will use the ethical ground question *'What ought I to do?'* as an instrument of medico–ethical clarification. The technical question is used only as a tool to describe what those crafting the Measure judge 'ought' to be done. This ground question is divided into four technical elements. These elements are used as guideposts when clarifying the medical and ethical realities at hand. Cf. Wernow, Jerome R, *This Vital Death: Toward Applying a Postmodern Reconstructed Christian Ethic to the Discussion of Forgoing Treatment in the Critically Ill Hospitalized Adult.* (Katholieke Universiteit Leuven: Dissertation, June, 1994), pp. 25–52.

4. I am using the phrase 'tradition bound' in the same sense as suggested by Alasdair MacIntyre in *Whose Justice? Which Rationality?* (Redwood Burn Limited, Trowbridge: 1988), p. 354: *The rationality of a tradition-constituted and tradition constitutive enquiry is in key and essential part a matter of the kind of progress which it makes through a number of well-defined types of stages. Every such form of enquiry begins in and from some condition of pure historical contingency, from beliefs, institutions, and practices of some particular community which constitute a given.*

5. Keisling, Phil (Secretary of State), 'Measure 16,' *Official 1994 General Election Voters' Pamphlet* (No Date), p. 121. The statement intimating this notion reads: *I understand the full import of this request and I expect to die when I **take** the medication to be prescribed* (bold mine).

6. My use of the term 'implicit' is in accord with the language adopted by the Justices of the Oregon Supreme Court in their discussion of this issue. The intent

of the writers regarding the identity of the one administering the medication for
the purpose of medicide appeared to be unclear to the Justices as well. In their
press release, proponents of the referendum argued against petitioner Kane's
proposition that 'give' should be used in the place of 'prescribe'. It is important to
notice the use of the term 'apparent' by the Judges in the following citation. This
term intimates an appeal to the clarity of the intent of the crafters and not the
restrictions of the Measure's language. The judges ruled that: '*Give' could be easily
read by a voter as indicating that the lethal medication would actually be administered by
the prescribing physician; that does not appear to be what is contemplated by the proposed
measure. Rather, the physician's role is limited to prescribing; the act of taking the
prescribed drug is to be that of the terminally ill person.* Cf. Oregon Supreme Court,
Henry Kane et al. v Theodore R. Kulongowski, (SC S41020) (SC S41022) (SC
S41024), April 14, 1994, p. 4 (underline mine).

7. Keisling, Phil (Secretary of State): 'Measure 16,' *Official 1994 General
Election Voters' Pamphlet* (No Date), pp. 123, 122. This implication can be found
under '3.13 Insurance or Annuity Policies,' *Neither shall a qualified patient's* **act of
ingesting medication** *to end his or her life in a humane and dignified manner have an
effect upon a life, health, or accident insurance or annuity policy.* (bold mine)

8. Coalition for Compassionate Care, *Questions and Answers About the Assisted
Suicide Initiative* (June 7, 1994), pp. 1–2.

9. See 'Allows Terminally Ill Adults to Obtain Prescription for Lethal
Drugs,' Keisling, Phil (Secretary of State), 'Measure 16,' *Official 1994 General
Election Voters' Pamphlet* (No Date), p. 121. The summary of the Act states:
*Allows terminally ill adult Oregon residents voluntary informed choice to obtain
physician's prescription for drugs to end life.* Oregon Right to Die. *Draft Explanatory
Statement.* (July 20, 1994) lines 1–5. *This measure would allow an informed and
capable adult resident of Oregon, who is terminally ill and within six months of death, to
voluntarily request a prescription for medication to take his or her life. The Measure
allows a physician to prescribe a lethal dose of medication when conditions are met. The
physician and others may be present if the medication is taken.*

10. Oregon Revised Statutes (ORS) 689005 (28), 1993-52–4.

11. Oregon Revised Statutes 677010 (6). Drug was further defined by ORS
689.005 (10) as: *Articles recognized as drugs in the official United States Pharmacopoeia,
official National Formulary, official Homeopathic Pharmacopoeia, other drug compendium or any supplement to any of them; (b) Articles intended for the use in the diagnosis,
cure, mitigation, treatment or prevention of disease in a human or other animal; (c)
Articles (other than food) intended to affect the structure or any function of the body of
humans or other animals . . .*

12. Keisling, Phil (Secretary of State), 'Measure 16,' *Official 1994 General
Election Voters' Pamphlet* (No Date), p. 123.

13. The lack of clarity in these two statements led influential panel members of
the Oregon State Extension Service to interpret the 'Act' as prohibiting 'lethal
injection' and 'mercy killing'. The ambiguity of Section 3.14 leaves the accuracy
of this interpretation in question. Cf. Hare, J; Gregerson, D; Pratt, C; Campbell,
C; Kliewer, David; Bruce, J, *The Oregon Death with Dignity Act.* EM 8569,
August 1994.

14. This interpretation is not a mere personal contrivance but rather a
suggested addition introduced by a Hemlock Society member for legislative
change sent to Dr Grant Higginson, Acting State Health Officer. The December
6, 1994 text reads: '*Prescription for Medication' means drugs in all doses, dosages forms
and routes of administration prepared and dispensed by a licensed pharmacist for the
purpose of self-administration to end life in a humane and dignified manner.* The citation
comes from closed task force implementation sessions and the identity of the
participants involved are confidential. The veracity of the text can be substan-
tiated through the public records on file at the Oregon State Board of Pharmacy.

It should be noted that this recommendation was modified into meaninglessness at a following meeting of this task force and was never implemented by the Oregon legislature.

15. Letter from Mr Eli Stutsman AAL to Jerome R Wernow, Ph.D., R.Ph. (September 14, 1994) p. 2.

16. Bates, Tom, 'Write to Die', *The Oregonian* (December 18, 1994), section A, p. 30. This expose gives a concise account of the historical background of those associated with the Measure and its crafting.

17. Ibid, section A, pp. 1, 30ff.

18. Under the rubric 'What the Oregon Death with Dignity Act Does Not Allow' the statement in bold reads: 'The Oregon Death with Dignity Act does not authorize lethal injection, mercy killing or active euthanasia' Cf. Goodwin, Peter (ed), *What Health Care Professionals Need to Know About the Oregon Death With Dignity Act.* (Authorized by Oregon Right to Die, No Date), inside panel 3.

19. Cf ABC News Nightline #3533 (December 7, 1994) pp. 2–3.

20. Humphry, Derek, *What's in a word? The results of a Roper Poll of Americans on how they view the importance of language in the debate over the right to choose to die.* (Euthanasia Research and Guidance Organization (ERGO): August, 1993), p. 2.

21. Bates, Tom, 'Write to Die', *The Oregonian* (December 18, 1995), section A, p. 30.

22. Maas, P J van der; J J M van Delden; and L Pijnenborg, *Euthanasia and other Medical Decisions Concerning the End of Life.* (Elesevier: Amsterdam, 1992), v. 2, p. 47.

23. The intent regarding the identity of the one administering the medication contemplated behind the Measure remained unclear to them as well In their press release they argued against petitioner Kane's proposition that 'give' a drug should be used in the place of 'prescribe.' It is important to notice the use of the term 'apparent' by the Justices. This term intimates an appeal to the clarity of the intent of the crafters and not the restrictions of the Measure's language. Cf. note 6.

24. Humphry, Derek, 'Letter to the Editor,' *New York Times,* (December 3, 1994) p. 14. Humphry suggests that he has data substantiating his opinion saying: *In October Dutch television aired a documentary showing the death of Cornelius van Wendel de Joode from injections of barbiturates and curare. This voluntary euthanasia was swift, painless and sure. Here is where the Oregon law, which forbids injections, could be disastrous. In a controlled study in the Netherlands, 90 people were given, at their request, nine grams of barbiturates by mouth. Sixty-eight died quickly — within two hours. The rest lingered as long as four days; In 15 instances the doctor gave a lethal injection because the oral drugs were causing protracted suffering to the patient, the family and himself.*

25. O'Keefe, Mark: 'Dutch researcher warns of lingering deaths', The Sunday Oregonian (December 4, 1994), p. 1. According to this source, Admiraal has found that 25 percent of those attempting suicide using the oral route linger *two days or longer.* He intimates that Oregon's law is a first step but uncivilized in its current form because of the unpredictability of outcomes after oral ingestion.

26. Humphry, Derek, *What's in a word? The results of a Roper Poll of Americans on how they view the importance of language in the debate over the right to choose to die.* (ERGO: No Date), pp. 2–3.

27. Ibid, p. 2.

28. Bates, Tom, 'Write to Die', *The Oregonian* (December 18, 1994), section A, p. 30.

29. Alexander, Leo, 'Medical Science under Dictatorship,' *The New England Journal of Medicine* (July 14, 1949), v. 241/2, p. 46.

30. Glare, P G W (ed), *Oxford Latin Dictionary.* (Clarendon: Oxford University Press, 1982) 2nd reprint, p. 88.

31. Simpson, J A; E S C Weiner; *et al*, (eds), *The Oxford English Dictionary*, (Oxford: Clarendon Press, 2nd edition, 1989), v. 1, p. 248.

32. Glare, P G W (ed), *Oxford Latin Dictionary*. (Clarendon: Oxford University Press, 1982), 2nd reprint, p. 1444.

33. Cf Bok, Sissela, 'The Physician as Moral Agent: Round Table Discussion.' *Philosophical Medical Ethics: Its Nature and Significance*. (eds) Stuart F Spicker and H Tristram Engelhardt, in the series *Philosophy and Medicine*, (Holland: D Reidel Publishing Co.: 1977), v. 3, p. 230; Beck, Lewis White, 'Agent, Actor, Spectator, and Critic,' *The Monist*. (April 1965), v. 49/2, pp. 168–169; Baier, Kurt, 'Action and Agent,' *The Monist*. (April 1965), v. 49/2, pp. 183–193; Boler, John F, 'Agency,' *Philosophy and Phenomenological Research*. (December 1968), v. 29/2, pp. 168–173.

34. Koch, Kathryn A; Meyers, Bruce W; Sandroni, Stephen: 'Analysis of Power in Medical Decision-Making: An Argument for Physician Autonomy.' *Law, Medicine, and Health*. (Winter, 1992), v. 20/4. pp. 320–326.

35. Section 301 (1) states that *The attending physician shall: (1) Make the initial determination of whether a, patient has a terminal disease, is capable, and has made the request voluntarily*. Cf. Keisling, Phil (Secretary of State): 'Measure 16,' *Official 1994 General Election Voters' Pamphlet*. (No Date), pp. 121–122. Beyond the difficulty of accurately predicting the timing of someone's death which is perhaps 4–8 months away, there is also the issue of class bias. It seems incomprehensible to deny medicide to an individual suffering from a grave illness whose prognosis is nine months. It is rather difficult to fathom a rational justification for denying the medicide of a mentally incompetent patient who has asked for its application in a health care advanced directive. In fact, the inability to draw the line was brought out in the April 18, 1995 hearing when Judge Hogan queried pro-medicide defence attorney Charles Hinkle regarding where the line should be drawn. The apparent answer was that, except for adult status, there is no line. Cf. Lee, et al. v Harcleroad: U.S. District Court of Oregon (Eugene) (94–CV–6467) April 18, 1995. The page was not available at the time of this text's drafting because the case report was under advisement of Judge Hogan at that time. Information was taken from my personal notes of the hearing.

36. Cf note 40. *Section 4.01(4)* reads: *No health care provider shall be under any duty, whether by contract, by statute or by any other legal requirement to participate in the provision to a qualified patient of medication to end his or her life in a humane and dignified manner. If a health care provider is unable or unwilling to carry out a patient's health care provider shall transfer, upon request, a copy of the patient's relevant medical records to the new health care provider.*

37. Orentlicher, David, 'The Illusion of Patient Choice in End-of -Life Decisions,' *The Journal of the American Medical Association* (April 15, 1992), v. 267/15, p. 2102. He states that *A number of studies suggest that physician values may be more decisive than patient values in end-of-life decisions.*

38. Ibid, pp. 2102–2103.

39. Abrams, Fredrick, R, 'Caring for the Sick: An Emerging Industrial By-product,' *The Journal of the American Medical Association*. (February 21, 1986), v. 255/7, p. 937.

40. Board of Pharmacy, *Oregon Revised Statutes* (Board of Pharmacy, 1993), p. 5.

41. Keisling, Phil (Secretary of State): 'Measure 16,' *Official 1994 General Election Voters' Pamphlet* (No Date), p. 123.

42. Memorandum to All Pharmacists sent in care of the Oregon State Pharmacists Association (Salem, Oregon) dated December 7, 1994.

43. Cf Maas, P J van der; J J M van Delden; and L Pijnenborg, *Euthanasia and other Medical Decisions Concerning the End of Life*. (Elesevier: Amsterdam, 1992), v. 2, p. 194; Alexander, Leo, 'Medical Science under Dictatorship,' *The New*

England Journal of Medicine. (July 14, 1949), v. 241/2, p. 45. The Dutch experience, documented in the first of these two citations, states that *physicians prescribe, supply or administer a drug with the explicit purpose of hastening the end of life without explicit request of the patient in somewhat more than one thousand cases annually (0.8% of all deaths).* Cf. p. 194. Alexander admonishes practitioners in the United States to shun a health care system based upon *utility, efficiency, and productivity.* Cf. Alexander, Leo, 'Medical Science under Dictatorship,' *The New England Journal of Medicine.* (July 14, 1949), v. 241/2, p. 46.

44. Governor Bill Hayden of Australia provides even greater reason for concern by stating, *Moreover, having had a full and satisfying lifetime, there is a point where the succeeding generations deserve to be disencumbered — to coin a clumsy word — of some unproductive burdens.* Cf. Netscape/Internet under the rubric DeathNet, *Online Library* ERGO, June 22, 1995. His opinion represents a logical extension of modernity's naturalistic utilitarian ethic.

45. Cf Wolfe, David L, *Epistemology: The Justification of Belief.* (Downers Grove, Ill.: Intervarsity Press 1982), pp. 44–45. I draw my metaphor of web from Quine. '*W V O Quine proposes that we think of our beliefs as forming a complicated, interconnected web of ideas. Some of the beliefs constituting this web lie at the edge of the web, very close to experience, other beliefs lie far from experience, more toward the interior of the web, so to speak. Like portions of a physical web, those interior portions of the web are essential to holding the web together. Logically they are part of a global set of beliefs about what reality is like. Let us call this, as I have earlier, an interpretative scheme or framework. It is the integrity of the web of beliefs which gives the inner beliefs their meaning. They have a function in the web which is not simply social or emotional, but cognitive. They are part of an interpretation of reality which seeks to come to terms with experience in a total rather than a piece meal fashion.*' I modify this statement by adding the adjectives 'sensory and ontological' to the beliefs experienced at the edge of the web, and hold that a mystical experience, rather than 'far from experience ' describes what lies closer to the centre of the web.

46. O'Keefe, Mark, 'Founding Father,' *The Oregonian,* (November 1, 1994), section A, p. 13.

47. Ibid.

48. Russell, O Ruth, *Freedom to Die: Moral and Legal Aspects of Euthanasia.* revised edition, (Human Sciences Press, New York, 1975), pp. 72–76.

49. Humphry, Derek, 'Why I Believe in Euthanasia: the case for rational suicide' (ERGO Information Center, 1995) religion section. His essay may be accessed through the InterNet using Netscape. Search *DeathNet* then *ERGO Information Center,* then Derek Humphry Essays.

50. Schaeffer, Francis A and Everett C Koop, *What Ever Happened to the Human Race?* in the series *The Complete Works of Francis A Schaeffer: A Christian View of the Church,* (Westchester, Illinois: Crossway Books, 1982), v. 4, p. 376.

51. O'Keefe, Mark, 'Founding Father,' *The Oregonian* (November 1, 1994), section A, p. 12.

11

North American Law and Public Policy

Arthur J Dyck, PhD

Is physician-assisted suicide favoured by a majority of Americans?
Will such a policy become legally permissible? Proponents of
legalizing physician-assisted suicide and euthanasia (mercy-
killing) would like all Americans to believe that the answer to both
questions is 'yes'! They use opinion polls as part of a major
strategy to convince their opponents and the voting public that
most Americans now favour the legalization of physician-assisted
suicide and mercy-killing, and that legalization of these practices is
inevitable. This can be a very effective strategy. If the American
public comes to believe that legalizing physician-assisted suicide
and mercy killing is desired by most Americans, and will
inevitably be realized, that same public will tend to view opponents of such practices very negatively. As representing a minority
viewpoint, opponents of physician-assisted suicide can be seen as
seeking to impose their own morality on their fellow citizens.
And, if such opponents invoke their Christian convictions, they
can be seen as pushing a particular religious viewpoint, not shared
by Americans generally, a viewpoint that is inappropriate as well
as irrelevant as a guide to what public policy ought to be.
Understandably, these Christians themselves are tempted by poll
data, and media use of them, to think that they represent a
minority opinion, an opinion that cannot, or perhaps should not,
prevail as the law of the land in a pluralistic, democratic country.

But Christian beliefs are relevant and appropriate to the shaping
of American public policy. Indeed, they are needed as never
before, particularly, though not exclusively, on such issues as
physician-assisted suicide and mercy killing. This is true for at
least two reasons: 1) Christianity, at its very core, affirms the
natural human proclivities and inhibitions that actualize the moral
bonds, the human relations, logically and functionally necessary
for the existence and sustenance of individuals and communities;
and 2) the whole way of thinking that currently challenges
existing laws against assisted suicide and euthanasia denies what
Christianity affirms. This perspective affirms instead that individuals naturally pursue egoistic desires at odds with what makes

communities possible and sustainable, and affirms, moreover, that the pursuit of such egoistic desires is a moral value, a basis for claiming individual rights, such as autonomy. This is a 'streamlined' version of John Stuart Mill. It is fairly pervasive in the bioethics literature and American courts.[1] It is an attack against the shared morality sustaining contemporary institutions and communities, as well as an attack against the Christian beliefs that instruct and motivate individuals and groups to embody this shared morality. In Christian parlance, this shared morality is the 'law written on the heart'. As the collapse of communism amply demonstrated, no community can long exist if this moral law is flaunted and those who honour it are suppressed. This is one Christian conviction absolutely essential to public policy in any community. Other religions share it. That laws and governments must share it as well is the central conclusion of the present analysis.

The analysis will proceed in three segments: 1) It begins with a brief assessment of public opinion toward physician–assisted suicide; 2) it proceeds to analyze the dominant set of concepts fuelling public opinion trends, largely found in a 'streamlined' version of Mill; 3) it concludes by arguing that Christianity is part of a longstanding consensus against physician–assisted suicide, and has a definite, positive role to play in shaping law in this and other areas. Since laws permitting assisted suicide are destructive of the moral bonds of community, and the shared morality that actualizes them, Christians have a moral responsibility to do what is in their power to maintain and strengthen the longstanding consensus underlying current laws prohibiting assisted suicide. To carry out this responsibility is not a power play or contrived strategy; it is rather the effort of Christians to practise love of one's neighbour, and to protect the very bases of neighbourliness.

WHAT WE KNOW ABOUT PUBLIC OPINION

To begin, then, what do we know about American public opinion regarding physician–assisted suicide? If those who use polls strategically to push for legalizing assisted suicide were to be believed, a clear majority of Americans side with these strategists. Examples of this strategic use of polls abound. Let one suffice for this presentation.

Two days before the vote on Washington State's referendum (Initiative 119)[2] — which if passed, would have legalized physician–assisted suicide and mercy killing — the *Boston Sunday Globe* published a major article under the bold print heading, 'Poll: Americans Favor Mercy Killing.'[3] According to this poll, 64 percent of the American public favour physician–assisted suicide and euthanasia; and 61 percent would vote for Initiative 119 if it were on the ballot in their state.[4]

But one should be sceptical of these poll data. Whereas the polls showed 61 percent in favour of Initiative 119, only 46 percent of Washington State's voters marked their secret ballots that way. The disparity between the public opinion polls and the results gleaned by secret ballot in California, was even greater one year later in 1992 as voters there defeated a referendum to legalize physician–assisted death by the same 54 to 46 percent margin.[5] Yet these polls are taken at face value even by people who should know better. The *Globe* confronted a medical ethics professor at Boston College with their poll results indicating that 71 percent of all Catholics would vote for the Washington Initiative. The professor gave them the quote they wanted: 'It's quite clear two–thirds of the Catholics don't believe what the bishops are teaching.'[6] No scholar has any basis for such a generalization from one poll, but this professor is far from alone in treating poll results as hard data.

Even though polls tend to exaggerate considerably the support that exists for legalizing physician–assisted suicide and euthanasia, the change in attitudes toward these practices is real. In 1994, the people of Oregon did approve a referendum legalizing physician-assisted suicide, albeit by a slim two percent margin. (Its implementation, however, has been blocked by the courts due to various problems with its formulation.)[7] Most significantly, public opinion has shifted over time. Surveys conducted in the United States during the period encompassing 1950 to 1991 asked the following question: 'When a person has a disease that cannot be cured, do you think doctors should be allowed by law to end the patient's life if the patient and his or her family requested it?' The percentage answering yes increased from 36 percent in 1950 to 63 percent in 1991.[8] Most of the change came before 1973, with 53 percent answering yes.[9] This shift in American public opinion paralleled changes in attitudes about religious practices, sexual morals, divorce, and abortion, mainly between 1965 and 1975.[10]

What we do know is that Americans are more inclined now than in the past to favour the abolition of present legal prohibitions of assisted suicide. What we do not know is how extensive and fixed such opinions are. The voting record of three states, Washington, California, and Oregon, suggests a fairly even split in the number of opponents and proponents of legalized physician-assisted suicide. Poll data suggest a trend favourable to proponents, at least at present. To enter into the debate over assisted suicide, it is vital to understand the kind of thinking that fuels such an apparent trend.

THE JUDICIAL THREAT TO HUMANITY'S SHARED
MORALITY

The debate over physician-assisted suicide is already being carried
on in American and Canadian courts. Although the voters of
Washington State turned down the legalization of physician-
assisted suicide, Justice Rothstein, writing for a U.S. district court
in Washington State declared that physician-assisted suicide is an
individual's constitutional right.[11] In turn, California's Ninth
Circuit Court of Appeals reversed this opinion.[12] As noted earlier,
Oregon's referendum approving the legalization of physician-
assisted suicide was immediately taken up by the courts. Canada's
Supreme Court has upheld the constitutionality of Canada's laws
but did so by a close five to four decision.[13] In these court
decisions the streamlined version of Mill, fuelling opinions that
favour the legalization of physician-assisted suicide, is clearly
evident and clearly stated; the consensus so far prevailing against
this viewpoint is equally clearly evident and clearly stated. An
analysis of certain court cases will suffice to bring the heart of this
debate into full view.

To begin with, consider the opinions in the case of Elizabeth
Bouvia.[14] Bouvia was a 28-year-old woman being cared for in one
of Los Angeles County's facilities. She has cerebral palsy, and her
disease had progressed to the point where she required supple-
mental nutrition in the form of a nasogastric tube. Removal of the
tube was expected to lead to death by starvation. The patient was
considered by all to be mentally competent, and beyond that of a
keen and lively mind. The tube was well tolerated physically.

In the court's unanimous view, her mental and emotional
feelings deserved respect. 'To the petitioner,' wrote the court, 'it is
a dismal prospect to live with this hated and unwanted device
attached. . . . She has the right to have it removed immediately.'[15]
The patient's interests and desires represented the key ingredients
in the decision. This decision was 'a moral and philosophical
decision that being a competent adult, [was] hers alone'.[16]
Furthermore, the court argued that Bouvia, lying helplessly in
bed, unable to care for herself, may consider her existence
meaningless. She cannot be faulted for so doing.[17]

So far all three judges agree. Moreover, they are making use of
Mill's calculus to paint a gloomy picture of Bouvia's life and its
prospects, and to decide what is right for her to do. Also, like
Mill, there is no natural, continuous desire to preserve one's life,
as in Hobbes and Locke: life may not retain its meaningfulness
when abilities are lost and/or pain enters the picture. And the
court is in agreement with Mill that decisions about one's health

and one's state of mind are private and 'require no one's approval'.[18]

But the court splits when it comes to interpreting what Bouvia wishes and what wishes of hers are to be free of government interference. Two of the three judges contend that Bouvia does not wish to commit suicide but wishes only to be free of her nasogastric tube. Judge Compton, however, in her concurring opinion, stated unequivocally that Bouvia had made a 'conscious and informed choice that she prefers death to continued existence in her helpless and intolerable condition. . . . [S]he has an absolute right to effectuate that decision.'[19] Judge Compton found her death by self-starvation inhumane and maintained that

> The right to die is an integral part of our right to control our own destinies so long as the rights of others are not affected. That right should, in my opinion, include the ability to enlist assistance from others including the medical profession, in making death as painless and quick as possible.[20]

Judge Compton was convinced that Bouvia wished to commit suicide. Accommodating her, in Judge Compton's view, should not trouble the medical profession because it has already abandoned the Hippocratic Oath in the matter of abortion. According to Judge Compton, '[i]f there is ever a time when we ought to get the government off our backs, it is when we face death — either by choice or otherwise.'[21]

Thus Judge Compton has incorporated still another element of Mill's thought, namely that

> [T]he only purpose for which power can be rightfully exercised over any member of a civilized community, against his will, is to prevent harm to others. His own good, either physical or moral, is not a significant warrant. He cannot rightfully be compelled to do or forbear because it will be better for him to do so, because it will make him happier, because in the opinion of others to do so would be wise or even right.[22]

To justify legalizing physician–assisted suicide, Judge Compton: 1) calculated the disutility of Bouvia's life in her circumstances and saw her pain and suffering as evil; 2) asserted the sovereignty of individuals over their own minds and bodies; and 3) prevented the state from interfering in harms or wrongs done by individuals wishing to do these harms or wrongs to themselves only. These three elements lifted from Mill are also found in other explicit defences of a constitutional right to physician–assisted suicide, such as the decision rendered by Judge Rothstein in Washington State, and in dissenting opinions by Judge Wright of California's

Ninth Circuit Court of Appeals and Judge McLachlin of the Canadian Supreme Court.[23]

Why call these formulations a *streamlined* version of Mill? The reason lies in Mill's view of justice as the name for stringent moral rules and the basis for human rights. Mills regards these rules as 'essentials of human well-being,' as those that 'forbid human beings from hurting one another,' and as those which make 'safe for us the very groundwork of our existence' and are the 'main element in determining the . . . social feelings of mankind'.[24] Those judges who articulate the streamlined version of Mill do not discuss this aspect of Mill's thought. They do not consider the possibility that harm to both oneself and others may consist of laws that undermine, or unduly weaken 'essentials of human well-being.' This neglected portion of Mill's thinking is not found in his essay *On Liberty* but in his essay on *Utilitarianism*. Mary Ann Glendon has noted that

> To a greater degree than any other, the American legal system has accepted Mill's version of individual liberty, including its relative inattention to the problem of what may constitute 'harm to others' and unconcern with types of harm that may not be direct and immediate. Indeed, we took Mill's ideas a step further than he did. For, when Mill's ideas about liberty of conduct were taken into American constitutional law, they underwent a sea change. His stern sense of responsibility to family and country, and his decided rejection of any notion that all life-styles were equally worthy of respect, largely dropped out of sight.[25]

Over against Compton's narrow understanding of what constitutes harm to self and others, the majority of the court in the Bouvia case upheld California's ban on assisted suicide, appealing to a previous California court decision, and to the sanctity of life.[26] Like other courts across America, they distinguished refusal of treatment from suicide. The irony in the Bouvia case is that while seeking to carry out her wishes, neither the majority nor Compton correctly characterized her wishes in 1986. Bouvia did not refuse the nourishment she needed to live. There is an article in 1992 that verifies her continued wish to live six years later.[27] The Bouvia court did not work with the Hobbesian and Lockean view that there is a natural striving to preserve ones own life; nor did they keep in view the natural, shared morality of all humanity which undergirds the sanctity of life. This shared morality is known to Christians as the law written on the heart. Bouvia and her caregivers remained under its influence. Their natural, God-given inhibitions against killing oneself and others, together with the natural, God-given proclivities to nurture life, were sufficiently strong to cope with and relieve a very difficult set of life-threatening and painful circumstances. It is this view of morality that belongs to the consensus that sustains individuals and communities, and not the special, sectarian theological anthropology of Mill that has entered the thinking and opinions of American courts and that has fuelled a more permissive attitude toward physician-assisted suicide.[28]

One of the most explicit affirmations of this consensus is found in the majority opinion of the Canadian Supreme Court in 1993 upholding the constitutionality of the Canadian law against assisted suicide.[29] The law was being challenged by Sue Rodriguez, suffering from Lou Gehrig's disease, and seeking a right to physician-assisted suicide. In her dissenting opinion, Justice McLachlin had invoked the streamlined version of Mill already sketched above. Justice Sopinka directly repudiated the notion that justice amounts to individual-based principles of privacy writing that 'respect for human dignity and autonomy' (her sole criteria) is but one component of justice 'upon which our society is based'.[30] Justice Sopinka portrayed justice as embodying the requisites of community, ironically citing a former (majority) decision of Judge McLachlin to that effect: 'The principles of fundamental justice are concerned not only with the interest of the person who claims his liberty has been limited, but with the protection of society.'[31] Thus, determining the content of justice in the context of assisted suicide required reference 'to the state's interest in protecting the vulnerable . . . and societal beliefs which are said to be represented by the prohibition'.[32] The purpose of the law against assisted suicide

> is grounded in the state interest in protecting life and reflects the policy of the state that human life should not be depreciated by allowing life to be taken. This policy finds expression . . . in the provisions of our Criminal Code which prohibits murder and other violent acts against others, notwithstanding the consent of the victim. . . . This is not only a policy of the state, however, but is part of our fundamental conception of the sanctity of human life . . . . Preservation of human life is acknowledged to be a fundamental value of our society.[33]

Judge Sopinka then underscored this conception of justice, which expresses the moral requisites of community, by outlining the history of suicide provisions, common law views of medical protection for the terminally ill, and legislation in other countries.

Finally, Judge Sopinka cut through the controversial distinctions between withdrawal of treatment and assisted suicide with the conclusion that

> [to] the extent that there is a consensus, it is that human life must be respected and we must be careful not to undermine the institutions that protect it. . . . In upholding the respect for life, [the law against assisted suicide] may discourage those who consider themselves to be a burden upon others, from committing suicide.[34]

In short, the majority opinion characterized justice as an ideal necessarily implying a moral responsibility of the Canadian state and community, and states and communities generally, to preserve, nurture, and sustain the sanctity of human life. Judge Sopinka painted a picture of justice that reaches out to those perceiving themselves as 'a burden upon others' and seeks to prove them wrong.

Consider briefly also the decision of California's Ninth Circuit Court of Appeals asserting the constitutionality of Washington State's law against assisted suicide.[35] Like the Canadian Supreme Court, the majority opinion written by Judge Noonan is firmly grounded in legislative and constitutional history:

> In the two hundred and five years of our existence no constitutional right to aid in killing oneself has ever been asserted and upheld by a court of final jurisdiction. . . . [A] federal court should not invent a constitutional right unknown to the past and antithetical to the defense of human life that has been a chief responsibility of our constitutional government.[36]

The court also takes aim against the streamlined version of Mill that led Judge Rothstein to ignore the harms to others the state seeks to protect through its laws against assisted suicide. Judge Noonan cites and discusses the following state interests:

1. The interest in not having physicians in the role of killers of their patients;
2. The interest in not subjecting the elderly and even the not-elderly but infirm to psychological pressure to consent to their own deaths;
3. The interest in protecting poor persons and minorities from exploitation;
4. The interest in protecting all people with disabilities from societal indifference and apathy.
5. An interest in preventing abuse similar to what has occurred in the Netherlands. Since 1984 legal guidelines have allowed voluntary assisted suicide and euthanasia. But in addition to the 1.8 percent of all deaths from these practices, .8 percent and arguably more come from direct measures to end life without the patient's contemporaneous request to end it.

Judge Noonan also faulted Judge Rothstein for failing to distinguish between actions taking life and actions by which life is not supported or ceases to be supported.[38] There is a right to be let alone and to do so by refusing treatment. But, as Judge Noonan maintained, the claim to a right to have someone licensed by the state help bring about your death is no longer seeking to end 'unwanted medical attention'. You are asking for 'the right to have a second person collaborate in your death. To protect all of the interests enumerated . . . above, the statute [law against assisted suicide] rightly and reasonably draws the line.'[39]

THE CHRISTIAN CONTRIBUTION TO POLICY

What do Christians have to contribute in this policy debate over physician-assisted suicide? How should Christians conceptualize their role?

To begin with, Christian beliefs support the longstanding consensus that puts a floor under the laws against assisted suicide. Christians affirm the natural and divine basis of laws that protect innocent human life. The philosophies of Hobbes and Locke, cited in American courts, do also. It is only what can be viewed as a sectarian, streamlined version of Mill that undercuts these affirmations. But Hobbes, Locke, and Mill all conspire to deny the natural basis of our responsibilities to one another. This threatens the longstanding consensus. The Christian belief that the moral law is written on our hearts is a belief in the natural basis of our inhibitions against killing, and of our propensities to procreate and nurture life. This belief is needed because it is realistic and true. This belief is needed because it is the basis of laws necessary to instruct and remind people of their responsibilities, and to curb the evil desires of those who ignore or violate the moral law.

Christians should not view themselves, nor should they be viewed by others, as seeking to impose their particular morality on society when they defend laws against assisted suicide. Rather, Christians should be joined by the whole society in defending the natural responsibilities to refrain from killing and to nurture life. These responsibilities are among the moral requisites of community. No community can come to be and sustain itself if the natural inhibitions against killing and the proclivities to procreate and nurture are weakened. In the Netherlands, the inhibition against killing has been weakened already to the extent that physicians do not even allow some patients and their families to choose life when they are severely ill. Given all the killing going on in the world, the inhibitions against it need all the encouragement of instruction and law that biblically faithful Christians have to offer.

Christians are followers of the Word, followers of Jesus Christ. In Matthew 5:17, Jesus, after calling upon his followers to be shining lights to others through their good works, says of himself, 'Do not think that I have come to abolish the law or the prophets; I have come not to abolish but to fulfil.'[40] Followers of Jesus Christ, faithful to his word, will stand for the moral law, teach it, and live it. In so doing, Christians, like the Good Samaritan of old, will love and save the lives of their neighbours. That is how and that is why Christians will support the laws against physician-assisted suicide.

NOTES

1. The pervasiveness of a 'streamlined' version of Mill in American courts is documented in Mary Ann Glendon, *Rights Talk: The Impoverishment of Political Discourse* (New York: Free Press, 1991). See especially pp. 49, 52–54, and 72.

2. Initiative for Death With Dignity, Washington Initiative No 119 (1991). Initiative 119, if it had been passed, would have made it legal for doctors to give patients who wished it a lethal injection or a lethal dose of drugs. At least two physicians must have diagnosed the patient as terminally ill, with six months or less to live, or as in a persistent vegetative state. Also, it would have been legal for patients to request in advance that life-sustaining care, including tube feeding and intravenous fluids, be withheld in the event that they are hopelessly ill or injured.

3. Richard Knox, 'Poll: Americans Favor Mercy Killing,' *Boston Sunday Globe* (November 3, 1991), p. 22.

4. Ibid.

5. The California Death With Dignity Act, California Proposition No.161 (1992).

6. Richard Knox, op. cit.

7. The Oregon Death With Dignity Act (1994); Lee v. State of Oregon, 869 F. Supp. 1491 (D. Or. 1994).

8. R J Blendon, U S Szalay & R A Knox, 'Should physicians aid their patients in dying? The public perspective', *JAMA*, vol. 267 (1992), pp. 2658–2662.

9. Ibid.

10. Paul J van der Maas, Loes Pijnenborg, & Johannes J M van Delden, 'Changes in Dutch Opinions on Active Euthanasia, 1966 Through 1991,' *JAMA*, vol. 273 (1995), p. 1414.

11. Compassion in Dying v. Washington, 850 F. Supp. 1454 (W. D. Wash. 1994).

12. Compassion in Dying v. Washington, No. 94-35534, 1995 WL 94679 (9th Cir. Mar. 9, 1995).

13. Rodriguez v. British Columbia, 107 D.L.R. 4th 342 (1993).

14. Bouvia v. Superior Court, 225 Cal. Rptr. 297 (Cal. Ct. App. 1986).

15. Ibid., p. 299.

16. Ibid., p. 305.

17. Ibid., p. 304.

18. Ibid., p. 301. Mill states it this way: 'Over himself, over his own mind and body, the individual is sovereign.' John Stuart Mill, 'On Liberty,' in Marshall Cohen (ed.), *The Philosophy of John Stuart Mill* (New York: The Modern Library, 1961), p. 197.

19. Ibid., p. 307.

20. Ibid.

21. Ibid., p. 308.

22. John Stuart Mill, op. cit. p. 197.

23. *Compassion in Dying*, op. cit. and *Rodriguez*, op. cit.

24. John Stuart Mill, 'Utilitarianism' in Marshall Cohen (ed.), op. cit. pp. 391–92, 385.

25. Mary Ann Glendon, op. cit. p. 72.

26. *Bouvia*, op. cit. p. 306.

27. Gail Diane Cox, 'Advocate Takes His Own Life,' *National Law Journal* (August 24, 1992), p. 6. This reference to Bouvia is in this article about the death by suicide of the lawyer who represented her in 1986.

28. The term 'sectarian' in this context means 'of limited scope.' Justice Stevens in the U.S. Supreme Court's decision concerning Nancy Cruzan had accused Missouri law reflecting a sectarian and hence, non-secular view. But Missouri is part of the longstanding consensus view of life's sacredness and Stevens is the sectarian. For the argument in detail, see Arthur J Dyck, 'Beyond Theological Conflict in the Courts: The Issue of Assisted Suicide,' *Notre Dame Journal of Law, Ethics & Public Policy*, vol. (No. 2, 1995), pp. 503–535.

29. *Rodriguez.* op. cit.
30. Ibid., p. 394.
31. Ibid., p. 395.
32. Ibid., p. 396.
33. Ibid.
34. Ibid., p. 406.
35. *Compassion in Dying*, op. cit.
36. Ibid., p. 591.
37. Ibid., p. 592–93.
38. Ibid., p. 594.
39. Ibid.
40. *NRSV.*

[12]

The Netherlands Experiment

Henk Jochemsen, PhD

On June 1, 1994 a new legal regulation of euthanasia, assisted suicide and life-terminating actions without a request became effective in The Netherlands. This regulation can be seen as an experiment. Will it be possible to tolerate and regulate euthanasia while at the same time keeping it under control and within specific boundaries? This chapter presents an evaluation of this experiment so far. It begins with a description of the Dutch experience to date and then provides an overview of the main arguments for and against (legalization of) euthanasia in light of that experience.

THE DUTCH EXPERIENCE

DEFINITIONS AND DISTINCTIONS

In The Netherlands euthanasia is today defined as: *the active killing of a patient, at his or her request, by a physician.* Thus, the request of the patient has become part of the definition of euthanasia. In the international literature one usually distinguishes between voluntary euthanasia, which fully corresponds with the above definition of euthanasia, non-voluntary euthanasia, which is the killing of a patient without an explicit request, and involuntary euthanasia which is the killing of the patient against his or her will. In The Netherlands non-voluntary euthanasia is called a life-terminating action.

For clarity in the discussion and evaluation here it is important to distinguish euthanasia from other actions of physicians that may appear to be euthanasia but are not. It has been agreed in The Netherlands that the following three categories of actions should not be considered as euthanasia.[1]

a) Stopping or not beginning a treatment at the request of the patient,
b) Withholding a treatment that is medically useless,
c) Pain and symptom treatment with the possible side-effect of shortening life.

We will briefly discuss the appropriateness of distinguishing these three courses of action from euthanasia.

Regarding a): No patients may be treated without their informed consent, and patients are entitled to refuse treatment or to withdraw consent. As a rule the physician should respect such a wish, granted that the patient is competent. The physician has a moral duty to try to convince a patient to undergo medically useful treatment and the physician should not stop such treatment right away, just because such is the request of the patient. Yet, when the physician respects the wish of a fully competent patient and the patient dies soon after the withdrawal of the refused life-supporting treatment, this is legitimately not classified as euthanasia. (I leave aside possibly difficult and ambiguous situations).

Regarding b): Treatment that is medically useless should not be provided and can or even should be withdrawn after it has been begun. This statement, of course, raises the question of what is medically useful treatment. Such treatment fulfils the following criteria: 1) the treatment is effective and proportional, which means that the expected benefits of the treatment outweigh its expected or possible risks and burdens for the patient, and 2) the evaluation of benefits, risks and burdens for the patient should take into consideration only medical criteria and should not be an evaluation of the value of the life of the patient. To be sure, the medical judgement of proportionality is not a value-free evaluation. To a certain extent such an evaluation is personal and subjective. That is why medicine is a moral enterprise in the first place and why medical practice cannot do without medical ethics. Stopping medical treatment that has become medically futile, after which the patient dies, has sometimes been called passive euthanasia. Such terminology is confusing. Stopping disproportional medical treatment has always been good medical practice. That it is often not easy in practice to determine when a treatment becomes disproportional does not rule out this principle. The withdrawal of futile medical treatment does not intend the death of the patient. Neither can the death of the patient in a moral sense be considered the result of such a withdrawal. In other words, there is morally a fundamental difference between 'killing' and 'letting die' in many situations.[2] Only when medical treatment that should be considered proportional is withdrawn, with the intention of bringing about the death of the patient, is 'letting die' the moral equivalent of killing.

Regarding c): Pain treatment aims at alleviating the patient's physical discomfort. It may, and in certain cases almost certainly will, shorten the life of the patient. However, it is acceptable to define actions according to their aims rather than their side effects. So the shortening of life as a side effect of proportional pain and symptom treatment is a morally tolerable action and should not be classified as euthanasia. In these cases the principle of double-effect applies.[3] According to this principle a person may be aware that a course of action has undesirable but unintended side effects. However, as long as the intended positive effects cannot be achieved without the foreseen but unintended side effects, he or she is not held morally responsible for them. It is obvious that in practice pain treatment can shift to the killing of the patient when the medication is gradually and intentionally increased beyond doses needed to treat the pain and symptoms effectively. In that case the principle of double effect would no longer apply.

DATA ON THE PRACTICE OF EUTHANASIA

Using these definitions and clarifications, we will look at the main quantitative data on the practice of euthanasia gathered by Van der Maas et al. for 1990.[4] We will assume that these data are representative of the annual picture. In that year there were 9,000 requests for euthanasia (termination of life on request). Of these, 2,300 resulted in patient death, which constituted 1.8% of the total number of deaths for that year (129,000). There were also 400 cases of assisted suicide in which patients used means supplied by physicians to commit suicide. In that same year there were 1,000 cases of life-terminating actions by physicians without specific request from patients (normally called non-voluntary euthanasia outside of The Netherlands). Furthermore, the survey found that in 7,100 additional cases physicians intensified pain and symptom treatment partly with the intention or with the explicit intention of shortening life. In 5,840 cases treatment was either not started or was withdrawn by physicians with the partial or explicit intention of shortening life.[5] In these last two groups where physicians partly or fully intended to shorten the life of the patient by either intensifying symptom treatment or withholding or withdrawing treatment, they had not obtained an explicit consent from 20% to 60% of their patients. These data raise several questions to which we now turn.[6]

The 1,000 cases of life-terminating actions without specific request caused some uneasiness in political and medical circles, because they were contrary to the established requirements. People liked to believe that these requirements were generally well-observed (see further discussion of the conditions for euthanasia below). In these 1,000 cases physicians distinguished life-terminating actions (killing of a patient without an explicit request) from the intensification of pain treatment with the explicit purpose of shortening life. Particularly problematic, about a quarter of these patients were competent to a certain extent but their lives were terminated by the physicians without an explicit request.

Another question concerns the intensification of pain and symptom treatment and forgoing medical treatment. Both can be good medical practice even where they may involve a shortening of life, as long as shortening of life is a side effect and not the intended result. Yet in quite a number of cases physicians reported that they intensified pain and symptom treatment, or stopped treatment (including tube-feeding) partly with the purpose or with the explicit purpose of shortening life. Many people insist that the intention to shorten life should not be part of the professional ethics of physicians. On the other hand the *intention* to shorten life, by itself, does not make the action euthanasia. Euthanasia is defined as the *actual intentional shortening of life* and not merely the intention. Since the survey did not ask the physicians what they really did and how far they considered their treatment proportional, it is unclear to what extent the actions aiming at the shortening of life are really cases of euthanasia.[7] This means that, in fact, we do not have a clear picture of the real practice of euthanasia. This lack of clarity will hamper effective control of the practice.

THE 1994 REGULATION

The genesis of the 1994 regulation was the Supreme Court's ruling that the physician who commits euthanasia can, in cases of an objectively established 'conflict of duties' appeal to a defence of 'necessity' (Penal Code art. 40). This conflict concerns, on the one hand, the duty to obey the law prohibiting euthanasia and assisted suicide (Penal Code art. 293, 294), and on the other hand, the duty to alleviate suffering.

The court ruled that the conditions establishing such a 'conflict of duties' are essentially: a free, well-considered patient request, unacceptable suffering, and consultation of a colleague by the physician. The government approved the Supreme Court's decision, thereby accepting euthanasia under certain circumstances. At the same time, however, the government sought to maintain its responsibility for the effective protection of human life by maintaining the prohibition of euthanasia and assisted suicide in the Penal Code. They tried to reconcile these two aims by giving a statutory basis to the procedure by which physicians report death in cases of euthanasia, assisted suicide and life-terminating actions without an explicit request, by amending the law on the Disposal of the Dead. So the new law is in fact not so much a regulation of euthanasia, as a regulation of a reporting procedure of euthanasia that already existed for a few years without a legal basis. In terms of this procedure, a physician who has terminated a patient's life informs the local medical examiner. The examiner then inspects the body externally and takes from the attending physician a statement which contains the relevant data (the patient's history, request, possible alternatives, the consultation of a second physician, intervention, etc.). This report, together with an evaluation by the local medical examiner, is checked by the Public Prosecutor, who considers whether or not the termination is contrary to the Penal Code as interpreted by the courts.

The wisdom of adopting the same procedure for reporting euthanasia and reporting life-terminating actions without a specific request has been debated fiercely. Critics say that this approach puts both kinds of actions morally on the same level, which they consider incorrect. The government's intention, on the other hand, is that the courts should make judgements about the physician's actions in both types of cases. For this to be possible, both euthanasia and life-terminating actions need to be reported. Whether or not such is likely to happen will be considered below.

QUESTIONABLE PRACTICES

Will the regulations of 1994 lead to better control of the practice of euthanasia? We will consider this question in light of how well the reporting procedures were followed in the survey by Van der Maas et al. We find first of all that beyond those cases in which the actions of physicians meet the criteria for euthanasia there is a large gray area between good medical practice and the intentional shortening of life with or without a request. It remains unclear from the survey what the physicians actually did in those cases where symptom treatment was intensified or where treatment was withheld or withdrawn with the ethically suspect intention to shorten life. Because these actions are not reported, government control on what is happening is impossible.

Even the majority of euthanasia cases were *not reported* in the 1990 survey.[8] Of the 1,000 cases of termination of life without a request, virtually none of them was reported. Thus it is impossible, in practice, for the legal authorities to evaluate what had happened in those unreported instances where physicians took intentional actions to shorten the life of their patients.

The 2,300 *reported* cases of euthanasia in 1990 represent those selected from all cases of euthanasia in which the requirements were met. Furthermore, when physicians report a case of euthanasia, they choose formulations which are known to satisfy the legal authorities, but which may conceal what has really happened.[9] Apparently the reporting procedure did not guarantee the effective control of life-terminating actions by the legal authorities in 1990. It is doubtful whether the new law will change this situation.

The 1994 procedure also raises questions about the position of the medical examiner. Medical examiners are supposed to sign a form stating that they have checked the notification of the physician who performed euthanasia and have found that the procedure has or has not been followed according to the rules. However, in most villages medical examiners are also working as family doctors. They are thus colleagues of the other physicians in the village with whom they collaborate regularly regarding weekend duties and other matters. In such situations medical examiners will experience strong social pressure to give their sanction to euthanasia cases even when they have doubts about the fulfilment of the requirements. Furthermore, it is impossible for medical examiners to check the most fundamental criteria after the patient is no longer alive, viz., whether the patient was suffering intolerably and whether the request was completely voluntary and well considered.

ASSISTED SUICIDE

The legislation of 1994 did not stop the discussions or the development of new parameters within which to permit euthanasia and assisted suicide. A landmark case was that decided by the Supreme Court on June 21, 1994.[10] This case concerned a psychiatrist, called Chabot, who assisted a woman in committing suicide. She was depressed because of very sad personal experiences, including the death of her two sons. One had committed suicide. The psychiatrist had reported his 'life-terminating action' and had been acquitted by two lower courts before the Supreme Court investigation. The Supreme Court decided that, in principle, a physician can also appeal successfully to 'necessity' after performing euthanasia or assisted suicide on patients who are not in a terminal stage and who are experiencing psychic rather than somatic suffering. However, a second psychiatrist must have seen the patient and confirmed that there are no other ways to alleviate the suffering. Chabot had not asked a colleague to investigate the patient. For this reason he was found guilty but not punished.

Chabot was also brought before the Medical Disciplinary Court in Amsterdam in February 1995.[11] This court rebuked Chabot for having assisted in suicide, but not on the ground that it is contrary to professional ethics. Instead, the Court's concern was that he had not tried hard enough to treat the patient for her depression. In fact the Disciplinary Court applied the earlier decision of the

Supreme Court that a physician can assist in suicide only when there are no medical possibilities to relieve suffering. Furthermore, the court was of the opinion that because of her depression this patient could not be considered fully competent and therefore Chabot should not have fulfilled her request without having treated that depression. The Disciplinary Court also rebuked Chabot for not observing sufficient professional distance from the patient.

The Dutch Cabinet has also adopted the Supreme Court Chabot decision that euthanasia and assisted suicide can be performed when a patient has psychic suffering deemed to have no possibility of alleviation. Consequently, the Public Prosecutor has dropped the prosecution of physicians who euthanized patients suffering somatic pain who were not yet in a terminal stage. The Cabinet did not change its position after the decision of the Medical Disciplinary Court that Chabot had not tried hard enough to treat his patient's depression.[12] The ministers of Justice and of Public Health also apply the rule that no euthanasia or assisted suicide is permitted when there are medical possibilities to alleviate the suffering of patients with somatic pain. Since parallel regulations have been evolving for cases of psychic and of somatic pain, it appears that, under certain strict conditions, euthanasia and assisted suicide have now become acceptable to government authorities in cases of non-terminal patients suffering from either somatic or psychic pain.

SEVERELY HANDICAPPED BABIES

The most recent significant development concerns the 1995 case of a severely handicapped baby who was killed by a physician at the request of the parents. The baby had spina bifida, hydrocephalus, a spinal cord lesion, and brain damage. The specialists decided not to correct the spina bifida, because of the bad prognosis. The baby appeared to be suffering severe pain that was hard to treat. The parents did not want the baby to suffer and asked for the termination of her life. Three days after the baby was born, she was killed. She died in the arms of her mother. The physician appealed to the defence of necessity, and the Court accepted this appeal. In its written opinion, the court formulated requirements that the physician should fulfil in order to appeal successfully to the defence of necessity in similar cases. These requirements are:[13]

- The patient/baby is suffering intolerably with no prospect of improvement; the suffering is incurable and cannot be alleviated, at least not 'in a medically useful way'.

- Both the procedure leading to the decision to terminate the patient's life and the life-terminating action itself should meet the requirements of carefulness and precision.
- The physician's actions should comply with scientifically responsible medical opinion and with prevailing standards of medical ethics.
- Life-terminating actions should be performed only at the explicit, repeated, and consistent request of the parent(s) as the legal representative(s) of the baby.

By referring to suffering that could not be alleviated 'in a medically useful way', the Court implies that killing patients is potentially acceptable when the only way to take away the suffering is to put the patient virtually in a state of coma. From the available data it is difficult to determine whether or not the present case truly fits this criterion. It seems unlikely that it did, but the available data do not give a full picture of the situation.

Overall, the killing of babies in certain cases is defended by two lines of reasoning that essentially equate killing with letting die. First, stopping or not initiating a treatment is directly construed as a decision for death and equated morally with a decision to kill the baby. Under certain circumstances one ought to do this, it is argued, in order to prevent the baby from more suffering. Second, the principle of double effect is rejected. Accepting that pain and symptom treatment will shorten life, so the line of reasoning goes, is not fundamentally different from intentionally shortening life by medication at a dosage calculated to kill the patient.

However, both arguments violate widely agreed upon parameters for physician actions as explained near the outset of this chapter. In fact, advocates of euthanasia and life-terminating actions are very ambivalent, if not self-contradicting, in putting forward these arguments. When they interpret the finding of Van der Maas et al., they do distinguish between euthanasia on the one hand and stopping or not starting a treatment or intensifying pain treatment with the (explicit) intention of shortening life on the other. If they did not make this distinction, the number of cases of euthanasia would be unpleasantly high. But why then do they deny the distinction between forgoing disproportional treatment and proportional pain treatment — and in this way morally equate unavoidable shortening of life with intentional killing? Is it because, in this context, blurring the distinctions is necessary to give unrequested euthanasia an appearance of ethical correctness? Though higher courts will still rule on this case, this judgement may well be a first step towards the formal acceptance of non-voluntary euthanasia, i.e., the killing of patients without their consent.

ARGUMENTS IN FAVOUR OF EUTHANASIA

AUTONOMY

A major argument of those who approve of euthanasia is the principle of autonomy, or human self-determination. More and more the right to self-determination is extended to the moment of death, including the way one is going to die.[14,15] Death is not to be awaited with fear and trembling while one's physical and mental condition is deteriorating; rather, death should be brought about wilfully by a 'free decision' of an autonomous person who has chosen to 'step out of this life'. The wide support for a recent proposal illustrates the rise of this mentality in The Netherlands. According to this proposal, people from a certain age should be able to obtain a 'euthanasia-pill' from their physicians by request. This would allow elderly persons to terminate their lives at a self-chosen moment.

This way of applying the autonomy principle, however, is not generally accepted internationally.[16]

HEALTH AND DEATH

In modern society health is understood more and more not only as the ability to function and to enjoy things, but also as an ideal of vitality, wholeness, even beauty and a sense of well-being. Health care and medicine are expected to maintain or restore this health as much as possible.[17]

Many people find it increasingly difficult to cope with incurable diseases and handicaps. When a certain state of health is the prerequisite for a meaningful life, then life loses its meaning when that condition has become unattainable. So, when a certain condition of illness, discomfort, and dependency has been reached and the burdens of life outweigh its benefits, the death of the sufferer is considered an advantage for everybody involved. Then, the question is asked, why not bring about death?

CONTROL AND MERCY

In modern medicine there is a drive to gain control over life.[18,19] The intention is to maintain life and health as much as possible. However, enormous technological capacities also make it possible to prolong the life of patients in a situation which turns out to be 'unbearable' for the patient. Such suffering toward the end of life is seen as dehumanizing. It should not be tolerated. Humans have a right to die with dignity, it is stated. The aspiration for control may lead to a choice for death. Killing the patient is then considered an act of mercy by the physician — an act of *beneficence* towards the patient.

ARGUMENTS AGAINST EUTHANASIA

The autonomy concept is inadequate. The concept of autonomy, so fundamental for the advocates of euthanasia, is based on a certain view of humanity. People are viewed basically as individuals, who by reason can decide their own norms and values. They can make decisions for their own lives independently. What makes human beings really human is, in this view, their reasoning ability. This anthropology fails to recognize the importance of the spiritual, historical and social dimensions of humankind. It thinks in terms of rights and duties and not in terms of care and responsibility. Thus the modern principle of autonomy contrasts with a Christian view in which all of these should have a place (see Cameron's chapter on autonomy in Part I).

The autonomy concept is also unrealistic, particularly in health care. Can a very ill person really make an independent and free request to be killed? A Dutch neurologist has argued that the very fact of being in a terminal state, as well as the medication that is often given in those situations, makes a clear and normal functioning of the brain almost impossible.[20,21] Furthermore, the patient is completely dependent on others, who through their attitude, gestures, tone of voice, etc. can suggest that the patient should ask for euthanasia. This is especially true for the physician and can even happen unconsciously if in the doctor's opinion euthanasia is considered to be a good 'solution' in some cases. Even if a truly voluntary request existed theoretically, in practice it would be difficult to ensure that a request was indeed voluntary.[22]

Furthermore, the autonomy of the patient alone cannot be the main reason for accepting euthanasia, since it is the physician who performs it. Euthanasia also requires the autonomous consent of the physician. When performing euthanasia, the physician freely and intentionally kills the patient. But one can argue that the free and intentional killing of another person, even with good intentions, will influence the attitude of the physician towards all his patients, both competent and incompetent. Therefore, euthanasia also affects other patients and cannot be considered as an affair between the individual patient and his or her physician alone.

A last, and for Christians most decisive, objection against the autonomy principle is the biblical teaching about God's sovereignty. God is the Creator and therefore the Lord of life. A human being is not allowed to terminate the life of another (Gen. 1:27;

4:9,10; 9:5,6). The best-known formulation of this outlook is the sixth commandment: 'You shall not murder' (Ex. 20:13).[23] In the New Testament this is one of the commandments Jesus explicitly radicalizes by extending it to cover attitudes and speech (Matt. 5:21–23). This commandment addresses all human beings. In the Christian view of life, the value of life is not determined by the functions or capacities that can objectively be verified. The value and the dignity of a person reside in being created by God and in being called to live in a relationship of love with God, one's fellow humans, and creation. In all these relations one's physical existence is fully involved. As long as there is a living human being — i.e., until total brain death occurs — her or his personhood remains. Personhood is rooted in one's relation with God, which cannot be measured medically.

INADEQUATE CARE

A request for euthanasia is very often a sign of inadequate care or attention. The patient feels uncomfortable, has pain, fears what may still happen, and worries about relatives or relationships. Such a request should be taken as an appeal to our responsibility to provide the needed care. 'Quality of life' should not be a criterion in considering whether life can be terminated, but should be understood as a call to social duty, not least by Christians. This is precisely what hospice care intends to do (see Twaddle's chapter on hospice in Part IV). Good care and attention by physicians and nurses, attention by relatives, and adequate pain treatment (today almost always possible) in most cases make a request for euthanasia disappear.[24,25] Exceptions to that rule may exist, but exceptions should not determine morality or legislation. Fortunately, the alternative of better care is getting more and more attention in The Netherlands.

SLIPPERY SLOPE

The practice of voluntary euthanasia will lead to non-voluntary euthanasia. Indeed, the Dutch data on euthanasia practice already suggest that one fundamental reason physicians terminate a patient's life is not just the patient's request but rather her or his condition. (cf. earlier discussion).

In those cases where the condition of the patient provides reason to perform euthanasia on request, the patient will often no longer be able to make a free request. However, since the condition may function as the fundamental ground for euthanasia, the fact that there is no request can readily be considered insufficient reason not to perform euthanasia. In this way the ideological background of voluntary euthanasia also provides a justification for non-voluntary euthanasia.

PHYSICIAN/PATIENT RELATIONSHIP

The acceptance of euthanasia will seriously change the physician/patient relationship for the worse.[26] 'There is an inherent conflict of interest between the beneficent healing and comforting role in which life and wholeness is sought, and one in which death is caused intentionally'.[27] The acceptance of euthanasia as a part of 'good medical practice' will definitely change the attitude of health care workers toward terminally ill patients, both competent and incompetent. Fenigsen has given several examples of the new mentality becoming manifest in The Netherlands: e.g. giving up patients unnecessarily, or withholding medically indicated treatment since the patient is 'just living by himself', or is already 70 yrs. of age.[28]

It may be granted that when the life of a patient is intentionally terminated, death itself is not the good that is sought; rather, the elimination of suffering is the goal. However, medicine should fight suffering because of the person rather than turning against the person because of his or her suffering. In extreme situations it is understandable that patients, in the experience of those involved, are almost completely identified with their suffering. However, such a conceptual identification is incorrect. This identification does not necessarily underlie withholding or withdrawing disproportional life-sustaining treatment, which need not intend the death of the patient. Yet this total identification of patients and their suffering is operative when patients are killed to end their suffering. Medicine thus becomes subservient to an undue aspiration for control: When the quality of *life* cannot be maintained at the desired level, the *situation* can be brought back under control by killing the patient.

Behind this way of proceeding appears to be an outlook in which medicine is made responsible for the relief or the alleviation of all suffering. All suffering is considered wrong and its relief is considered the highest value. More and more this suffering includes that caused to the parents by the birth of a child with severe handicaps, even apart from the suffering the child experiences. A misunderstanding of the character and an overestimation of the task of medicine are involved here. The results include the danger of overtreatment on the one hand and making killing a task of medicine on the other.[29] Both involve a dehumanization of medicine.

It is very important that physicians are able and willing to recognize the limitations of medicine in fighting death, and to accept that at a certain stage death becomes inevitable. It then becomes very important not only to care for the patient, but also to help him or her, as well as the family, to accept that death is imminent.[30,31]

CULTURAL SUICIDE

Accepting (nonvoluntary) euthanasia assumes that some people will decide about the lives of others. This entails acceptance of the concept of 'human life that is not worth living', with the implication that such a life may be terminated.

Polish philosopher L Kolakowski has argued that the unique and irreplaceable character of each human being has long been a fundamental value in European culture. Accepting that it is right to kill certain people would be a denial of this value and would mean 'cultural suicide'. The consequences would be incalculable, but would certainly include serious risk to the lives of certain groups of people. Kolakowski acknowledges that this conviction about the sanctity of human life cannot be proven.[32] Like every ethical position, it is ultimately based on certain basic beliefs. In the biblical Christian view of life, respect for human life irrespective of its conditions is grounded in the existence of a personal God and the creation of human beings in the image of God (Gen. 1:26).

CONCLUSION

The Dutch experiment of trying to regulate euthanasia while at the same time keeping it under control has arguably failed. The experiment has demonstrated that once euthanasia is officially approved and practised, the practice develops a dynamic of its own that resists effective control and tends to expand. While the experiment has failed, its consequences will be irreversible, at least for quite some time.

It is astonishing that so many people in The Netherlands do not seem to realize how much the present situation corrodes the basis of the Dutch constitutional state. Fortunately, the number of initiatives in hospice care, which may provide an alternative to euthanasia, is also increasing. Christians have been actively involved in this movement.

The Word of God is not just for the private lives of those who believe in God. God's commandments apply to all people (Eccl. 12:13), because such parameters enable all life to flourish. When life presents us with situations so hard that there seems no good solution, it makes sense to look to the One who made and understands everything in order to find the way to go.

NOTES

1. H J J Leenen, 'Dying with Dignity: developments in the field of euthanasia in The Netherlands'. *Medicine and Law* 8 (1989), pp. 520–526.

2. Cf. D Callahan, 'Can we return death to disease?', *Hastings Center report* 19 (1989) no.1, special supplement, pp. 4–6.

3. See W Reich (ed.),'Acting and refraining', in: *Encyclopedia of Bioethics*, (New York: Free Press, 1978), pp. 33–35; also T L Beauchamp, J F Childress, '*Principles of biomedical ethics*', (New York: Oxford University Press, 1983, 2nd ed.), pp. 113–115.

4. P J van der Maas, J J M van Delden, L Pijnenborg, 'Euthanasia and other medical decisions concerning the end of life', *Health Policy* 22 (1992) nr.½), pp. 1–262; also published in hardback by Elsevier Science Publishers, Amsterdam 1992.

5. The latter two numbers are not given in the report of Van der Maas et al., but are calculated from their data; see Van der Maas et al., note 4, Table 8.14 and ch. 17.4.

6. For a more detailed discussion of the data and of the new regulation see: H Jochemsen, 'Euthanasia in Holland: an ethical critique of the new law', *J Med Ethics* 20 (1994), pp. 212–217.

7. That the physicians estimated life to have been shortened by more than one day by their action in about 75% of these cases makes most of these cases look like euthanasia. Even so, in their actual effect, those actions may not have been different from adequate pain treatment. The question that should also have been asked is: What medication would you have given, had the shortening of life not been your intention?

8. In 1989, 336 cases were reported in 1990, 454; in 1991, 590; in 1992, 1318; in 1993, 1303; and in 1994, 1417. *Source: Year Report Public Prosecutor 1994*. It is not clear, however, whether the total number of cases of euthanasia has also increased since 1990.

9. G van der Wal et al., *Medisch Contact* 47 (1992) nr.2, pp. 43–47; *Medisch Contact* 47 (1992) nr. 31/32, pp. 905–909; *Medisch Contact* 47 (1992) nr.36, pp. 1023–1028.

10. This decision has been published in: *Ned Juristenblad* 69 (1994) afl.26, pp. 895 ff; for an extensive personal presentation of this case, see: H Hendin, 'Seduced by death: doctors patients and the Durch cure', *Issues in Law & Medicine* 10 (1994) nr.2, pp. 23–168.

11. 'Psychiater berispt voor hulp bij zelfdoding', (*Psychiatrist rebuked for assisted suicide*), *Medisch Contact* 50 (1995) nr.21, pp. 668–674.

12. Letter of the Minister of Justice and the Minister of Public Health, Welfare and Sports, d.d. 16 September 1994, to the Second Chamber, concerning the consequences of the decision of the Supreme Court of 21 June 1994, for the prosecution of euthanasia.

13. Decision District Court Alkmaar d.d. 26 April 1995 (parketnr. 14.010021.95) regarding mr H Prins, pediatrician.

14. Leenen, see note 1.

15. J H P H Willems, 'Euthanasie en noodtoestand', *Ned. Juristenblad* 22 (1987), pp. 694–698.

16. Cf. 'The Appleton International Conference: developing guidelines for decisions to forgo life-prolon ging medical treatment', *Journal of Medical Ethics* 18 (1992, supplement), pp. 3–5.

17. D. Callahan, *What Kind of Life – the limits of medical progress*. (New York: Simon and Schuster, 1990), ch. 2.

18. K Jaspers, 'The physician in the technological age', *Theoretical Medicine* 10 (1989), p. 262.

19. Editorial, 'A new ethic for medicine and society', *California Medicine* 113 (1970) nr.3, pp. 67, 68.

20. B P M Schulte, 'Over euthanasia en in het bijzonder over de relatie tussen hersenfunctie en vrijwillig heid bij euthanasie', *Vita Humana* XV (1988) nr.1, pp. 9–12.

21. M Hunt, 'Sick Thinking', *New York Times* March 1, 1988, who quotes dr E Cassell, clinical professor of public health: 'Sickness changes people's ability to make decision. They become dependent on the doctor and others to take care of them and focus on themselves rather than the outside world. . . . . . they no longer reason like well people'.

22. D Callahan, 'When self-determination runs amok', *Hastings Center Report* 22 (1992) nr.2, pp. 52–55.

23. For an instructive discussion of the meaning of the 6th commandment for the euthanasia issue, see: P Saunders, 'Thou shalt not kill', *Journal of the CMF* 38.3 (July 1992), pp. 3–11.

24. H L van Aller, et al., '*Stervensbegeleiding*' (Utrecht: Bunge, 1990), Chapter 6. (This is a publication on care for the dying, prepared by a working committee of two Dutch associations of physicians).

25. J M M Michels, 'De symptomatische behandeling van terminale patiënten' (the symptomatic treatment of terminal patients), *Vita Humana* XIV (1992) nr.1, pp. 5,6.

26. P A Singer, M Siegler, 'Euthanasia — a critique', *New Engl J Med* 32 (1990) nr.26, pp. 1881–1883.

27. W Reiche, A Dijck, 'Euthanasia: a contemporary moral quandary', *The Lancet* ii (1989), pp. 1321–1323; quote p. 1322.

28. R Fenigsen, 'A case against Dutch Euthanasia', *Hastings Center Report* 19 (1989) nr.1, special supplement, pp. 22–30.

29. For a further elaboration of this point see: H Jochemsen, J Hoogland, S Strijbos, 'The medical profession in modern society — the importance of defining limits', In: J F Kilner, Nigel M de S Cameron, D L Schiedermacher (eds). *Bioethics and the future of medicine: a Christian appraisal* (Grand Rapids MI: Eerdmans, 1995), pp. 14–29.

30. National Association of Health Authorities, '*Care of the dying*', Birmingham 1987.

31. R G Twycross, '*The dying patient*' (London: CMF Publications, 1986).

32. L Kolakowski, 'Het doden van gehandicapte kinderen als het fundamentele probleem van de filosofie' (The killing of handicapped children as the fundamental problem of philosophy), *Rekenschap* 19 (1972), pp. 35–49.

[PART IV]

Constructive Alternatives

[13]

Hospice Care

Martha L Twaddle, MD

The 1980s in the United States was the decade of health — health clubs, health foods, 'work-out-clothes' fashion. The consumption of red meat, whole milk, and fatty foods declined; grocery shelves and glossy magazines sported 'fat free' this and 'lite' that. Smoking was no longer the fashion. We jumped and jogged, drank sparkling water and consumed large quantities of vitamins and fibre. Medical technologies extended our age expectations; medical breakthroughs staggered our imagination. And still we died.

Jim Fixx, Arthur Ashe, Jackie Kennedy, the young and the old among us still succumbed to ageing, death, and disease. AIDS loomed large and could not be thwarted. Stories of death and pain haunted popular literature and our conversations.

Then came the 1990s: Jack Kevorkian and assisted suicide have appeared repeatedly in our morning papers, best seller books have included such titles as *Final Exit* and *How We Die*. Legislation and debates continue to reflect great controversy regarding physician-assisted suicide, the rights of patients and families, the fight for control. It seems we have come face to face with the enemy. If we *must* die, can we control the process? If *I* must die, can I control the when and how?

DYING WITH DIGNITY

In truth, the number one fear of most individuals is not the fear of public speaking, nor cancer, nor pain, but rather the loss of control. Throughout time, the energies of many have been focused, often in desperation, on controlling the world around them — the political tides, the process of life. As elusive as these areas are to define, so are they to control. We desperately desire to maintain autonomy and self-direction in health and illness; we speak thus of 'dying with dignity'. A more appropriate term, however, may be to die 'with integrity', that is, to die as we have

183

lived, with interpersonal relationships, spirituality, and a sense of self intact.

Sadly the process of illness can rob us of control. The fast paced world of acute care medicine, the loss of bodily functions, the effect of medications may blunt our sensorium and take away our choices. Thus the request for suicide in this setting is often a frantic and misdirected attempt to control a life experience. There is a better choice. There exists a highly developed programme of support for those whose lives are threatened by incurable and end stage illnesses. There is a specialized discipline of medicine focused on the relief of symptoms and maintenance of the highest level of function for the individual whose time is limited. There is a government-recognized, insurance-reimbursed programme that provides support to patients, caregivers, and families. There is a service organization focused on whole-person-care, stressing life in the process of dying, with vast provisions to make that journey with integrity. There is Hospice.

As early as the 1950s, Dame Cicely Saunders recognized the beginnings of the gross divergence of medical care for the curable and for the dying. The ability to diagnose, intervene, and technologically support patients was growing exponentially. However, whole-person-care, particularly for those individuals who were unresponsive to interventions, was losing priority, if not reimbursement. Dame Saunders, trained as a nurse, social worker, and physician, envisioned a team approach to patient care, with emphasis on patient-directed goals and quality of life. Her vision led her to founding St. Christopher's Hospice in London, England. St. Christopher's opened its doors in 1967 as an inpatient facility with a mission to care for the dying patient. Hospice care optimized symptom control and provided social and spiritual support to the patient and family through the last months of an illness.[1]

HOLISTIC PAIN MANAGEMENT

Spurred by the advent of hospice, the specialty of palliative medicine was born. Research and anecdotal evidence bolstered increasing expertise in providing patients with symptom relief in the face of malignant and non-malignant illnesses. Symptom relief became one of the foundational goals of good hospice care. 'Pain nails you to your body' said Saunders and others. If patients were to have the freedom to see death and dying in the context of a complete life experience, or to contemplate the 'whys' of life, they must be freed from the physical symptoms that bind them to the present.[2] The symptoms of pain became a topic of high priority.

Perhaps the most feared of physical symptoms, it was often the most destructive of human spirit. Ever new information regarding pain pathophysiology and treatment filled peer-review journals dedicated to its study. Substantial advancements in understanding of pain medications included discoveries that there is no ceiling dose for the pain relieving qualities of the medications, and that there is a minimal (less than 1%) chance of addiction when they are used for the relief of pain. New pharmaceutical preparations that allowed simple oral administration also were a welcome development.[3]

Together with the better understanding of the physical dynamics of pain came a new appreciation of the pain experience. Saunders spoke of 'total pain', composed of the physical aspects of disease, but as importantly, of the psychological, social, and spiritual dimensions of pain. The meaning of the pain mattered; the pain of labour symbolized a promise of new life, the pain of metastases embodied the approach of an ending. Attending to all aspects of pain was imperative to the goal of whole-person-care. Hospice, by its team structure and approach to care, was and is uniquely capable of assessing and managing total pain (Figure 1).[4]

FIGURE 1
TOTAL PAIN MODEL

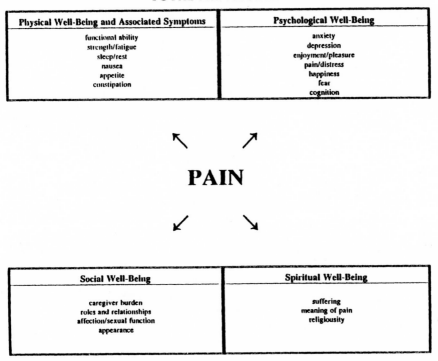

Physical Well-Being and Associated Symptoms	Psychological Well-Being
functional ability strength/fatigue sleep/rest nausea appetite constipation	anxiety depression enjoyment/pleasure pain/distress happiness fear cognition

PAIN

Social Well-Being	Spiritual Well-Being
caregiver burden roles and relationships affection/sexual function appearance	suffering meaning of pain religiousity

THE HOSPICE TEAM

The caregiver structure of hospice is a team — not multi-disciplinary, but interdisciplinary in nature. Composed of nurses, physicians, social workers, chaplains, volunteers, and others, the team provides a broad assessment of patient and family care needs. The assessments of each discipline are shared at team meetings; the plan of care is built on the input of many and shaped by the patient's specific goals. Conventional medical care is hierarchical, with a physician directing a plan of care. In hospice care, the physician is no more the determination of 'what is best' than the chaplain. Ideally, 'what is best' is patient-defined. By prioritizing patient-defined goals, a sense of control and personal direction is re-achieved. This, in itself, facilitates the beginning of total pain control. The contributing expertise of each team member is vital for the delivery of whole-person-care.

The hospice nurse is a remarkable person — one who combines a big picture perspective with an attention to detail. The role challenges the professional to be a combination of 'the Lone Ranger' and a team player. The patient-nurse interface is critical, as good hospice care must involve excellent physical care. Nurses often function as a 'voice' for the patient and family — noting changes in the patient's condition, informing the physician of such changes, suggesting adjustments in the management of the patient, etc. The 'tone' of the nurse-physician relationship in hospice care is a particularly good one. Moreover, certified nursing assistants necessarily join nurses as important members of the team, for attending to basic human needs facilitates the patient's ability to look beyond the immediate.

Ideally, the patient's primary care physician remains actively involved in this phase of medical care, becoming a 'member' of the interdisciplinary team. A good patient-physician relationship is worth at least 10 mg of morphine, as presence alone can ease the anguish of fear. Physicians must be skilled in palliative medicine. Unfortunately this knowledge base in not ubiquitous. Thus, the hospice medical directors provide valued consultation in this vital discipline. The physician is committed to relief of symptoms and the provision of choices. Options in care exist even in this domain. Allowing patients choices, even as simple as 'would you prefer a pill or a liquid?', helps restore a sense of self. Hospice physicians often describe their role as 'coming alongside' dying patients and accompanying them through the death process.[5] Easing the journey through medications, explanations, and presence might be thought of as thanatologic midwifery.

Social workers may be involved in the therapy of talk, or actively seeking resources in the community to assist patients and families. Proactive involvement with the caregiver and family, particularly children, may avoid unresolved misunderstandings burdening the future. It is now understood that children must be involved in the death experience; isolation is perceived by them as punitive and a sense of guilt may haunt them for a lifetime. Again, early and honest explanations may ease the pain of family suffering, present and future.[6,7]

The realm of suffering is vast, and poorly understood. Certainly, in the world of secularized medicine, little attention is given to the state of the soul; nor are there adequate means to measure its distress. Hospital chaplaincy is an acknowledgment of the importance of this aspect of care. Hospice care might be thought of as the return of the soul to medicine. Again, the stated purpose of palliative care in hospice is to allow the individual support and freedom to find spiritual healing, even in the face of physical death.[8] The focus of hospice care is not dying, but healing for families, patient, and all involved in the end-of-life journey. Healing in this arena does not connote restoration of bodily health but resolution of spiritual angst. Chaplains play an important role in helping patients and others address such angst — though all hospice team members ideally are alert to spiritual issues that arise in the process of caregiving.

Hospice in the US is the only government-supported type of health care requiring volunteer involvement for certification. Volunteers provide several critical dimensions to care, including affirming a patient's continued social worthiness. The tendency when one is ill is to become isolated and, even more problematic, to feel useless and burdensome. A volunteer may help one weakened by disease to accomplish concrete goals, or the volunteer may simply convey by quiet presence the intrinsic worth of the dying individual. Volunteers often assist in what is known as 'biography therapy' — the creation of a scrapbook, tape recordings, a collection of letters, etc. — that allows the patient to see death in the context of life and not as an isolated experience. Patients may more readily share fears and questions with their volunteer than with the medical staff. When the volunteer communicates to other team members the patient's fear of taking medication, concern for family and other caregivers, and spiritual pain, the interdisciplinary approach to whole-person-care is greatly enhanced.

A 'good' death, exemplified by comfort and symptom control, is most often as important for friends and families as for the dying patient. The witnessed death experience becomes a living memory for the survivors; a comfortable death can often facilitate closure for a grieving family. Certainly not all deaths bring closure and resolution, however. Grief issues for survivors may be complex, even painful. Hospice provides bereavement support for over a year following the patient's death through personnel trained in grief counselling.[9]

The highly developed caregiving team of hospice can and does facilitate 'a good death', the true meaning of the word 'euthanasia'. With such provisions, the need for a quick exit via physician-assisted suicide is generally deemed unnecessary and unacceptable.

CHANGING THE MODEL OF CARE

Surprisingly, even though excellent hospice care is widely available in many countries of the world, a 'good death' is still more the exception than the rule, particularly in a hospital setting. The reasons for this state of affairs appear to be that the concept of hospice remains poorly standardized and its practice exists, even now, outside of mainstream medicine. As figure 2 illustrates, the current medical model prioritizes palliative care only after curative measures are exhausted.[10] Patients are the losers as pain is insufficiently managed and end-of-life issues are insufficiently

FIGURE 2
THE CURRENT CONTINUUM OF CARE

Continuum of Care

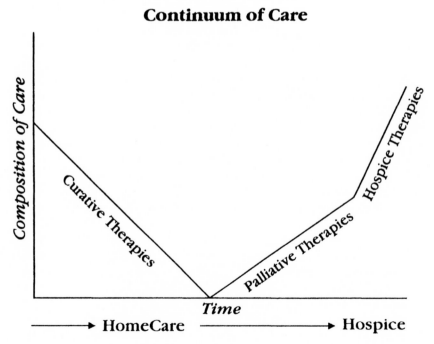

FIGURE 3
THE EMERGING CONTINUUM OF CARE

Continuum of Care

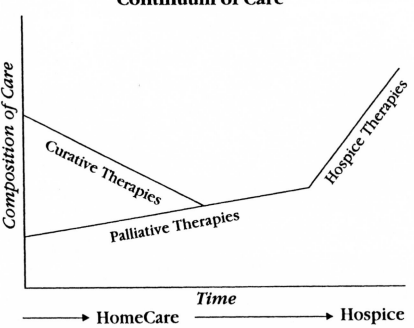

addressed. A referral to hospice often depends on a well-informed, proactive family and a self-abasing physician. The art of symptom control and the recognition and treatment of total pain are not a part of medical school curricula. Current health care reforms threaten the economic viability of the programme.[11]

Nevertheless, the hospice philosophy remains committed to whole-person-care. Hospice physicians and nurses, independently and through their academies, are striving to insure that every dying person has a right to a 'hospice' death and access to effective palliative care. The discipline of palliative medicine has begun to permeate medical training programmes and to redefine the medical model (Figure 3).[12] Patients and families are the winners as patients' pain is effectively managed, families receive support throughout the course of treatment, and end-of-life planning is not postponed to the last possible minute. A move towards standardization and accreditation in palliative medicine is gaining momentum. Certification in hospice nursing has been possible since 1994.

Hospice would ideally be the standard of care for treating all patients with advanced terminal illnesses, regardless of their diagnosis or ability to pay. If this high standard were applied and hospice care were made available to all patients, the current clamour for physician–assisted suicide would all but evaporate. We can live until we die, and we can make that transition with integrity.

NOTES

1. Saunders C, Summers D H, Teller N, *Hospice: The Living Idea* (Edward Arnold, 1981).

2. Sauders C, Baines M, *Living with Dying: The Management of Terminal Disease* (Oxford University Press, 1989).

3. Twycross R G, Lack S A. *Therapeutics in Terminal Cancer* (Churchill Livingstone, 1990).

4. Ferrell, B, PhD, FAAN, City of Hope Medical Center, 1500 E. Duarte Road, Duarte, CA 91010.

5. Byock, Ira MD, Hospice Medical Director of Partners in Home Care, Missoula, Montana.

6. Grollman E A, *Explaining Death to Children* (Beacon Press, 1987).

7. Jarratt C J, *Helping Children Cope with Separation and Loss* (Harvard Common Press, 1984).

8. Twycross, R, *Definition of Palliative Care*.

9. Rando T A, *Treatment of Complicated Mourning* (Research Press, 1993).

10. McDonald, Neil, MD, Montreal, Canada. Center for Bioethics, Clinical Research Institute of Montreal, Quebec, and Edmonton General Hospital.

11. The AMA initially did not consider hospice a core medical service, BlueCross Blue Shield of Illinois does not currently provide a hospice benefit, numerous insurance companies strive to reimburse by 'unbundling' the team approach to a homecare model.

12. McDonald, Neil, MD, Montreal, Canada. Center for Bioethics, Clinical Research Institute of Montreal, Quebec, and Edmonton General Hospital.

[14]

Long-Term Care

James R Thobaben, MPH, MDiv, PhD[1]

While it is apparent that many chronically disabled persons have long-term care needs, exactly what those needs are and how best to meet them is not as clear. Some seriously disabled persons need supervision; others can live 'independently'. Some require traditional institutions; others are best served through more flexible support networks. Unfortunately, even in a country as wealthy as the United States, the current mechanisms for addressing these diverse needs are inadequate. On occasion, this inadequacy becomes a significant factor in the decision of seriously disabled persons to ask for physician-assisted suicide.

Christians may well wish to advocate against physician-assisted suicide and other forms of euthanasia for the chronically ill (causing death for 'well-intentioned' reasons). If so, it is morally necessary that they also advocate for improved alternatives in care and living options for the seriously disabled. Certain specific changes must occur within Christian healthcare institutions and among Christian practitioners — not to mention their secular counterparts. This claim is based on an analysis of disability in the United States, so the present chapter begins with a brief overview of that analysis. The chapter then compares categories of chronically ill persons in long-term care settings with categories used to justify euthanasia. This comparison is provided as a means of explaining how easily the institutional boundary between care for the chronically disabled and toleration of euthanasia can be transgressed when those in certain categories of disability are, by definition, 'euthanizable.' The third section examines in greater detail the social process of euthanizing the disabled. The remainder of the body of the chapter then presents 'Seven Intentions' for Christians and Christian institutions. These are offered as suggestions for an institutional response which, in turn, is but a portion of a broader Christian reply to the societal toleration of the devaluing of the disabled.

AN OVERVIEW OF DISABILITY IN THE UNITED STATES

Disability, in one form or another, is an integral part of the lives of vast numbers of people in the United States. Perhaps they carry a grandmother up and down stairs. Perhaps they live with acute pain. Perhaps they bathe a father's foot. Perhaps they live with a hearing impairment, or blindness, or mobility limitations. Though it may seem paradoxical, while each person's circumstances are unique, they are not especially exceptional.

It is conservatively estimated that 34–35 million, or 14% of the national census population, is disabled to the degree that it 'interferes with life activities'.[2] Two million of these persons are in long-term care facilities, with 3/4 of those in nursing homes. Over 19 million are defined as having a severe limitation.[3] These are persons with chronic but not terminal negative health conditions. If the disabling condition is life-long, the person and his or her family may have developed coping mechanisms that allow participation in a society which does not consider them 'normal.' If the disability is acquired, it often severely disorders the life of the disabled person and the lives of his or her family until some process of adjustment has been negotiated. 'Going on' with a disability is not a matter of heroism on the part of people with disabilities; it is a part of daily existence. Disability does not mean death is imminent nor does it mean that life is meaningless.

Increasingly, however, persons are being convinced or are convincing themselves that living with severe disability is, at best, a supererogatory act and, consequently, is not morally required. In other words, portions of this very large segment of the American population are being persuaded or are persuading themselves that they cannot live with chronic conditions unless they are heroes and, so it is argued, no one should be forced to be a hero. This is all the more strongly argued when the disabled person is likely to require some sort of long-term care, in or out of an institution, and must thus pay a high financial cost to be a hero.

Western secularized, pluralistic, privatized societies are struggling with the entire concept of being disabled.[4] In the U.S., for example, the Americans with Disabilities Act, supported by most advocacy groups, promotes greater acceptance and mainstreaming.[5] At the same time, pro-euthanasia efforts and some health care cost restrictions push persons with disabilities to believe that their lives are, literally, not worth as much as the lives of those who are not disabled. The initial Quality-Adjusted-Life-Years (QALY)-based rationing programme proposed by the state of Oregon, for example, ran into conflict with the A.D.A. because it devalued people whose quality of life is limited by a disability.

The mixed signals of society force disabled persons, especially those newly disabled, to ask, 'My life is so different, would I not be fulfilling myself and serving my loved ones, as well as the greater good, if I terminated my life?' Unquestionably, daily existence is forever changed for those with acquired disabilities. This change is not only a change from the personal past, it is a change from societal norms. The latter, the experience of being different, is often an on-going phenomenon for those with disabilities associated with congenital impairments.

In the modern West, this kind of being 'different' quite quickly transforms into being 'unworthy'. Disabled people are defined less frequently as 'unclean' (one of the traditional cultural interpretations) and increasingly as useless or of diminished social efficiency. The personal dilemma is framed by the political debate which simultaneously declares the supremacy of autonomy while using the reasoning of a crass utilitarianism. How can pleasure and profit be maximized while pain and loss are minimized for the patient, the family, the society?

The suffering associated with a diminishing (or perceived diminishing) of social worth is amplified by the western emphasis on individual accomplishment. The one universal moral assertion of the secularized, pluralistic, privatized society is the right of personal autonomy; and the one clear positive duty of the state is to provide the tools to do something with autonomy. Some persons with disabilities seem to be convinced — existentially — that no one *really* 'lives' with a severe disability because somehow such a person has lost the autonomy needed to be human. Without autonomy one cannot accomplish; without accomplishment, one is worthless. Such persons are truly without hope, not simply depressed.

Post-traumatic depression is frequent among persons with recent disabling injuries. Persons can be clinically depressed following a new injury, emotionally worn-out by a chronic condition, or mentally exhausted by a severely impaired son, daughter, wife, husband, or child. These persons, it can be argued, need time and care in order to adjust. But what of those who assert a right to 'rational suicide?' What of that person who is not simply depressed, but who, apparently (perhaps with the agreement of family members), rationally concludes that life with a serious disability is utterly pointless? Such a person is calmly determined to eliminate the disability, even if death is the only mechanism through which that can be accomplished. This person is alienated with no sense of anger; anomic with no sense of desperation.

From this perspective, such a person has virtually ceased to exist. The person — as that person — is all but gone. When the autonomous self is severely restricted, the social identity is obliterated. If one cannot live autonomously, then one can at least die autonomously. The so-called beneficence of inadequate health care and sparse independent living alternatives is rejected. The guilt of choosing euthanasia is negated by the categorizing of the chronically ill/disabled person as non-human (or nearly so). In fact, euthanasia becomes desirable since a non-human should not consume health care and other resources that might be used for a human.

CANDIDATES FOR LONG-TERM CARE OR EUTHANASIA

Basically, there are seven categories of disabled persons receiving or needing long-term care. These categories are fluid. The health care institutions established to meet the needs of disabled persons needing long-term care vary widely depending on funding, region, and availability. Still, a working categorical table is useful:

1) the near-term dying (< 1 year): hospice, nursing homes, hospitals, home health;
2) the intermediate-term dying (1–3 years): nursing homes, home health; occasionally hospitals;
3) the long-term dying (> 3 years): nursing homes, home health, independent living support; occasionally residential programmes, hospitals;
4) the chronically disabled (mild to moderate/not dying): independent living support; occasionally home health, residential programmes;
5) the chronically disabled (moderate to severe/not dying/not cognitively or affectively impaired): nursing homes, home health, independent living support; occasionally transitional facilities, residential facilities;
6) the chronically disabled (moderate to severe/not dying/ cognitively or affectively impaired): nursing homes, home health; occasionally transitional facilities, residential facilities, independent living support;
7) those in ongoing comas and persistent vegetative states: hospitals (rarely including coma stimulation programmes), nursing homes; occasionally home health.

This analysis is restricted to categories 3, 4, 5, and 6. These are not persons with recognizably terminal conditions whose deaths will occur in the foreseeable future; those are best treated through hospice-type programmes. These are not those very few persons in persistent vegetative states or near PVS; such persons are a very small minority of the chronically ill. The far greater social problem (and personal problem for those involved) is what happens to people who are severely disabled, who are aware of it to one degree or another, and who will live for years. Larry McAfee, Elizabeth Bouvia, and, perhaps, Michael Martin, are a few persons within these categories.

In the first great push toward the legalization of euthanasia in the U.S. and Europe, four categories of people were suggested as likely candidates for voluntary or involuntary euthanasia. The same categories appear in the current bioethics literature, though with a refinement in terminology.

The euthanasia categories are:

A. The terminally ill
B. Persons in significant and irresolvable/intractable pain
C. Persons who are severely impaired mentally[6]
D. Persons in long-term coma or a persistent vegetative state

There is considerable overlap between the euthanasia categories and the categories of chronically ill persons who are not terminally ill.

When comparing the two lists, it is evident that the terminally ill euthanasia category (A) coincides with the first and second categories of disabled persons needing long-term care. The second euthanasia category (B), irresolvable/intractable pain, is partially coincident with categories 1, 2, 3, 5, and 6 of persons needing long-term care. The category of persons who are euthanized because of mental impairment coincides with category 6 of those needing long-term care. In The Netherlands, psychological disorder has served as the primary justification for euthanizing and has been a contributing factor in decisions to euthanize in the United States. For instance, children who are likely to be diagnosed as mentally retarded are at higher risk for non-care at birth. The final category of persons who are euthanized (D) coincides with category 7 of disabled people requiring long-term care.

It can be argued that persons very near death should not be subjected to treatments intended to extend life, if that is their desire. Unfortunately, some of the typical characteristics of the persons in category 1 (e.g., pain, mobility impairments, lack of clarity in thinking) are declared the primary reasons that death is to be allowed. It is then assumed that these same characteristics justify the euthanizing of others with similar characteristics, both those who are and those who are not near death. As the categories used, formally or informally, to define disability coincide to a greater and greater degree with those used to justify euthanasia, the euthanizing of the non-terminally ill disabled becomes more and more likely. Since the categories are seen as simply two ways to describe the same thing, the 'disabled' become the 'euthanizable'. The possibility that partial coincidence in the categories might indicate that other significant factors, including institutional, social, and cultural factors, inordinately influence the decision for euthanasia is submerged beneath the fearful image of endless physical pain and suffering in a dismal institutional setting.

The category of intractable pain is extremely susceptible of being a catch-all. In fact, some argue that the emotional pain of disability is itself severe enough to justify euthanasia on the grounds of non-treatable suffering. As the experience in Michigan with Dr Jack Kevorkian demonstrates, chronic disability and pain are sometimes considered justifiable reasons for euthanasia in the U.S. Similarly, the Dutch experience indicates that mental impairment as a source of pain can be deemed a sufficient cause, at least on occasion.

THE SOCIAL PROCESS OF HEALTH CARE AND DECISIONS FOR EUTHANASIA

While this kind of thinking does not seem to be shared by the vast majority of persons with disabilities, it does appear that this view, or an approximation of it, is held by many decision-makers. Bach, Campagnolo, and Hoeman surveyed 82 ventilator-assisted persons with Duchenne Muscular Dystrophy (DMD). They found that persons with DMD reported nearly the same rate of life satisfaction as the general population. They assert that:

> Clinicians should be cognizant of their inability to gauge disabled patients' life satisfaction and refrain from letting inaccurate and unwarranted judgment of these subjective factors [affect] patient management decisions.
> This latter point is potentially tragic because the physician's judgment of the patient's quality of life and about the relative desirability of certain types of existence appear to affect the likelihood of a patient receiving life-sustaining therapeutic intervention.[7]

Paris determined that medical students and health professionals viewed disabled persons' quality of life in a far more negative way than did the disabled people themselves.[8] According to Gerhardt, Koziol-McLain, Lowenstein, and Whiteneck, while 98% of non-disabled emergency room (ER) providers believe that they themselves are persons of worth and 95% of quadriplegic spinal cord injury survivors believe the same about themselves, only 55% of those same ER providers declared they would be persons of worth if they were to sustain a disabling spinal cord injury (SCI). This constitutes a phenomenal difference of 40% from those who are actually disabled by spinal injuries.[9] The same discrepancies exist when health professionals and persons with disabilities are asked about having a positive attitude toward life and feelings of failure. Gerhardt and Corbet go so far as to suggest that these health professionals may well bias the decision-making of, or for, vulnerable persons.[10]

Such bias is structurally manifest in long-term care. The limited institutional long-term care that is available is usually in the form of nursing homes in which persons are not encouraged to achieve any significant level of independence. Alternatively, care may be provided in the form of home health care, but again without mechanisms (transportation, daily living support, etc.) for achieving independence. In both cases, vocational, recreational, and transportation services tend to be grossly under-funded or simply unavailable.

The following is a chart of the rehabilitation and long-term care continuum in which persons with disabilities must seek care and services. The post-acute column on the matrix receives the least funding per charge, the acute column the most. There is reimbursement for high tech acute treatment and some for home health, but far less reliable coverage for rehabilitation, and hardly any for transitional living and respite care. The general approach to a disabling injury or illness is high care or no care.[11] In a managed care environment, high tech care may decrease, but there is not sufficient evidence to assert that rehabilitation, transitional living, and respite care will increase. Indeed, the opposite appears to be the case.

The system functions the way it does, in part, because reimbursement (or resource allocation more generally) validates the prevailing attitudes of health care providers, insurers and policy-makers about how they think they would personally respond to a disabling event. Apparently, social decision-makers are disproportionately made up of persons who believe in autonomy and personal success as proof of one's moral worth.

OPTIONS FOR THE CHURCH: SEVEN GOOD INTENTIONS

The church in the West has essentially abdicated its responsibility and role in health care to the funding sources (either the welfare state or the insurance companies) and professional guilds. This abdication need not continue. The church can and should 'minister' to persons in need. The church should offer charity, not in a paternalistic or condescending manner, but in the sense of *caritas* or *agape* — serving love rendered in recognition of one's own brokenness and God's mercy. Such service includes, but also goes beyond, attending to the rights of the disabled to care.

When considering this service, it is helpful to keep in mind the hardest case — that person who chooses 'rational' suicide. The question of strategies is transformed when one realizes that the person advocating euthanasia is sometimes the very person one

FIGURE 1
THE REHABILITATION AND LONG-TERM CARE CONTINUUM[12]

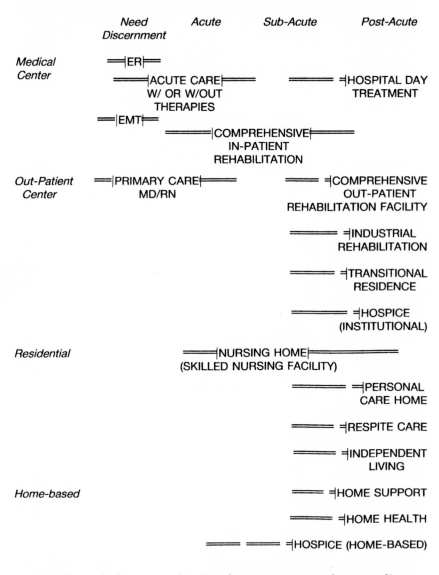

	Need Discernment	Acute	Sub-Acute	Post-Acute

would like to help. It is a fine line between care and paternalism, a line made even thinner by practitioners who promote autonomy as the ultimate value and then define autonomy in terms of a proper, educated, and ever-so-tasteful hedonism.

Seven specific institutional 'intentions' for Christian organizations and practitioners are here offered. It is unlikely that these could be implemented in secular institutions or in those (so-called) 'Christian' institutions that identify with other healthcare providers or organizations in the marketplace more consistently than with the church. Also, these intentions do not exclude other approaches or responses.

The seven intentions should not be called strategies because organizational strategies should be institutionally specific in order to fit the particular social environment. In other words, a certain moral allometry is required. Institutional type and size depends on the different types and sizes of problems.

The Seven Intentions are:

- Improve staff education in the sociology of healthcare and culture of disability
- Improve staff moral education and development
- Begin formal patient and family moral education
- Begin educating managed care case-managers and insurers about the need for increased funding of rehabilitation and long-term care alternatives
- Develop facilities for transitional and open residential living
- Develop in-home transitional and independent living support
- Develop respite care

INTENTION I: IMPROVE STAFF EDUCATION IN THE SOCIOLOGY OF
HEALTHCARE AND CULTURE OF DISABILITY

The healthcare workers described above indicated a greater willingness to devalue a life with disability than did people who are disabled. This is true in spite of the fact that such workers are better informed about particular aspects of health care than the general public. There appears to be a large gap between personal assumptions and actual facts about disability and long-term care. Apparently, some make practice decisions on the basis of the societal bias against the disabled. In reference to a particular disability, SCI, Gerhardt and Corbet put it this way:

> In the days and weeks following a severely disabling injury, individuals may die for the wrong reasons — they may die because of what they don't know rather than what they do know. That this happens on an individual level is concerning, and, at least in some cases, seems to speak of the failure or inadequacy of informed consent. However, much more alarming are the pervasive societal ramifications. Each time a newly-spinal-cord-injured person chooses death over life — and is allowed to die — society is shown 'proof' that it's better to be dead than disabled.[13]

Of course, there are many caring persons working throughout the health care sector, but these persons are not impervious to the devaluing of disabled persons prevalent in society. Consequently, the starting point for any long-term care strategy must be educating providers. This education should be multifaceted, including education on the sociology of healthcare in the U.S. (e.g., managed care, governmental activities, the role of quasi-governmental accrediting bodies), on the sociology of healthcare organizations (e.g., organizational process, the history of the institution as Christian), and on the cultural and social aspects of disability (e.g., the sick role, cultural degradation, the self-help movement).

Attitudes toward treatment and interpretation of dysfunction are intimately related. To a great degree, they are shaped by what is taught both through the information provided and as an expression of what is institutionally expected. Frequently, negative attitudes toward disabled persons are not based on accurate portrayals of life with a moderate to serious disability, but nonetheless lead to decisions for death.

One good tool for teaching medical professionals about the social and cultural aspects of chronic conditions is the International Classification of Impairments, Disabilities, and Handicaps (ICIDH) from the World Health Organization (WHO). Impairments are anatomical or physiological losses or disorders; for instance, a C-5 spinal cord lesion. Disabilities are the functional problems that are the result of the impairment; for instance mobility difficulties due to the quadriplegia associated with a C-5 injury. Handicaps are the limits created by social, psychological, and cultural barriers; for instance, a 7 centimetre concrete step that prevents a C-5 quadriplegic person using an electric wheelchair from entering a church.

Some sub-categories offered in the ICIDH model are awkward and imprecise, but the general structure is quite useful. The distinctions help patients and family members, but they are especially useful for health professionals attempting constructively to analyze what can be changed and what cannot. This understanding, in turn, increases the possibility that long-term care in the home, nursing home, or transitional living facility will be a functional success since caregivers can more intelligently respond to needs.

Certainly, it would be wonderful if an impairment could be cured and the affected people could get up and walk. However, if they learn how to use a wheelchair effectively, then mobility is regained even if limb movement is not. Functionality overcomes disability. If they were unable to get into a church building and the barrier at the door is corrected, then community participation is increased. Access overcomes a handicapping barrier.

INTENTION 2: IMPROVE STAFF MORAL EDUCATION AND DEVELOPMENT

Along with educating staff on the social analysis of chronic disorders comes moral training. All institutions are legally permitted to hold and express values. Private, not-for-profit institutions are allowed to have specifically religious values that are a manifestation of a particular moral anthropology. Any Christian institutions that do not explicitly state that all persons are persons of worth and that their centre is a refuge for at least some of those who are devalued by society do not deserve to bear the name 'Christian.'

The staff members, including professionals practising therein, should either share the core values of the institution or at least be willing to act in a manner consistent with those values. This may require both formal and disciplinary education. Persons must be instructed that cynicism about and disrespect toward disabled persons is unacceptable. Eventually, employees should achieve a greater awareness of the particular difficulties faced by persons with disabilities. For example, if an 'able-bodied' employee of a Christian rehabilitation hospital parks in a space reserved for persons with mobility impairments, that person should be warned — but only once. If the worker cannot or will not change, then the employment relationship should be terminated. Christian institutions should promote 'virtuosity' among providers and one of the virtues that ought to be most sincerely desired is the 'prudence' to recognize what behaviours are and are not appropriate.[14]

This moral education may even lead to outright advocacy. The only way any long-term care alternatives will be successfully developed is if they have advocates within the professional communities who will push for institutional change. For example, it will take clinical and administrative personnel to point out to insurers and managed care case managers that a critical path (the standard treatment pattern) for a spinal injury or for severe rheumatoid arthritis or a serious traumatic brain injury or multiple sclerosis is a dead-end, if it does not include some institutional mechanism for community re-entry.

INTENTION 3: BEGIN FORMAL PATIENT AND FAMILY MORAL EDUCATION

In a pluralistic society, patients are entitled to believe what they want and so are their families. But a long-term care facility also is entitled to have beliefs or foundational values which guide daily practice. If long-term care is to make any real sense, then it is necessary for such institutions to realize that they cannot be, nor should they pretend to be, value neutral.

Rehabilitation, transitional living, and other forms of long-term care exist because of a specific moral assertion: people with chronic disabling conditions are still people. They are not refuse to be discarded by society. They are not shameful aberrations to be hidden away or, worse, eliminated. They do not need to be ashamed of themselves or to see themselves as useless.

Self-valuing must be taught to injury survivors and persons with chronic diseases. The potential for the future and the worth of disabled persons must be conveyed to their family members. The disability may change life, it may make life relatively 'un-normal,' but it does not necessarily destroy it. Life can be reordered. Such a notion is quite compatible with the Christian theme of redemption. It also stands in direct contradiction to the movement in the U.S. that would devalue any human life that is not 'independent' (as if any life is really independent). Such a view implies that disabled life is not human life. In an ironic weaving together of the American myth of autonomous individualism and contemporary moral relativism, an individual can assert that disabled life is not human life *in his or her individual case.* If the family agrees, then the people paying the bills are likely to assert the same since it saves them money. With no apology, Christian institutions and Christian providers should attempt to transform that attitude when it is possible to do so within the limits of a patient's rights.

INTENTION 4: BEGIN EDUCATING MANAGED CARE CASE-MANAGERS AND
INSURERS ABOUT THE NEED FOR INCREASED FUNDING OF REHABILITATION
AND LONG-TERM CARE ALTERNATIVES

Insurers and case managers (including those working for the government) need education on the continuity of care required for functional recovery. The structures of long-term care will change very slowly, if at all, as long as the society in general and the health care decision-makers in particular (especially the insurers and the employers that select health care plans for employees) continue to view disability as a curse worse than death or a rarity.

The current lack of continuity in funding long-term care pushes people to view chronic disability as an unresolved crisis. The perceived options are full 'normal' life, or death — anything else is medical purgatory. The only way around this predicament is to bring the insurers into the education loop as both students and teachers: the former, so they can understand the long-range implications of treatment choices; the latter, so they can teach providers about less expensive but equally effective alternatives.

For better or for worse, long-term care requires money. What insurers need to recognize is that, in most cases, if the patient continues to live, a strategic approach is necessary. It is ultimately less expensive to train that patient's family, help with employment, purchase a higher quality wheelchair, obtain attendant support, etc. than to pay for treatment made necessary by inadequate personal training or equipment. For instance, the costs of sufficient family and patient teaching and a high-quality wheelchair seat cushion are significantly less than the expense of one extra hospitalization to treat skin decubiti. Of course, all this assumes that one does not believe that killing disabled (or any other) persons is preferable simply because it is cheaper. The termination of life is admittedly far less costly *in financial terms* than is helping someone continue with life.

INTENTION 5: DEVELOP FACILITIES FOR TRANSITIONAL AND OPEN RESIDENTIAL LIVING

There are few transitional living facilities in the U.S. and those that do exist are usually run by for-profit organizations which do not provide significant non-reimbursed treatment.[15] Since few insurers cover sufficient stays in these facilities, a transitional period is usually possible only if one is wealthy or has well-to-do relatives. Some institutional mechanism to make the transition back into society should be available which does not financially destroy families or survivors.

Christian organizations (e.g. large churches, annual conferences, judicatories) should consider developing transitional living facilities. These could be small (4–10 residents) and located near a church with a parish nursing programme. The effort would require money, since residential facilities are not inexpensive. However, development is not cost-prohibitive. The small facilities could be operated by churches in the same way as small foster facilities. To do this, governmental waivers and insurance protection may be necessary.

When the possibility of institutional development is suggested, it is often met with dismay or dismissed as infeasible. A realistic approach to such an endeavour is certainly essential. However, the effort has to start somewhere. As was learned with abortion, if Christians are going to take a stand, then the church should 'put its money where its mouth is'. A recognition that barriers exist does not render institutional development untenable.

For reasons similar to those underlying the development of transitional living facilities, Christian organizations should help develop permanent residences. Currently, most residential facilities are nursing homes, since skilled nursing facilities generally receive the best reimbursement. Besides these, there are group home facilities for persons with developmental disabilities, but few for those with acquired chronic disorders. The only other significant type of residential facility is a personal care home. Something more is needed.

Ideally, residential facilities should be places that include work and education opportunities. The facilities could be located in rural areas for gardening and recreation or in small towns or urban areas so that residents could interact with neighbours and have access to community resources. The facilities may have to have some specificity (i.e., be oriented toward a particular condition such as traumatic brain injury, mobility impairment, or cerebral palsy).

INTENTION 6: DEVELOP IN-HOME TRANSITIONAL AND INDEPENDENT LIVING SUPPORT

Currently, transitional living support usually takes the form of temporary independent living assistance — which is often a government-supported programme to assist persons with disabilities. Unfortunately, the funding of the programmes is limited and the availability of services is often restricted to urban areas. In some instances, the independent living programmes are also constrained by excessive bureaucracy. There is no reason why such services could not be supplemented by churches. In some cases, the church might develop a formal programme; in others, the church might choose to develop a reliable network to meet the needs of particular parishioners or neighbourhood residents. A church of any size could participate in the latter.

Particularly useful would be help from lawyers, small business owners, accountants, and social workers. These professionals could provide assistance in teaching how to handle bills (especially those from providers and insurers), instructing how to interact with state rehabilitation departments and divisions, developing home employment opportunities, etc. Churches could expand parish nursing and/or voluntary home aid services. These efforts strengthen the congregation by broadening its participating membership to include persons with disabilities, who may well have other extremely valuable abilities or who strengthen the fellowship simply by being present. This is an area ripe for church participation.

One additional means of assisting with the transition back into the community is accessible housing. It is possible to build housing for persons with disabilities in cooperation with Habitat for Humanity and similar organizations. This simultaneously provides needed accessible housing, legitimates concern for disabled persons who have been disenfranchised, and allows interaction with a family that lives with disability.

INTENTION 7: DEVELOP RESPITE CARE

Often forgotten in the period of acute hospitalization is the family. While usually drawn into the conversation during rehabilitation, families are frequently forgotten again when patients return to the community. This is unfortunate since the disabling event is just as real for the family members as for the injury or illness survivor. Further, a lack of respite services (formal or informal) can be detrimental to the patient. The best thing for a person with a chronic disability, after faith in God, is a supportive family and care-giving network. Yet, without respite care, the family can be overwhelmed to the point of destruction.

The church community can provide respite care as a sort of 'health care Sabbath'. Any church can assist with this in the home. Institutional respite care could also be developed by churches, though it probably should be offered in conjunction with a group residential or transitional living home.

CONCLUSION

These are Seven Good Intentions — but everyone knows *what* is paved with good intentions. In this case, failing to act upon at least some of these intentions is the road to death for seriously disabled persons as well as the road to hell for . . . perhaps for churches in the U.S. if nothing is done to serve those disenfranchised by physical impairments, disabilities, and handicaps. Jesus did, after all, identify with the sick in his parable of the sheep and the goats and, in so doing, directed his church into active concern.[16]

Far too often decisions for death are made because no potential is seen for the future. Long-term care has been shaped by attitudes about disability and reinforced by funding sources without sufficient consideration of the transition back to the community and respite care for family providers. The continuum of care should demonstrate a recognition of the intrinsic worth of disabled persons as community members.

The common response of Christians looking at euthanasia is to assume that some policy change, new law, or court ruling will solve the problem. It will not. The Baby Boom cohort is ageing. People now survive violence and motor vehicle accidents, thanks to emergency transport and care, at a phenomenal rate. Technology, good nutrition, and medications are increasing the length of life for elderly persons. Chronic severe disability is a problem that will not go away with a change in the law.

Protest must be matched by real, enacted concern. Christians can complain as much as they want to about abortion — they can even change national policy — but, until sufficient supportive care exists, women who sense they have no alternative will choose abortion. Some seriously disabled persons and their families will make analogous choices for death. Alternatives need to be provided so the choice is not between death and a nursing home hundreds of miles from family.

It is unlikely, even if other institutional alternatives exist, that the option of 'rational' suicide will always be rejected. However, it often will be. Certainly laws and regulations to protect disabled persons from 'suicide doctors' should be sought. Still, legal victories will be hollow unless Christians serve as they would desire to be served, through the provision of alternatives to being 'shut up and shut away' or being killed.

Living with no desirable alternatives in a society that puts a premium on 'autonomy as self-sufficiency', some chronically disabled persons understandably choose death. Such choices will only become more frequent in our increasingly disconnected society unless clear institutional alternatives become available.

NOTES

1. During the editing of this chapter, James Thobaben also assumed the position of Associate Professor of Social and Medical Ethics at Asbury Theological Seminary, Wilmore, Kentucky.

2. Andrew M Pope and Alvin R Tarlov, eds. *Disability in America: Toward a National Agenda for Prevention* (Washington, D.C.: National Academy Press, 1991) p. 1.

3. Robert C Ficke, *Digest of Data on Persons with Disabilities, 1992* (National Institute on Disability and Rehabilitation Research: Washington, D.C., 1991), pp. 5–7.

4. Ravi Zacharias, 'Human Dignity' (video and audio tape available from The Center for Bioethics and Human Dignity, Bannockburn, Illinois, 1995).

5. Whether the American with Disabilities is 'abused' by persons without serious disabilities and whether it contains too much room for the assertion of unintended 'rights' are matters to be considered in another context.

6. In the earlier euthanasia movement, which sometimes had eugenic undercurrents, this category included 'incurable idiots'. See references to Karl Binding and Alfred Hoche and their 1920 (Leipzig) work, *Die Freigabe der Vernichtung lebensunwerten Lebens. Ihr Mass und ihre Form.* [The permissibility of terminating life unworthy of life: its proportion and form] in Michael Burleigh, *Death and Deliverance: 'Euthanasia' in Germany 1900–1945*, (Cambridge: Cambridge University Press, 1994).

7. John R Bach, M.D., Denise I. Capagnolo, M.D., and Shirley Hoeman, Ph.D. 'Life Satisfaction of Individuals with Duchenne Muscular Dystrophy Using Long-Term Mechanical Ventilatory Support' *The American Journal of Physical Medicine and Rehabilitation* Vol.70, No.3, (June 1991), p. 29–135.

8. Mary Jean Paris, 'Attitudes of Medical Students and health-Care Professionals Toward People with Disabilities' Archives of Physical Medicine and Rehabilitation Vol.74, No.7 (August 1993) pp. 818–825.

9. Kenneth A Gerhardt, Jane Koziol-McLain, Steven R. Lowenstein, and Gale G Whiteneck, 'Quality of Life Following Spinal Cord Injury: Knowledge and Attitudes of Emergency Care Providers' *Annals of Emergency Medicine* Vol.23, No.4 (April 1994), pp. 807–812.

10. Kenneth A Gerhardt and Barry Corbet, 'Uninformed Consent: Biased Decisionmaking Following Spinal Cord Injury' *HEC Forum*, vol.7: nos.2–3 (March–May 1995), pp. 10–121.

For a partial counter argument in reference to the terminally ill [disability categories I & II] see Lawrence J Schniederman, Richard Kronick, Robert M Kaplan, John P Anderson, and Robert D Langer, 'Attitudes of Seriously Ill Patients toward Treatment that Involves High Costs and Burdens on Others' *The Journal of Clinical Ethics* Vol.5: No.2 (Summer 1994), pp. 109–112.

11. George J Agich, *Autonomy and Long-Term Care* (New York: Oxford University Press, 1993). Cf. John F Kilner's chapter on 'Forgoing Treatment' in the present volume.

12. This matrix runs institutional location on the Y-axis and level of medical intervention on the X-axis. The matrix was developed with assistance from Mark Adams, CEO of Mississippi Methodist Rehabilitation Center and Lois Willis, also of MMRC.

A presentation by Harriet S Gill (for Fowler Healthcare Affiliates, Inc.: Atlanta, Georgia), *Subacute Rehabilitation* (National Association of Rehabilitation Facilities, 1993) includes a 'Spectrum of Rehabilitation Care', a model of the continuum of care. Conversation based on that presentation triggered the ideas used in this matrix, although the matrix itself is original.

13. Kenneth A Gerhart and Barry Corbet, 'Uninformed Consent: Biased Decisionmaking Following Spinal Cord Injury' *HEC Forum*, vol.7: nos.2–3 (March–May 1995), pp. 110–121.

14. Edmund D Pellegrino and David C Thomasma, *The Virtues in Medical Practice* New York: Oxford University Press, 1993).

15. I am unaware of any studies that directly report on the charitable activities of for-profit transitional living facilities. The evidence is anecdotal. However, it has been demonstrated that not-for-profit acute care facilities do tend to have lower costs and tend to provide more charity care than for-profit hospitals. This has been recently re-confirmed in a study conducted in Virginia ('Virginia not-for-profits charge less, offer more charity care' *Modern Healthcare* (July 24, 1995). This fact, the anecdotal evidence, and the limited supply relative to demand make extrapolation to transitional living facilities reasonable.

16. Matthew 25:31–46. The Old Testament contains references indicating that disabled persons were not appropriate for service in the Temple, but it also includes warnings to protect the weak, the sojourner, the socially disenfranchised. The New Testament raises the disabled to a category of equality. While there is debate as to whether or not there should be deference for the poor, the sick, etc., it is clear that any lower or degraded status relative to others in the faith community is entirely inappropriate (i.e., sinful).

[15]

Wise Advocacy

James S Reitman, MD

Over the last two decades several countries have been rapidly redefining the standard of care for patients with intractable suffering, as is evident, for example, in the current U.S. debate over physician assisted suicide.[1] This evolving standard is exemplified by the outcomes of an increasing number of court decisions and published accounts of individuals who have made appeals to relieve their suffering by hastening death.[2] Before developing a biblical model of care for intractable suffering, this analysis will summarize two such cases and demonstrate that the ethical foundation for the disposition of these two cases seriously overlooks certain moral and existential issues that characterize the dilemma of intractable suffering. These issues must be clearly identified and cogently addressed by any model that attempts to define morally appropriate care for intractable suffering.

The two cases selected have become virtual paradigms for the care of individuals with intractable suffering:

Elizabeth Bouvia is a woman with severe lifelong neuromuscular impairment from cerebral palsy who at one time was able to control a motorized wheelchair and even completed college. After several psychosocial crises in her mid-20's, she became depressed and entered a hospital in California expressing a desire to commit suicide. Her request to be allowed to starve herself was denied, and a judge permitted the hospital to tube feed her. Three years later she filed suit to have her feeding tube removed and to be treated for any discomfort as she starved. The trial court asserted that such a request was tantamount to 'suicide by starvation' and denied her petition, but the decision was reversed by the Court of Appeals, which declined to label her request suicide, since her life 'has been physically destroyed and its quality, dignity and purpose gone'. After the decision, she chose to live.[3]

'Diane' had a family history of alcoholism and a past history of vaginal carcinoma and depression, when she was diagnosed with leukemia by her physician, Timothy Quill. When he referred her to an oncologist, she became enraged at the apparent presumption that she should accept his offer of chemotherapy. Convinced she would die, she expected the worst and repeatedly expressed her need to be 'in control', as well as her fear of becoming progressively dependent on others. When Dr Quill was convinced it was the only way she could 'maintain dignity and control', he referred Diane to the Hemlock Society and ultimately prescribed a fatal dose of barbiturates. A few months later, Diane finally said good-bye to Dr Quill, family, and closest friends, then took the pills and died.[4]

INTRACTABLE SUFFERING AND ETHICAL INDIVIDUALISM

The outcome in both of these cases is based on an ethic of *radical individualism* which rationalizes the use of medical 'care' to relieve intractable suffering by hastening death. The *contractual model* of care is based on this ethical individualism and holds the right to self-determination to be paramount in decision making; the caregiver then owes certain correlative 'duties', such as *confidentiality* and *informed consent*, to guarantee the free exercise of the right to self determination.[5]

Among the purported *derivative* rights that are becoming increasingly accepted by physicians and ethicists is the so-called *right to die*,[6] which was determinative in the disposition of these two cases. However, these cases raise the very troubling question of what *other* correlative duties might then be required of the physician to guarantee the free exercise of this right to die; for if it is also asserted that the highest goal of medicine is the relief of suffering,[7] then the condition of *intractable* suffering places the physician who subscribes to this widely held assertion on the horns of a dilemma: Would the *prerogative* of relieving suffering then become a *duty* to relieve that suffering when asked to do so, even if it meant eliminating the one suffering?[8]

When incurable disability or progressive illness prevents the patient from being able to maintain control in life, the patient could exercise the right to self-determination (via the derivative 'right to die') by requesting the physician to assist in suicide. The contractual model would then require that the caregiver be 'assured' that the patient was not depressed.[9] If depression could be ruled out, the physician could then fulfil his or her 'duty' by relieving the intractable suffering, either by withdrawing life support, as in the case of Bouvia, or by prescribing lethal 'therapy', as requested by Diane. Arguably, the two responses would be morally equivalent forms of assisted suicide.[10]

There are, however, key moral and existential questions that are left unidentified and unanswered by the contractual model. The issues raised by these questions help set the parameters for building an ethical model capable of redefining morally appropriate care for people who are intractably suffering.

• *Do we adequately understand the nature of intractable suffering?*

Why do some people, like Diane, choose to die, while others choose to endure intractable suffering?

- *What is the moral value of preserving dignity and control while life remains?*
Does the right to self-determination really trump other values such as respect for human life and potential?

- *How does intractable suffering influence rational decision making?*
Can we be sure that requests to hasten death reflect reasoned consideration of potentially meaningful alternatives, even if depression has been excluded by psychiatric evaluation?

- *What is the ultimate role of the caregiver?*
When cure is not possible, is this role in fact to relieve suffering? Are there no *other* prerogatives open to the caregiver?

THE 'WISDOM MODEL'

The framework for decision making proposed here is based on the Old Testament Wisdom literature. This literature effectively identifies and addresses the key moral and existential issues and provides the basis for redefining morally appropriate care for people with intractable suffering.

The book of Job furnishes a quintessential example of the sufferer's confrontation with the moral and existential questions we have raised. Job's desperation — manifested by his repeated expressions of the appeal of death — places the intractable sufferer's profound need for morally responsive care in stark perspective. The extended dialogue between Job and his friends shows how the deepest existential needs of the intractable sufferer may remain unmet by even well-meaning 'caregivers' and thereby serves as a negative paradigm for the morally appropriate care of intractable suffering.

The book of Ecclesiastes tackles the key question facing the sufferer who has lost hope: What is the point of continuing to struggle through life when life itself seems so meaningless? By addressing the four questions raised above in light of this basic dilemma, the book provides an ethical framework for decision making that takes seriously the moral and existential issues surfaced by the questions.

THE NATURE OF SUFFERING

DO WE ADEQUATELY UNDERSTAND THE NATURE OF INTRACTABLE SUFFERING?

What is it about suffering that makes the prospect of hastening death seem eminently reasonable to some, while others are able to endure continued, even intractable, suffering? What makes still others like Bouvia change their minds, and how can we possibly determine beforehand who will and who will not? Job's example provides us with a helpful starting point.

Left with a miserable, incurable illness after losing his entire fortune and all his children, Job exemplifies in his poignant 'death wish' the naked despair which often accompanies intractable suffering:

> Why is light given to him who is in misery,
> And life to the bitter of soul,
> Who long for death, but it does not come,
> And . . . are glad when they can find the grave?
> For my sighing comes before I eat,
> And my groanings pour out like water.
> For the thing I greatly feared has come upon me,
> And what I dreaded has happened to me.
> I am not at ease, nor am I quiet;
> I have no rest, for trouble comes (Job 3:20–26).[11]

Note how Job's despair encompasses the appeal of death, and that it seems to be based on the expectation that his worst fears have been realized; there is a deep, inexorable unease over the profound erosion of vitality brought on by the trouble that has 'come upon' him. This portrayal of the existential impact of severe, intractable suffering is remarkably consonant with Eric Cassell's definition:

> Suffering occurs when an impending destruction of the person is perceived; it continues until the threat of disintegration has passed or until the integrity of the person can be restored. . . . It follows . . . that although it often occurs in the presence of acute pain, . . . suffering extends beyond the physical. . . . [S]uffering can be defined as the state of severe distress associated with events that threaten the intactness of the person.[12]

Such dread of impending *personal disintegration* and the associated loss of hope also characterized the despair of Diane and Elizabeth Bouvia in their desire for death. Considering what they faced, we feel fortunate that we have not been afflicted in the same way — in fact, we *might* even be persuaded to agree that life in that condition is not worth living. It is not surprising then that those charged with caring for an individual suffering so intensely would also be susceptible to such empathic identification with the sufferer's despair. The potential for such caregiver 'contagion' by despair is reflected by the response of the author of Ecclesiastes when confronted by deep suffering in others:

> And look! The tears of the oppressed,
> But they have no comforter —

On the side of their oppressors there was power,
But they have no comforter.
Therefore, I praised the dead who were already dead,
More than the living who are still alive (Eccl. 4:1–3).

Most people have seen or heard of patients whom they felt were better off dead, just because of the *sheer intensity* of their suffering. The point comes when nothing seems more appropriate than to help them preserve what little control or dignity remains in life, even if it means hastening death.

The author of Ecclesiastes soon discovers, however, that a deeper question lies beneath the more obvious concern for the relief of intractable suffering: Would it be possible to endure even intractable suffering if life could still have some meaning? In other words, what is more important in life, freedom from suffering or true meaning? This is the question addressed in the author's next observation, '*If a man begets a hundred children and lives many years, so that the days of his years are many, but his soul is not satisfied with goodness, . . . I say that a stillborn child is better than he*' (Eccl. 6:3–4).

It seems not so much the *suffering* per se that makes life unlivable as the perception that life has no 'goodness', which in Ecclesiastes carries the nuance of 'satisfying meaning'. Many people have committed suicide, even when they appeared to have everything they could want in life. Rather than asking, 'How intense or intractable is the suffering?' perhaps we should ask, 'Where can one find new meaning in life, even when suffering — however profound it may be — cannot be avoided?'

Ironically, our author shows how the very despair precipitated by this kind of suffering can provide just this opportunity to discover new meaning:

Sorrow is better than laughter,
For by a sad countenance the heart is made better.
The heart of the wise is in the house of mourning,
But the heart of fools is in the house of mirth (Eccl. 7:3–4).

The phrase '*by a sad countenance*' literally means 'by misery on the outside'. In other words, honest mourning over the circumstances of suffering can help the sufferer accept the lack of control and dignity that characterizes their mortal existence. So spending time in '*the house of mourning*' — whether it be in an ICU, hospice, nursing home, or funeral parlour — can 'do the heart good', by serving as a *turning point* to new sources of meaning, even in the midst of intractable suffering.[13] This insight parallels the pivotal conclusion of Moses, who reflected deeply about his mortality. '*Teach me to number my days, that I may gain a heart of wisdom*' (Ps. 90:12), Moses prays — implying that authentic mourning in the face of one's mortality can foster *wise stewardship*.

What if an individual responds to this awareness of mortality by refusing to accept the limitations imposed by one's illness on the capacity to maintain 'control and dignity' in life? What if that person insists on exercising self-determination by choosing to 'end it all' and then requests assistance in carrying out that choice? What interest should the caregiver have in trying to influence such an individual to engage in 'authentic mourning' — why not simply resign oneself to a difference in moral values and just 'live and let die'? This quandary for the caregiver leads directly to the next moral issue.

PRESERVING CONTROL AND HUMAN DIGNITY

WHAT IS THE MORAL VALUE OF PRESERVING DIGNITY AND CONTROL WHILE LIFE REMAINS?

Is the logic of self-determination compelling enough to trump other values which might otherwise be explored by the caregiver? And if a caregiver does help a suffering patient to die in the interests of 'maintaining control and dignity', who remains morally *accountable* for that choice? What other moral values might lend hope to continuing such an existence?

The author of Ecclesiastes bluntly affirms that the goal of preserving self-determination in life is a complete illusion:

> Whatever one is, he has been named already,
> For it is known that he is man;
> And he cannot contend with him who is mightier than he. . . .
> For who knows what is good for man in life, all the days of his vain
> life which he passes like a shadow?
> Who can tell a man what will happen after him . . .? (Eccl. 6:10, 12).

The text portrays an individual desperately 'contending' against life's circumstances. She or he is unable to escape human limitations and ends up shaking a fist at God or fate. But the notion that one can forge meaning out of one's own existence by controlling circumstances, so well depicted in the cases of Bouvia and Diane,[14] is *totally illusory*; for even if it were possible to marshal the resources required to accomplish one's own agenda, one could still never determine beforehand which choices would end up being 'good' or meaningful in life.

However, even if we accept the author's argument that the value of 'maintaining control' is thus diminished by the constraint of existential uncertainty, we are still confronted with an implication even more disturbing than the illusion of control in the midst of suffering: What hope of any meaning in life could possibly be left for those faced with the intolerable *indignity* of depending on others for everything, including toileting and feeding? It seems cruel to passively allow their last vestige of dignity to erode by doing nothing to relieve an already intolerable suffering that is only aggravated by such progressive, all-encompassing dependency.

This dilemma of 'indignity' is directly confronted in a remarkable verse that challenges the very core of the 'death with dignity' argument: '. . . *[F]or him who is joined to all the living there is hope, for a living dog is better than a dead lion*' (Eccl. 9:4). There is no apology here for placing the value of one's hope in living — even in a 'degraded' condition — above the value of 'death with dignity'. The option of actively hastening death would thus appear to be foreclosed in the Wisdom Model, even when life appears to have lost all dignity as dignity is commonly understood.

However, we are immediately faced with another quandary: What, exactly, is meant by a 'living dog'? Does one have to meet criteria for *brain death* to be considered 'dead', according to this Wisdom? The verses that immediately follow furnish our author's criteria for who may be considered 'dead':

> For the living know that they will die;
> But the dead know nothing,
> And they have no more reward,
> For the memory of them is forgotten.
> Also their love, their hatred, and their envy have now perished;
> Nevermore will they have a share
> In anything done under the sun (Eccl. 9:5–6).

According to our text, then, 'life' is worth supporting when there remain the capacities for *cognition, 'rewarding' relationship, emotional expression*, or *volition*. One could label these existential capacities the 'living dog' criteria.

Hope remains, then, for patients who retain full cognitive function, as did Diane and Bouvia. So, at least for anyone who meets these 'living dog' criteria, the caregiver would appear to be enjoined by Wisdom against hastening death, even when requested to do so, and even when assured that the patient is not depressed and therefore (supposedly) capable of autonomous choice. The logical question for advocates of 'death with dignity' to ask at this point would then be, How can anyone claim to respect autonomy by refusing to help patients in intractable suffering who have made up their minds to die?

Perhaps the question should be reframed by asking, Who should remain *morally accountable* for the choice to hasten death in such a patient? The author of Ecclesiastes establishes a foundation for moral accountability under just these conditions:

> [F]or every matter there is time and judgement,

Though the misery of man increases greatly.
For he does not know what will happen;
So who can tell him when it will occur?
No one has power . . . to retain the spirit,
And no one has power in the day of death (Eccl. 8:6–8).

Although there is an appropriate 'time' for everything that
happens, including death, we cannot presume to know when that
will be, thus making suicide a *presumptuous act*, whenever death is
not imminent. Moreover, since 'there is judgement', one is
accountable for one's autonomous choices, even in the midst of
intractable suffering (*'Though the misery of man increase greatly'*).[15]
This would imply that the caregiver who accedes to a request to
assist in a suicide — either by withdrawing life support or by
providing lethal drugs — would share in the moral culpability of
the presumption behind the choice to commit suicide.

How then *should* the caregiver respond when a patient or
surrogate makes such radical requests? The answer depends first
on an understanding of how intractable suffering may influence
rational decision making.

SUFFERING AND RATIONAL DECISION MAKING

HOW DOES INTRACTABLE SUFFERING INFLUENCE RATIONAL DECISION MAKING?

Even when significant depression has been ruled out, can we be
sure that requests to hasten death reflect truly reasoned consideration of other meaningful alternatives? Is there a moral basis for
attempting to influence such an individual to make more meaningful choices, without being guilty of coercion?

The author of Ecclesiastes appears to presuppose that one's
choices might well be adversely influenced by suffering, apart
from suffering-related depression. Wisdom clearly hangs in the
balance:

Sorrow is better than laughter,
For by a sad countenance the heart is made better.
The heart of the wise is in the house of mourning,
But the heart of fools is in the house of mirth.
It is better to hear the rebuke of the wise
Than for a man to hear the song of fools . . .
Surely oppression destroys a wise man's reason,
And a bribe debases the heart
(Eccl. 7:3–4, 5, 7).

The first two verses are the same ones we examined when looking
at despair as a *turning point to meaning*; the point to be emphasized
in this connection is the extent to which the benefit of mourning

depends on wise reasoning. Suffering may have such a deleterious effect on reasoning capacity, that the 'rebuke of the wise' may be required to restore some wisdom to decision making.[16] In other words, the sufferer's choices may need to be challenged by someone wiser before the dividends of mourning can be realized. Such a challenge could appropriately be labelled *'wise advocacy'*.

By contrast, the 'song of fools' only *appeases* suffering by offering the false promise of relief. Rather than 'making the heart better' by promoting authentic mourning, it actually 'debases the heart'. That is to say, 'bribing' the sufferer with the too eager promise of relieving his or her suffering only *subverts* the potential benefit (of wise stewardship over one's choices) that authentic mourning is capable of yielding in response to the despair precipitated by that suffering.

Sufferers thus have two choices: They can respond to the wise advocacy of others and benefit from new meaning in life through mourning; or they can listen to the 'Siren song' of dignity, which serves only to further entrench them in a disposition of radical self-determination and thereby limit any potential for further meaning in life to that of a 'dignified death'. Adopting such a disposition, however, brings with it certain unfavourable consequences, among which alienation from community may be the most keenly felt by the sufferer. The question thus arises: Are people really capable of living out the meaning of life apart from organic involvement in community?

The author of Ecclesiastes has already warned the reader of the alienation which characteristically accompanies a posture of radical self-determination:

> There is one alone, without companion:
> He has neither son nor brother.
> Yet there is no end to all his labours. . . .
> This . . . is vanity and a grave misfortune.
> Two are better than one,
> Because they have a good reward for their labour.
> For if they fall, one will lift up his companion.
> But woe to him who is alone when he falls,
> For he has no one to help him up (Eccl. 4:8–10).

There are clear benefits to depending on community in a 'fallen' condition like that of intractable suffering. Decision making with the support of a 'community' under such conditions holds the promise of greater benefit, especially that of wise advocacy, which is sadly forfeited by insisting on one's own way, 'without companion'.

Given the alienating effect of a self-determined disposition such as that manifested by patients like Bouvia and Diane, how far should a caregiver go in challenging their choices with such 'wise advocacy'? Once it became evident how determined they were, would not such a challenge be tantamount to *coercion*? Before reaching such a conclusion, perhaps we should first consider how often a person's request for aid in dying might be a test of whether an uninvolved community can rise to the challenge to 'help him up'. Such a test carries with it the implied dare of a kind of *Russian roulette*: 'If you dare to challenge my decision to die when you see how desperate I am, then maybe I will have a *reason to live*; if instead you help me die, at least I will be *out of my misery*.'

If indeed the stakes are this high when patients request assistance in hastening death, then 'wise advocacy' is all the more critical to restoring sound reasoning, and we are confronted with a final question, perhaps the most difficult of the four to answer.

SUFFERING AND THE ROLE OF THE CAREGIVER

WHAT IS THE ULTIMATE ROLE OF THE CAREGIVER?

Is this role indeed to relieve suffering at all costs? Should a physician or nurse ever become involved in wise advocacy? Why not stick to medical care and leave such risky 'advocacy' to others in the moral community?

In order to gain some insight into the wider range of opportunity which does in fact exist for those who dare to care in a deeper, more substantive way for those who are intractably suffering, it is instructive to study the response of Job's 'caregiver' friends when they were challenged by his suffering. All the dynamics of suffering we have seen addressed so far by the Wisdom Model are exemplified in the dialogue between Job and his friends, as Job's intractable suffering began to take its toll.

Consider again Job's initial soliloquy of despair in order to absorb the tone and mood with which Job initiated his uncomfortable dialogue with his friends:

Why did I not die at birth?
Why did I not perish when I came from the womb?
. . . For now I would have lain still and been quiet,
I would have been asleep;
Then I would have been at rest (Job 3:11, 13).

Imagine how Job's friends must have felt when he said these things. The risk of *contagion* by the sufferer's despair (cf. discussion of Eccl. 4:1–3 above) confronts anyone who would dare to be a wise advocate. This risk was apparently too great for Job's friends, who immediately tried to relieve his suffering with the false assurance that God would promptly restore him in exchange for his repentance (Job 4–5). But Job only became more agitated:

> To him who is afflicted, kindness should be shown by his friend . . .
> My brothers have dealt deceitfully . . .
>
> For now you are nothing,
> You see terror and are afraid.
> Did I ever say, 'Bring something to me'?
> Or, 'Offer a bribe for me from your wealth'?
> Or, 'Deliver me from the enemy's hand'?
> Or, 'Redeem me from the hand of the oppressors'? (Job 6:14–15, 21–22).

Rather than seeing their attempts to mitigate his suffering as 'kindness,' Job considered them a mere 'bribe' to appease his suffering — it was their own terror at the prospect of sharing the burden of despair that drove them in desperation to try to relieve the suffering that led to the despair. But if there was no possible assurance, just what kind of 'kindness' *was* Job seeking from his friends?

Interestingly, Job recognized his own need for wise advocacy (cf. discussion of Eccl. 7:5,7 above). After rebuking his friends, Job openly challenged them to risk facing him as advocates without first trying to mitigate his despair.

> Teach me, and I will hold my tongue; Cause me to understand wherein I have erred.
> How forceful are right words!
> But what does your arguing prove?
> Do you intend to reprove my words,
> And the speeches of a desperate one, which are as wind? (Job 6:24–26).

Instead, Job's friends continued to find ways to distance themselves from his despair, and he finally called them 'worthless physicians' (Job 13:4) and 'miserable comforters' (Job 16:2). Why weren't they able to furnish the kindness he so desperately sought? Job finally tells his friends just how they were lacking in kindness toward him:

> I also could speak as you do,
> If your soul were in my soul's place . . .
> But I would strengthen you with my mouth,
> And the comfort of my lips would relieve your grief (Job 16:4–5).

The word translated 'comfort' here is literally 'quivering' — 'the *quivering* of my lips would relieve your grief.' By demonstrating true empathy in this way, his friends might have earned moral standing as truly wise advocates who could legitimately challenge his choices.

Are Job's epithets — 'worthless physicians', 'miserable comforters' — prophetic of our current generation of caregivers? There are clear occasions when the physician is indeed the most appropriate member of the 'moral community' to provide 'wise care'. Yet the prospect of facing the sufferer with this level of empathy can be quite daunting for the contemporary caregiver; as John Kilner has stated, '[C]aregiving . . . can be a heavy burden, particularly if it involves efforts to help the patient bear the burdens of suffering . . . [T]he personal and vicarious suffering of the caregiver may prove valuable only after an extended period of uncertainty or even despair.'[17]

WISE CAREGIVING

The 'contractual model' for decision making is ill-suited to identify or effectively address the unique moral and existential problems that are presented by patients in intractable suffering who desire to hasten death and request assistance in doing so. The Wisdom Model not only identifies these issues but provides a viable ethical framework for decision making which promotes a morally appropriate response to the true needs of such patients. It is crucial that greater efforts be made to educate physicians about the nature of suffering and its impact on decision making.[18] Such education must address the qualities that characterize truly humane medicine, especially *empathic presence*,[19] which can bring more effective care to the sufferer.

However, there is no doubt that many caregivers will remain incapable of rising to the challenge of such empathic presence. It is entirely appropriate under such circumstances to enlist alternative forms of 'wise advocacy' to meet the needs of patients. We would be well-advised, for example, to re-evaluate the best ways to utilize the newer models for ethics consultation,[20] the techniques of hospice,[21] and other approaches commended in this volume in order to best enhance the process of moral deliberation and decision making for patients within a caring community. The ethical framework supplied by the Wisdom Model promises to guide the wise and morally appropriate use of approaches such as these to maximize the fruitful care of those who are intractably suffering.

NOTES

1. Sidney H Wanzer et al, 'The Physician's Responsibility Toward Hopelessly Ill Patients: A Second Look', *New England Journal of Medicine* 320 (1989), pp. 844–49; Timothy E Quill, Christine K Cassel, and Diane E Meier, 'Care of the Hopelessly Ill: Proposed Clinical Criteria for Physician-Assisted Suicide', *New England Journal of Medicine* 327 (1992), pp. 1380–84; Martin Gunderson and David J Mayo, 'Altruism and Physician Assisted Death', *Journal of Medicine and Philosophy* 18 (1993), pp. 281–95; American Health Consultants, 'Ethicists strive for acute ideological changes in care for the dying', *Medical Ethics Advisor* 11

(1995), pp. 13–19; Franklin G Miller and Howard Brody, 'Professional Integrity and Physician-Assisted Death', *Hastings Center Report* (May/Jun. 1995), pp. 8–17.

2. George D Lundberg, ' "It's Over, Debbie" and the Euthanasia Debate', *Journal of the American Medical Association* 259 (1988), pp. 2142–43 (cf. the anonymous account, 'It's Over, Debbie', *Journal of the American Medical Association* 259 [1988], p. 272); Stanley S Herr, Barry A Bostrom, and Rebecca S Barton, 'No Place to Go: Refusal of Life-Sustaining Treatment by Competent Persons with Physical Disabilities', *Issues in Law & Medicine* 8 (1992), pp. 3–36; Peter A Ubel, 'Assisted Suicide and the Case of Dr Quill and Diane', *Issues in Law & Medicine* 8 (1993), pp. 487–502.

3. Bouvia v Superior Court, 179 Cal App 3d 1127; 225 Cal Rptr. 297, 1986. Synopsis distilled from the discussions in Gregory E Pence, *Classic Cases in Medical Ethics* (New York: McGraw-Hill, 1990), pp. 25–44, and Herr, Bostrom, & Barton, 'No Place to Go', pp. 7–10.

4. Synopsis distilled from Timothy E Quill, 'Death and Dignity: A Case of Individualized Decision Making', *New England Journal of Medicine* 324 (1991), pp. 691–94.

5. For a discussion of the strengths and weaknesses of the contractual model, see generally William F May, 'Code and Covenant or Philanthropy and Contract', in Stephen E Lammers & Allen Verhey (eds), *On Moral Medicine* (Grand Rapids, MI: Eerdmans, 1987), pp. 83–104; Baruch Brody, *Life and Death Decision Making* (New York: Oxford University Press, 1988), pp. 56–64.

6. See the excellent discussion of the evolution of this 'right' by J Daryl Charles, 'The "Right to Die" in the Light of Contemporary Rights-Rhetoric', in *Bioethics and the Future of Medicine: A Christian Appraisal* (ed John F Kilner, Nigel M de S Cameron, and David L Schiedermayer, Grand Rapids, MI: Paternoster/Eerdmans, 1995), pp. 263–78.

7. So according to Eric J Cassell, *The Nature of Suffering and the Goals of Medicine* (New York: Oxford University Press, 1991), p. 249. Consider the well-articulated corrective to this view by Stanley Hauerwas, 'that medicine is a profession determined by moral commitments to care for the ill. . . . [S]uch a claim appears so obvious one can only wonder why anyone should think it interesting or important. However, . . . the ability to sustain such care in the face of suffering and death is no easy enterprise, for *the constant temptation is to try to eliminate suffering* through the agency of medicine rather than let medicine be the way we care for each other in our suffering' (from 'Introduction', in Stanley Hauerwas, *Suffering Presence* [Notre Dame, IN: University of Notre Dame Press, 1986], pp. 16–17, emphasis added).

8. This is the logical conclusion of the arguments of Howard Brody, 'Assisted Death — A Compassionate Response to Medical Failure', *New England Journal of Medicine* 327 (1992), 1384–88; Timothy E Quill, 'Doctor, I Want to Die Will You Help Me?' *Journal of the American Medical Association* 270 (1993), pp. 870–73; Timothy E Quill and Christine K Cassel, 'Non-abandonment: A Central Obligation for Physicians', *Annals of Internal Medicine* 122 (1995), pp. 368–74, cf. Edmund D Pellegrino, 'Nonabandonment: An Old Obligation Revisited', *Annals of Internal Medicine* 122 (1995), pp. 377–78.

9. See the discussions of the ambiguities involved in determining whether depression is present in patients who request assisted suicide in Yeates Conwell and Eric D Caine, 'Rational Suicide and the Right to Die: Reality and Myth', *New England Journal of Medicine* 325 (1991), pp. 1100–03; David C Clark, ' "Rational" Suicide and People with Terminal Conditions or Disabilities', *Issues in Law & Medicine* 8 (1992), pp. 147–66; Herbert Hendin and Gerald Klerman, 'Physician-Assisted Suicide: The Dangers of Legalization', *American Journal of Psychiatry* 150 (1993), pp. 143–45; Mark D Sullivan and Stuart J Youngner,

'Depression, Competence, and the Right to Refuse Lifesaving Medical Treatment', *American Journal of Psychiatry* 151 (1994), pp. 971–78.

10. The morally relevant issue is not the *means* by which death ensues, but the *intent* to hasten death by *whatever means* may be employed to create an imminent, irreversibly dying condition which did not already exist. This point is convincingly argued by Robert N Wennberg, *Terminal Choices: Euthanasia, Suicide, and the Right to Die* (Grand Rapids, MI: Eerdmans, 1989), pp. 30–38,136–42; Howard Brody, 'Causing, Intending, and Assisting Death', *Journal of Clinical Ethics* 4 (1993), pp. 115–117; Allen C Snyder, 'Competency to Refuse Lifesaving Treatment: Valuing the Nonlogical Aspects of a Person's Decisions', *Issues in Law & Medicine* 10 (1994), p. 316. The pitfalls of invoking the 'double effect' in this regard are aptly discussed by Timothy E Quill, 'The Ambiguity of Clinical Intentions', *New England Journal of Medicine* 329 (1993), pp. 1039–40.

11. All Scripture citations are taken from the *New King James Version* of the Bible.

12. Cassell, *The Nature of Suffering*, p. 33.

13. This truth is captured nicely by C Stephen Evans, *Existentialism: The Philosophy of Despair and the Quest for Hope* (Dallas: Probe Books, 1984), p. 42: 'Thus, in our journey through the valley of despair, we encounter evidence . . . that despair is not a dead end to which we are inevitably driven, but is in some cases the prelude to a fuller understanding of human existence . . . that lends hope that here at least is a pathway to hope.' See also, Stanley Hauerwas, *Naming the Silences: God, Medicine, and the Problem of Suffering* (Grand Rapids, MI: Eerdmans, 1990).

14. For an outstanding analysis of this disposition of 'control' in the case of Diane and Dr Quill see Patricia Wesley, 'Dying Safely', *Issues in Law & Medicine* 8 (1993), pp. 467–85. Hauerwas, *Naming the Silences*, p. 62, describes how such a disposition translates into the typical modern response to severe suffering: 'Sickness should not exist because we think of it as something in which we can intervene and which we can ultimately eliminate. [It] challenges our most cherished presumption that we are or at least can be in control of our existence.' For an excellent extended analysis from a secular perspective see Daniel Callahan, *The Troubled Dream of Life — Living with Mortality* (New York: Simon & Schuster, 1993).

15. The wisdom of this assertion — as well as that of the related previous point concerning the presumption inherent in suicide — is cogently expressed in an outstanding essay by Stanley Hauerwas, 'Rational Suicide and Reasons for Living', in Stanley Hauerwas, *Suffering Presence* (Notre Dame, IN: University of Notre Dame Press, 1986), pp. 100–13.

16. This is essentially the main point argued by Wesley, *Dying Safely*, in the case of Diane and Dr Quill. Along similar lines of reasoning, see Sullivan and Youngner, 'Depression, Competence, and the Right to Refuse', p. 976; Donald A Redelmeier, Paul Rozin, and Daniel Kahneman, 'Understanding Patients' Decisions: Cognitive and Emotional Perspectives', *Journal of the American Medical Association* 270 (1993), pp. 72–76; Edmund D. Pellegrino, 'Compassion Needs Reason Too', *Journal of the American Medical Association* 270 (1993), pp. 874–75; Eric D Caine and Yeates C Conwell, 'Self-Determined Death, the Physician, and Medical Priorities: Is There Time to Talk?', *Journal of the American Medical Association* 270 (1993), pp. 875–76; Snyder, 'Competency to Refuse Lifesaving Treatment'.

17. John F Kilner. *Life on the Line* (Grand Rapids: Eerdmans, 1992), p. 105. For a similar emphasis see Steven H Miles, 'Physicians and Their Patients' Suicides', *Journal of the American Medical Association* 271 (1994), pp. 1786–88; Susan D Block and J Andrew Billings, 'Patient Requests to Hasten Death: Evaluation and Management in Terminal Care', *Archives of Internal Medicine* 154

(1994), pp. 2039–47. Yet, contrast the concern over whether truly empathic care of this kind is even *desirable*, as expressed by Howard Curzer, 'Is Care a Virtue for Health Care Professionals?' *Journal of Medicine and Philosophy* 18 (1993), pp. 51–69.

18. Stanley Hauerwas, 'Medicine as a Moral Art', in Stanley Hauerwas, *Suffering Presence*, Part One, pp. 21–83; Eric J Cassell, 'The Importance of Understanding Suffering for Clinical Ethics', *Journal of Clinical Ethics* 2 (1991), pp. 81–82; Eric H Loewy, 'The Role of Suffering and Community in Clinical Ethics', *Journal of Clinical Ethics* 2 (1991), pp. 83–89.

19. Edmund D Pellegrino, 'Educating the Humanist Physician: An Ancient Ideal Reconsidered', *Journal of the American Medical Association* 227 (1974), pp. 1288–94; Leon R Kass, 'Ethical Dilemmas in the Care of the Ill: I. What is the physician's service?'; 'II. What is the patient's good?' *Journal of the American Medical Association* 244 (1980), pp. 1811–16;1946–49; Stanley Hauerwas, 'Medicine as a Moral Art'. See also, Stanley Hauerwas, 'Care', in Stephen E Lammers & Allen Verhey (eds.), *On Moral Medicine* (Grand Rapids, MI: Eerdmans, 1987), pp. 262–66; Richard M Zaner, 'Medicine and Dialogue', *Journal of Medicine and Philosophy* 15 (1990), pp. 303–25; Howard Brody, *The Healer's Power* (1992); William Zinn, 'The Empathic Physician', *Archives of Internal Medicine* 153 (1993), pp. 306–12.

20. Margaret U Walker, 'Keeping Moral Space Open: New Images of Ethics Consulting', *Hastings Center Report* (Mar/Apr. 1993), pp. 33–40; Timothy J Keay, 'Ethics Committees and Family Ghosts: Case Studies', *Journal of Clinical Ethics* 5 (1994), pp. 19–22; Richard M Zaner, *Ethics and the Clinical Encounter* (Englewood Cliffs, NJ: Prentice Hall, 1988); Troubled Voices (Cleveland: Pilgrim Press, 1993); and 'Voices and Time', *Journal of Medicine and Philosophy* 18 (1993), pp. 9–31.

21. Courtney S Campbell, Jan Hare, and Pam Matthews, 'Conflicts of Conscience — Hospice and Assisted Suicide,' *Hastings Center Report* (May/Jun 1995), pp. 36–43.

16

Parish Nursing

Norma R Small, RN, PhD

Churches are expected to minister to the spiritual needs of their members while other institutions in society are expected to minister to their medical, psychological and social needs. Increasingly, however, communities of faith are returning to their historical roots of ministry to the whole person: body, mind, and soul. Congregations are becoming places of healing, of restoring to health, throughout the stages of life from birth to death. Nurses are also returning to their Christian roots as part of this movement. Compassionate care for the weak, ill, and dying was a significant expression of discipleship in the early church.

Now parish nurses are helping to restore the ministry of care and healing to the congregation. This chapter will discuss parish nursing as one strategy for ministry to dying persons that involves walking with them to a peaceful death, the last stage of life. The discussion begins by considering the origins of the parish nurse movement and what nurses bring to the position of health minister. Next we consider a holistic definition of health that undergirds ministry to the dying even when death is inevitable. The chapter then concludes with a consideration of the specific roles of the parish nurse as they relate to issues of death and dying.

ORIGINS OF THE PARISH NURSE MOVEMENT

The idea of parish nursing originated in the Lutheran Health Care System. Rev Granger Westberg envisioned churches becoming part of the health care system by bringing a nurse onto the ministry staff of the congregation. He saw this as the way to integrate the art and science of medicine and nursing with the theology of health and healing.[1] The titles 'parish nurse' or 'health minister' may not be appropriate for all denominations and faith communities. But every congregation stands to benefit by identifying a person with responsibility for integrating faith beliefs and health practices in the work and worship of that congregation.

Issues related to health are best addressed within one's values and belief system. These issues include choices of lifestyle and behaviour such as nutrition, exercise, substance use, and risk-taking behaviour that account for the majority of chronic illnesses and premature death; and treatment decisions in illness and in dying. Since faith communities have been responsible for teaching values and beliefs, they should promote positive lifestyle choices and health care decisions based on these values. In doing this they are indeed reclaiming their historical position as places of healing and centres for health.

By returning to the church as the base for their work, nurses are themselves returning to the roots of nursing. Nursing developed from charitable ministries of the early church that were often focused in the orders of widows and deaconesses. Later, religious orders of men and women were the only source of care for the sick outside the family. Modern nursing began with Florence Nightingale in the 1800s. She was inspired by the revival of deaconess orders associated with the Lutheran Church in Germany. The Nightingale model, while borrowing from the deaconesses, located the work of nurses outside the church's oversight. In the congregation, nursing reclaims its heritage as the faith community again becomes a practice site.

The turning of nurses to the church as a place for ministry can truly be called a movement. Programmes for preparing nurses to work as parish nurses are springing up across the country, some in colleges and universities, and others in free-standing centres. A yearly conference brings these nurses together to learn from one another.

Why has there been this surge of interest in parish nursing? The incongruence between nursing as taught and nursing as practised in the current health care system has resulted in an identity crisis for the profession as a whole and for individual nurses as well. The current health care systems require the nurse's time and energy to support the goals and values of the health care agency. These employing institutions reward nurses for emulating the biomedical approach of sickness care, leaving little time for integrating the emotional, spiritual, and social care for patients and their families. Numerous attempts have been made to clarify nursing's identity and to define the essence of nursing practice. While describing the holistic nature of nursing and what nursing should be as a distinct health care profession, these definitions have had little influence on the real priorities of the workplace where nursing is practised and rewarded. When health care is returned to the congregation, nurses find themselves released to practise nursing in a holistic way that is satisfying to both nurses and patients.

WHAT NURSES BRING TO THE CHURCH

In 1961 the International Council of Nurses asked Virginia
Henderson to write a definition of nursing. This definition became
the standard on which later formulations were based. She wrote:

> The unique function of the nurse is to assist the individual, sick or
> well, in the performance of those activities contributing to health
> (what the patient lacks to make him complete, whole or independent)
> or its recovery (or to a peaceful death) that he would perform unaided
> if he had the necessary strength, will or knowledge and to do this in
> such a way as to help him gain independence as rapidly as possible.[2]

Her definition identified key concepts that define nursing practice
as distinct from medical practice. Nursing substitutes for what
individuals cannot do for themselves. Nurses also have a role
along the entire health–illness continuum, from wellness through
physical death. Henderson defined health as completeness, wholeness, and independence and identified the promotion of health as
one function of nursing.

> Think how rare is 'completeness' or 'wholeness' of mind and body.
> . . . [the nurse] must, in a sense, get 'inside the skin' of each of her
> patients in order to know what he needs. She is temporarily the
> consciousness of the unconscious, the love of life for the suicidal, . . .
> the 'mouthpiece' for those too weak or withdrawn to speak, and so
> on.[3]

Recently much thought and writing has been given to the idea
of *caring* as the essence of nursing. Benner and Wrubel describe
caring as follows:

> Caring is the essential requisite for all coping. . . . [It helps a person]
> to recover, to appropriate meaning, and to maintain or reestablish
> connection. . . . From the place of care, the person can neither claim
> complete autonomy nor be the absolute source of meaning. Involve-
> ment and caring may lead one to experience loss and pain, but may
> also make joy and fulfillment possible. Caring is primary because it
> sets up the possibility of giving help and receiving help.[4]

The concepts Henderson identified in her definition of nursing,
together with Benner and Wrubel's concept of caring, characterize
the essence of parish nursing. This characterization balances the
science of nursing with the art of nursing, the conscious use of
skill and creative imagination with theology and caring. Parish
nursing is a response to Christ's command for the church to carry
out his healing ministry by being a caring community. It is a
fulfilment of the vocation to which nurses were called by Christ's
command 'to heal the sick . . .' (Matt. 10:8).

A NEW DEFINITION OF HEALTH

To make dying with dignity possible a new definition of health must be found — one that goes beyond the absence of disease to a more holistic understanding of health. As defined within the context of a faith community, health means wholeness; integration of body, mind, and spirit; and meaning and purpose in life. Illness, on the other hand, refers to brokenness; disintegration of body (disease), mind (depression), and spirit (hopelessness); alienation and lack of community; and death. Just as the strength of a building depends upon the pillars supporting it, the health of an individual depends on the integrity of the person's physical, psychological, sociological, spiritual, and environmental supports. Every individual is somewhere on a continuum of health going from brokenness and illness to wholeness and health. Furthermore, each of the supporting pillars of health has its own continuum, as displayed below.

The Pillars of Health: The Health-Illness Continuum

```
BROKENNESS—<disintegration>——>integration>—WHOLENESS
ILLNESS————<symptoms>————>intervention>————HEALTH
DEATH——<disease>———PHYSICAL——>medicine>———CURE
DEPRESSION————————PSYCHOLOGICAL————OPTIMISM
ALIENATION————————SOCIOLOGICAL————BELONGING
SEPARATION—<sin>—SPIRITUAL—>forgiveness>—SALVATION
HOPELESSNESS————————————MEANING/PURPOSE
DISHARMONY————————ENVIRONMENTAL————HARMONY
```

While disease may weaken a pillar from within or stressors may weaken it from without, the strength of other pillars may prove sufficiently strong to support it. The ill individual can then be healed and become whole. Only when medical intervention, positive attitude, personal relationships, and meaning and purpose in life are not strong enough to shore-up the weakened or broken physical pillar does disintegration and illness lead to death. One who is ill may be cured of physical disease but not be healed or restored to health and wholeness. For example, surgery may seem successful and yet without the will to live the patient dies for reasons not explained physiologically. A disintegration of one or more of the supporting pillars has occurred. Yet, another individual having the needed supports may experience healing but not be cured from physical disease. For example, patients with terminal cancer may experience the process of dying and yet be whole persons. They are whole because they have found meaning and purpose in their suffering, a sense of belonging to a loving family and a caring community, an optimistic acceptance of their physical limitations, and the hope of eternal life.

This holistic understanding of health supports the prevention of disease, the striving for wholeness, and the healing of brokenness even when cure is not possible and physical death is inevitable. Thomas Droge writes:

> The 'something more' beyond the eradication of disease has to do with healthy attitudes and behavior, healthy communities, spiritual values, a purpose for living, and social justice for the poor and undeserved. Who is better situated to promote this 'something more' than congregations'?[5]

The importance of treating the whole person to promote health is gaining broad acceptance. Bernie Siegle[6] and Norman Cousins[7] stand at the forefront of the secular whole person health movement. Kenneth Bakken[8] and Thomas Droge[9] apply the biblical concepts of health, wholeness, integration, shalom, and salvation to the ministry of the Christian church today.

This holistic approach stands in contrast to much of what occurs in current health care where the physician treats the body, the psychologist treats the mind, and the clergyperson treats the soul. This disconnected approach has resulted in highly specialized health care providers who tend to view the person as a machine with broken parts in need of fixing rather than as an integrated whole being with worth and dignity. While addressing the challenges to cure disease, replace diseased body parts and extend longevity, present health care systems typically fail to consider the person as whole. When health is defined as the absence of disease, death is viewed as a treatment failure. There is no more to be done for failures. The caring healing congregation, however, has much more to offer through the ministry of the parish nurse.

ROLES OF THE PARISH NURSE

When a parish nurse enters the lives of dying patients and their families as a minister of the congregation, it is her or his goal to promote health, healing and wholeness by garnering resources for strengthening the supporting pillars of health. Parish nurses, licensed by the state, work with a health committee or council of the church that may include other health care providers, educators, and lay persons. In their ministry, parish nurses carry out six roles: health assessor, health educator, health promoter, health counsellor, trainer of volunteers, and health advocate. Nurse practice acts in each state recognize these roles as the independent practice of nursing. We will examine each of these roles as they concern the congregation's ministry of maintaining dignity for those who are dying.

Prior to implementing any congregational health programme, it is essential to assess what is already being done and what is needed and wanted by the members related to death and dying. The needs and interests of all age groups from adolescents to older adults should be considered, since life-threatening injury or illness can strike at any stage of life. Issues of death and dying concern people not only as individuals but also as family and community members.

Each person has a unique perspective on dying based on his or her spiritual maturity, prior experience with death and dying, family and community support, and proximity to death. Many Christians embrace the prevailing American view that defines a person's worth in terms of youth and productivity and denies death by refraining from discussing it and withdrawing from those who are dying. Teaching and preaching in a faith community should prepare individuals and families to face death, the dying of loved ones and their own dying.

Gathering information concerning the congregation's readiness to become a place of healing and wholeness is done in both formal and informal ways. Talking with various individuals and groups and observing participants in learning forums such as Christian education classes are example of informal assessment. More formal assessments include structured surveys, interviews, and gathering statistical and demographic information about the congregation. Learning about the surrounding community is also important since the members of a caring healing church will reach out to their neighbours as well.

In the role of *health educator*, the parish nurse starts with what people know and what they want to know. He or she then progresses to raising awareness of issues and creating a desire to learn more about needs and issues needing to be addressed. The health educator seeks to provide information appropriate to the level of understanding and the learning styles of the participants. He or she knows, for example, that because of differences in educational experiences older adults learn differently from adolescents, who are accustomed to multimedia productions.

Educational topics concerning dignity and dying may include the worth of each individual, pain and suffering, the dying process, advance directives, funeral planning, estate planning, and characteristics of a caring congregation. Teaching should include current information, be factual, and incorporate biblical teaching and faith practices. Recruiting teachers from within the congregation who have expertise and experience in specific areas, when possible, is wise. Many congregations have such potential teachers who have never before been called upon to integrate their vocation and their faith.

In this role of *health promoter*, the parish nurse goes beyond merely giving information to providing experiences whose goal is to change the lives of those who participate. For example, in workshops participants learn how to write advance directives, plan their estates, and make funeral arrangements. Support groups may serve the needs of those who are experiencing pain and suffering, facing death, giving care, and experiencing bereavement. Topical Bible studies on themes related to suffering, death, and dying aim to lead participants to new insights and spiritual growth. The parish nurse may not lead all the Bible studies, workshops, or support groups. However, she or he participates in the planning to insure integration of the holistic approach and understanding of health, illness, and dying.

Parish nurses serve also as *health counsellors*, having knowledge of the physical progress of disease and dying, the necessity of caring relationships and community, the importance of positive self-esteem and optimism, and the need to find meaning in one's pain and suffering. In this role parish nurses act as good listeners and develop caring relationships with people facing death and dying — those dying themselves and those who love them. Within this relationship of care the nurses impart strength through prayer and presence, conviction through encouragement and empowerment, and knowledge through sharing of information. They do this so that patients and their loved ones can make informed health care decisions. In the words of Henderson, '[the nurse] gets inside the skin of each patient in order to know what he needs.'[10]

Perhaps the major role of the parish nurse is to be a *trainer of volunteers*. A parish nurse cannot physically or emotionally meet all the health needs of the congregation or of the community it serves. Volunteers, lay ministers, are called to use their time and gifts for specific aspects of the health ministry of the church. Frequently it is volunteers who provide the connection between a dying person and the caring community. This essential connection promotes the continued sense of worthiness for the dying one that is a tangible example of Christ's healing even in the face of physical death. Volunteers support the dying person in many ways: personal presence, telephone reassurance (especially during the darkest parts of the journey), friendly visits, respite for caregivers, household chores, meals, recreational activities, and transportation to appointments. As a trainer of volunteers, the parish nurse inspires members of the congregation to become committed to this work, provides the needed skills and knowledge, and, most importantly, serves as an ongoing resource and encouragement to volunteers. When volunteers run into problems beyond the scope of their training, the parish nurse provides support.

Finally, in their role as *health advocates* parish nurses bring their knowledge of and acceptance by the larger health care system. In this unique position they are privileged to be 'the mouthpiece for those too weak or withdrawn to speak'[11] — advocates for vulnerable people. They speak for those who lack the strength, will, and knowledge to express their desires and concerns about treatment during terminal illness and the dying process. The parish nurse assists patients and families in seeking appropriate medical intervention for adequate control of pain and anxiety. If the patient's environment, such as an intensive care unit or nursing home, fails to promote dignity, self-worth, and respect, the parish nurse may advocate for changes. Sometimes parish nurses advocate within families and the caring community for the healing of broken relationships and for the strengthening of the dying person's sense of belonging. They may even engage in the ultimate advocacy by organizing prayer chains on behalf of patients and families.

CONCLUSION

For its members and neighbours, the faith community seeks to promote movement from the end of the health continuum where fear of illness/brokenness, disintegration, hopelessness and death reign, toward the desired goal of health as wholeness, integration, and salvation motivated by hope. Because current health care systems typically do not address these issues, Christian churches must reclaim their historical role in health, healing, and dying. The Bible refers many times to health, healing, wholeness, salvation, and physical health as God's plan for creation. It offers life eternal as the hope for believers. All the gospels are about health and healing.[12] The great commandment, 'You shall love the Lord your God with all your heart, and with all your soul, and with all your mind, . . . and you shall love your neighbour as yourself' (Matt. 22:37–39), sums up the imperative for Christians to develop a whole heart (healthy body), a whole mind (optimism), and a whole spirit (meaning and purpose) as essential aspects of loving God, self, and neighbour.

The failure of Christians to live as role models of their calling to love has caused many to call for laws preserving the right to die with dignity. 'Now abide faith, hope and love, but the greatest of these is love' (ICor. 13:13). Empowered by the Holy Spirit we are to 'bear one another's burdens, and thus fulfil the law of Christ' (Gal. 6:2). Christ teaches us his law of love by his example and by his teaching. He teaches us to reach out to neighbours in the parable of the Good Samaritan (Lk. 10:25–37) and to those in the congregation in the parable of the separation of the sheep and goats. 'To the extent you did it to one of these brothers of mine, even the least of them, you did it to me' (Matt. 25:32–40). Christians have a responsibility to reach out to each other and to their neighbours as instruments of Christ's love and caring during crucial stages at the end of life by supporting dying people through a peaceful, natural death as ordained by God.

How well churches carry out their health ministry to those who are dying may be influenced by parish nurses in their roles and by others whom they inspire to share in this health ministry. Parish nurses both provide and teach tangible ways to touch those who are experiencing the physical pain of disease, the emotional pain of feeling worthless, the pain of alienation and lack of caring relationships, and the spiritual pain that comes from a lack of meaning and purpose in life. By reaching out holistically to their brothers and sisters, to their neighbours, and especially to those dying without dignity and hope, parish nurses and all those who participate in the health ministry of the congregation act as caring disciples of Christ.

NOTES

1. G Westberg, *The Parish Nurse* (Minneapolis: Augsburg Press, 1990).

2. V Henderson, *Basic Principles of Nursing* (London: International Council of Nurses, 1961), p. 42.

3. *Ibid.*

4. P Benner and J Wrubel, *The Primacy of Caring: Stress and Coping in Health and Illness* (Menlo Park, CA: Addison-Wesley Publishing Co., 1989), p. 2.

5. T Droege, 'Congregations as Communities of Health and Healing', *Interpretation* 49 (Apr. 1995), p. 118.

6. B Siegel, *Love, Medicine & Miracles* (New York: Harper and Row, 1986).

7. N Cousins, *Head First: the Biology of Hope* (New York: E.P.Dutton, 1989).

8. K Bakken, *The Call To Wholeness: Health as a Spiritual Journey* (New York: Crossroad, 1987).

9. T Droege, *The Faith Factor in Healing* (Philadelphia: Trinity Press International, 1991).

10. Henderson, p. 42.

11. *Ibid.*

12. M Marty, *Striving for the Fullness of Life: The Church's Challenge in Health* (video, part 1. Chicago: Wheat Ridge Foundation, 1991).

17

Congregational Ministry

Dennis Hollinger, MDiv, PhD

Neither the church nor society is well-prepared to deal with the moral dilemmas surrounding death. The problem is not merely a lack of moral clarity to guide our thinking, though certainly that is the case. But a compounding conundrum is that the very notion of death makes most of us uncomfortable. Medical personnel, clergy, and laity find themselves ill at ease when the death bell tolls, whether it be for friend, family or casual acquaintance.

Daniel Maguire describes our discomfort well:

> The average person . . . would rather forget it. This is especially true if the average person is an American since in this happiness-oriented land, death (outside of a military context) is seen as something of an un-American activity. It happens of course but it is disguised. . . . When the unmentionable happens, the deceit goes on as the embalmers embark on their post mortem cosmetics to make the dead man look alive. Mourners, chemically fortified against tears that would betray the farce, recite their lines about how well the dead man looks when, in point of fact, he is not well and does not look it.[1]

Our coping mechanisms are illustrated in a 'Kudzu' comic strip. A layman says to the clergyman at the end of the funeral, 'Your language discriminates against the funeral honoree . . . The word "dead" is so . . . so negative . . . so final! I personally refer to them as the "pulseless" . . . or "people of passivity"!'

Though Christians are armed with a theology to make sense of death and have the hope of eternal life to soften its sting, we too find death a foreboding reality. This was brought home with force a number of years ago when I was a full-time seminary professor. A visiting chapel speaker once spoke on the subject of death, and began his sermon by asking each of us to look at the person to our left and say, 'Someday I am going to die.' I was rather surprised at the discomfort many of the students and some of my faculty colleagues displayed during this simple little exercise. Some looked down, some mumbled under their breath, and some chose not to participate at all. In just months or a few short years many of these seminarians would be counselling families in bereavement, offering words of hope in funerals, and pronouncing benedictions at grave sides. But the reality of their own death was a source of intense anxiety and embarrassment.

It is perhaps this sense of personal anxiety which contributes to our difficulty in facing the moral dilemmas surrounding death, whether it be euthanasia, treatment termination, or defining death. Yet death is the one great certainty we all must face, and the church in particular must be equipped to shepherd people into the 'valley of the shadow' with hope, and to provide direction for the ethical issues that often accompany its haunting face.

What should the church do in the face of ethical issues that confront us? What is the church's unique role as we encounter a world bent on control not only of life itself, but control of the cessation of life, including its timing and the means by which it occurs? Or to put it more baldly, how can the church be salt and light in a culture that most certainly is moving towards an acceptance of assisted suicide or voluntary euthanasia[2] — a move that signals not a coming to terms with death, but rather a continual denial of all that surrounds this mystery which every person must face.

In light of these cultural shifts, many in the church today opt for a response that is applied to a host of socio-cultural issues: the politicized response. Over the past several decades Christians, especially evangelical Christians, have moved from the periphery of society to its centre in terms of personal identity and social position. They have discovered that they have clout when it comes to shaping the political contours of American society. Thus many individual believers and churches have argued that the most effective way to save America from cultural disaster and moral suicide is to become a political block which can directly influence the outcome of political elections, legislative process, and judicial proceedings. Political strategists have quickly learned that they dare not neglect the political force and ideology of certain Christian groups.

I have long been a proponent of Christian social action and the need to uphold the cultural mandate of the Bible along with the great commission. But I must confess to some reserve about the politicization of Christianity in which the church becomes so self-assured in questions of public policy strategy and becomes an overt political force in the name of Christ.

Certainly there are clear Christian principles that must guide our thinking and actions, but it does not follow that there is only one public policy strategy that can implement those principles. Moreover, the very nature of public policy, with its need for give and take or compromise, has a way of stripping the church of its unique role within the world when it becomes an intentional political block. Whenever the church, or Christian groups identified with the church, have opted for explicit politicized approaches to social and cultural problems, they have tended to become just another of the many interest groups vying for power in the public square. History has demonstrated again and again that when the church, or groups identified with the church, become primarily preoccupied with political realities (whether it be the politics of the left or the right), they lose their unique role and often fidelity to the gospel, despite their good intentions.

It is ironic that in a time when many social commentators and politicians are questioning the state's ability to solve our most grievous social and cultural maladies, some Christians are placing most of their moral eggs in the political basket. The *Washington Post* writer and syndicated columnist William Raspberry recently wrote a stirring essay precisely on this point. He acknowledges that it may seem a strange message from 'a not particularly religious writer in an utterly secular newspaper,' but Raspberry claims he is struck by two phenomena: 'The first is the growing sense that America's major failings are not political or economic but moral. The second is the discovery that the most successful social programs are those that are driven . . . by moral or religious values.' The church, says Raspberry, has a unique role to play in curing what ails America. 'And still the church, like a seven-foot-tall basketball player shooting jump shots [from the chest], persists in playing away from its strength — its potential for spiritual regeneration.' Raspberry chastises the church for neglecting what it can do best, namely bringing a unique spiritual perspective and power into a society that heretofore has tended to seek political answers for its most vexing problems.[3]

The church and individual Christians should of course not turn their backs on the public policy issues and retreat into oblivion. There is a proper role for Christians in the public arena, including the biomedical arena with issues such as assisted suicide. But what does the church do best? What is the church's unique calling in the face of the cultural malaise which faces us today?

I want to suggest that the church has two primary responsibilities in facing the moral quandaries surrounding death and dying. These responsibilities are rooted in biblical mandates for the church, but also respond to specific changes in society that make euthanasia an ever increasing option for many people.

A COMMUNITY OF PROCLAMATION

The first response we need in the church is to be a community of proclamation. The proclamation of the eternal verities of God has long been understood as one of the *notae* or key marks of the church.[4] Unfolding the meaning of God's unchanging Word and applying it to the ever changing realities of our personal and social lives is a sacred task given to the church for the sake of guiding believers in their spiritual and moral journeys, and for the purpose of communicating to nonbelievers the grace of God offered through Jesus Christ. Proclaiming God's truth in the world is a task that no other institution in society can do, for no other social institution has received and been vested with the Word of God.

The church's unique role of proclamation is particularly needed as a response to changing world views which have precipitated the growing demand for control over the termination of one's own life. Euthanasia is not isolated from larger cultural and world view shifts which emanate from both the tenets of modernity and now more recently post modernity. The modern world since the Enlightenment has taught humans that they are the masters of their fate, the arbiters of their own freedom, and the owners of their own personal bodies. The technological advances of the modern world, which have enriched our lives on the one hand, have also led us to believe that we can control the formation of life, its cessation, and everything in between. Thus, as Larry Churchill notes, death has been moved 'as a human experience from the moral to the technical order.'[5]

The post modern world has lost confidence in the rational coherence that was thought to accompany the control of the modern world. While many still want control over birth, life and death, there is no longer the assurance that such control operates within an intelligible moral framework. Subjectivity has replaced rationality as the *modus operandi* of human decision making, and there are no external criteria by which humans can judge what is morally right and wrong. The pluralism of our age only confirms the post modernist contention that with the plethora of moral and philosophic choices we have today, there is no possibility of speaking of truth or of universal moral goodness.

It is from the residual forces of modernity and the more recent tenets of post modern thinking, that advocates for assisted suicide or euthanasia tend to build their case. Personal freedom, autonomy, and the right to a life free of suffering are often coupled with the assumption that ethical norms are local or parochial constructs that we devise to guide a profession, institution or our personal lives.

Biomedical ethics as merely the voice of an historic community is well illustrated in an article in a recent issue of *The Hastings Center Report*. Franklin Miller and Howard Brody argue for the possibility of voluntary physician-assisted suicide as a last resort on the grounds of a professional ethic of integrity. They contend that 'the internal morality of medicine and the virtue of professional integrity is [are] needed to supplement appeal to the

principles, rules, and virtues of our common morality,' and such
an internal morality of medicine and its professional ethic does not
preclude voluntary euthanasia.[6] But as Steven Miles argues in a
response article, this approach tends to move the authority for
such an act 'to a medical judgment of death as therapy.'[7] The
thinking of Miller and Brody is mild and nuanced compared to
many advocates of euthanasia today, but it reflects the kind of
shifts that have taken place in human perceptions of reality. The
assumption is that we can control life and death, and that moral
reflection is limited to historic, cultural and professional bound
norms that have no legitimacy beyond ourselves.

The church's proclamation then should come, in part, as a
response to world view shifts in our culture concerning the nature
of human life, death, suffering, and God. When for example
suffering is seen as an absolute evil which must be eradicated by
voluntary death,[8] this is a major shift from the Christian view that
suffering results from the Fall, but nonetheless in the providence
of God has potential for growth, witness, and power to endure
from beyond ourselves. Or when freedom is defined as the essence
of humanness with ethics being little more than subjective
reflection, it is a world view shift from the premise of Jesus that
'you will know the truth, and the truth will set you free' (Jn. 8:32).

In the midst of such world view shifts[9] that contribute to the
push towards euthanasia, the proclamation of God's truth plays a
unique role. State and civil laws probably cannot stem the tide of
such cultural shifts, for they are not well-suited to change the
thinking and character of the human self. Social and legal
inducements of course play a kind of minimalist role in shaping
human behaviour, character and thinking, but their power to
change world view is not nearly as powerful as the role of
mediating, voluntary institutions in society like the church.
Gertrude Himmelfarb makes a similar point in her recent work,
*The Demoralization of Society: From Victorian Virtues to Modern
Values.* Describing the Victorian approach to building virtuous
character she writes:

> They recognized the need for whatever inducements or sanctions —
> social, religious, legal, ultimately physical — might be required to
> encourage virtue and discourage vice. But they wanted to make those
> sanctions as painless and noncoercive as possible. The more effective
> the voluntary exercise of morality on the part of each individual, the
> more internalized that morality in the self (in the form of conscience,
> character, habit, or religion), the less need there would be for the
> external, punitive instruments of the state.[10]

The church through its divine gift and mandate of proclamation
has greater possibility of encouraging that voluntary exercise of
morality than any other institution. Thus when the church trades

its unique role in culture shaping for the less effective political power role, it is abandoning what it does best. It has traded its 'birthright for a mess of pottage,' though of course that mess of pottage has a role to play. But when the church plays down its vocation of proclamation, it abdicates a task that no other institution in society is empowered to perform, to herald the Word of our eternal creator, redeemer, sustainer.

The church's proclamation must always be geared in two directions. First, it is directed to the body of Christ itself. The acids of modernity and post modernity have corroded the moral and theological certitude of contemporary church members. Thus, I find whenever I have been asked to address issues of bioethics in the context of the church, there are always some whose world views have been conformed to the image of this world with reference to euthanasia. The church must clearly articulate to its own members biblical and theological understandings of human life, death, suffering, human agency and divine providence in such a way that believers will be equipped cognitively and practically to find their way through the cultural maze. Then believers will in the words of the apostle Paul, 'No longer be infants tossed back and forth by the waves, and blown here and there by every wind of teaching. . . . Instead speaking the truth in love, we will in all things grow up into him who is the head, that is Christ' (Ept. 4:14–15).

But there is a second direction for our ministry of proclamation, the larger society itself. On the one hand this embodies heralding the gospel message, for it more than any other factor has the power to change thinking and actions relative to the cultural allurements of our time. The church dares not lose sight of the role of conversion in its social and cultural impact on issues like euthanasia.

At the same time the church needs to nurture thinkers and practitioners who can engage in moral dialogue on such issues in the larger society. The church through well-informed leaders does need to address the public arena, whether that be in the polis or various institutions in society such as our health institutions. In the public debates, we are not so much seeking to be a political power block (the politicized approach) as a leavening process (to use Jesus's metaphor) within the culture.

To effect change in this manner we will often need to become bilingual, speaking a language that can be understood by modern unbelievers who do not share our world view, but who might through persuasion be convinced of our moral position on euthanasia or other moral issues. The language of Zion will guide and direct our deepest moral character, thinking and conversation within the church, but we will need to learn a broader language to be understood in Babylon. The broader appeals and arguments are not a capitulation to the larger culture, for our foundations, motives and guiding vision are rooted in explicit theological norms and the whole of the biblical story. But we will sometimes set aside the explicit language of Zion and adopt broader modes of discourse, with clarity, conviction and love, in order to make some dent in the cultural thinking and moral responses of our society.

A COMMUNITY OF CARE

It is not enough for the church to be merely a community of proclamation in its response to death and dying issues; it must also be a community of care. This too is part of the vocation of the church, for as Paul reminded the Body of Christ at Corinth, their own experience of God's mercy and care through Jesus Christ was to overflow in expression to others:

> Praise be to the God and Father of our Lord Jesus Christ, the Father of compassion and the God of all comfort, who comforts us in all our troubles, so that we can comfort those in any trouble with the comfort we ourselves have received from God. For just as the sufferings of Christ flow over into our lives, so also through Christ our comfort overflows (2 Cor. 1:3–5).

Such compassion cares not only for the human soul, but the whole person whose emotional, physical, social and spiritual dimensions are deeply intertwined.

The social shift that particularly beckons the church to be a caring community is the evaporation of natural support networks in our communities. The mobility of the modern world means that countless humans now face the end of life alone, and without the close family or friendship systems that once helped buffer the fears, sufferings and uncertainties surrounding death. As the late Paul Ramsey, former ethicist at Princeton University, put it, 'If the sting of death is sin, the sting of dying is solitude. Desertion is more choking than death, and more feared. The chief problem of the dying is how not to die alone.'[11]

Much of the interest in euthanasia today is fuelled by the modern pattern of dying. When people come to the end of life alone, suffering and fear hasten the desire for a quick final exit. All of this is couched in the language of compassion, kindness or beneficence for the dying patient, but the pleas really reflect the larger issue that many patients today face: they die alone and without care. When this reality is coupled with the changes of world view noted earlier, it is understandable that people want a quick way out before their time has come. Many today proceed, as John Kilner puts it, 'From the mistaken assumption that what matters in life is the quality of one's life and that some lives are not worth living. Such views reflect utilitarian and hedonistic presuppositions that people's lives must be justified by what they contribute to others or at least by the pleasure they provide to themselves.'[12]

When humans face death without personal support and care, they are more prone to believe that their life lacks meaning and is not worth living. Thus the emergence of the euthanasia movement is directly related to the lack of personal and social networks that can walk with the suffering patient down into the dark valley of death. As Cicely Saunders, the founder of the hospice movement in England, puts it, 'When someone asks for euthanasia or turns to suicide, I believe in almost every case someone or society as a whole has failed that person.'[13]

Of course nonbelievers and institutions other than the church can provide care for the dying patient in ways that help thwart the desire for euthanasia. But the church by its very nature, as a community grounded in the ultimate care of the cross, and guided by a world view rooted in truth, certainly has a prime opportunity to express care in such a way that the desire for assisted suicide is diminished. Its offer of grace in Christ and its manifestation of grace and mercy in actions can play a significant role in providing sustenance and hope for patients who otherwise might succumb to the temptation to end it all.

The church's involvement may be in a dying person's home or in other settings. Home health care, for example, is a form of ministry that warrants much greater attention. As Leslie Coomer explains, not only does church-provided home health care help meet the physical and emotional needs of people, but it also often provides an opportunity to discuss a Christian ethical position in support of life, the theological convictions underlying that position, and the patient's personal ownership of those convictions.[14] Home health care may be a ministry of a church denomination, a para-church organization, or a local congregation.

However, care for very sick patients in particular is by no means limited to the home setting. Larry Richards and Paul Johnson in their book *Death and the Caring Community* tell the following story that illustrates so well the kind of multi-setting care that ought to accompany the process of dying.

> As Cathy's cancer grew worse, and the treatment more and more draining, she simply had to stay at the hospital. But her last months were far from lonely.
> About four years before her illness, Cathy had become a Christian through a women's Bible study group started by a Young Life leader.

When that group grew into a church the next year, Cathy was one of the original members of the fellowship. Of course, Bob hadn't come, except to the dinner parties the members of the Fellowship gave. He and her grown children weren't Christians, and had no interest in the faith. And then the cancer came.

Cathy died. But she didn't die alone. Day after day, for a period of months, brothers and sisters from her Fellowship drove the 35 miles from their mountain community to the Denver hospital. No one told them they should. No one organized shifts. But all during the days and the evenings, brothers and sisters who loved Cathy were with her. And when she had a particularly difficult time, there would be those who stayed through the night.

Back at home people gathered around Bob, too. The men took him out to lunch, and insisted he go with them to play tennis. . . . Cathy, and Bob too, were surrounded by a supportive love that told each of them: you are significant. You are important to us, and to God.

When Cathy died over a dozen of her friends were there to see her off.

It had been a difficult time for Cathy. She'd known the same feelings and doubts and fears that others know as they pass through a terminal illness. But for Cathy there was something different than many others' experience. There was a surrounding warmth and love that flowed from a supportive community of those who cared.[15]

When the church cares in this manner there is no cry for euthanasia.

In order for the church to be a caring community there must be a supporting ecclesiology focusing the church in that direction. Some churches in their own self-identity have lost the biblical imagery of body, family, or people of God. These images have been replaced by institution, efficiency, management, and growth of head count. While these images have their place, the church is most faithful to its Lord and most effective in making assisted suicide a mute point, when it lives what it is, the body of Jesus Christ. And in his body, 'If one part suffers, every part suffers with it' (1 Cor. 12:26a).

The church as a caring community needs to extend beyond the personal and group care of suffering patients to institutional care as well. Church-related health institutions such as hospitals, nursing homes and hospices, can only justify their existence as distinct from other facilities only when Christian care is evident. The health institutions of our larger society have tended in their bureaucratic structures to strip the patient of personal identity and dignity.[16] Often the patient has even lost her name and becomes a number or 'the patient in room 207.' In light of the economics of contemporary health care, now is not an opportune time for churches and denominations to begin health care facilities. But when they do and for those that exist, it is the distinctive care emanating from their spiritual commitments which provides a significant part of their reason for being. It is such Christian care that can help nurture a climate in which there are fewer compelling reasons for active, voluntary euthanasia.

CONCLUSION

The world in which we live is simultaneously death denying and death desiring. It is death denying in that it cannot face with peace the reality that we are all appointed once to die and after that, judgement. Ironically, at the same time western society appears to be death desiring in its growing attempts to control the final exit and legally affirm the right to physician assisted suicide. The contradictions stem from the fragmented world view that many now embrace in the post modern world, a perception of reality that finds truth unwelcome and moral character to be subjectively defined. When coupled with increased social mobility which robs suffering and dying patients of a caring network, society will probably continue to exhibit the contradictions surrounding death and dying. The calls for voluntary euthanasia will only increase.

The church's role in responding to the crisis is unique. As a community of proclamation and care it provides what no other community can: a life-shaping story to make sense of it all, hope, meaning, forgiveness, a Saviour, and a caring group of brothers and sisters to send us off when it is time to go.

Though he lived in another era long before the onslaught of modern and post modern pressures which make euthanasia appealing, John Donne, the 17th-century English writer and clergyman, understood something of the world view and care we need in our own era when he wrote:

> No man is an island, entire of itself; every man is a piece of the continent, a part of the main. If a clod be washed away by the sea, Europe is the less. . . . Any man's death diminishes me because I am involved in mankind, and therefore never send to know for whom the bell tolls; it tolls for thee.[17]

NOTES

1. Daniel Maguire, 'The Freedom to Die,' in *Bioethics* ed. Thomas A Shannon (Ramsey, NJ: Paulist Press, 1981), p. 210.

2. I am using the terms 'assisted suicide' and 'voluntary euthanasia' as essentially interchangeable throughout this article. Active voluntary euthanasia is not the same as treatment termination (sometimes unfortunately called passive euthanasia). Though there are various forms of active euthanasia, the most called-for expression today is physician assisted suicide in which the person voluntarily and actively induces death through the aid of a certified assistant.

3. William Raspberry, 'The Moral Center,' *The Washington Post* (February 8, 1995):A–19.

4. For a discussion of this concept see G C Berhouwer, *The Church* (Grand Rapids: Eerdmans, 1976), pp. 13–16. The Roman Catholic Church in the Middle Ages spoke of four *notae* or marks of the church (unity, catholicity, holy, and apostolic), but at the Reformation the focus came to be more centered on the Word and its faithful proclamation, along with the sacraments.

5. Larry Churchill, 'The Amoral Character of Our Attitudes About Death: Some Implications,' *Journal of Religion and Health* 17,3 (1978):169.

6. Franklin G Miller and Howard Brody, 'Professional Integrity and Physician-Assisted Death,' *Hastings Center Report* 25–3 (May-June, 1995):9.

7. Seven H Miles, 'Physician-Assisted Suicide and the Profession's Gyrocompass,' *Hastings Center Report* 25–3 (May-June, 1995):18.

8. Marvin Kohl comes close to this perspective in his various writings where he opts for voluntary beneficent euthanasia on the grounds that suffering is pointless and that we have a prima facie duty to treat others with kindness. See for example his, 'Voluntary Beneficent Euthanasia,' in *Beneficent Euthanasia*, ed. Marvin Kohl (Buffalo: Prometheus Books, 1975):130–141.

9. The modern and post modern changes in world view and culture are of course complex in nature. While they are powerful forces, many in western culture have resisted their power or have appropriated them in inconsistent fashion, leading to a fragmented perception of reality. We must also understand that these major changes do not imply that earlier western culture was explicitly Christian in nature. Rather, it is best to see these earlier cultural expressions as simply more compatible with Christian outlooks, though falling far short of biblical norms in both thought and action.

10. Gertrude Himmelfarb, *The Demoralization of Society: From Victorian Virtues to Modern Values* (New York: Knopf, 1994), p. 51.

11. Paul Ramsey, *The Patient as Person* (New Haven: Yale University Press, 1970), p. 134.

12. John Kilner, *Life on the Line* (Grand Rapids: Eerdmans, 1992), p. 122.

13. Cicely Saunders, 'Caring to the End,' *Nursing Mirrors* 4 (September, 1980).

14. Leslie Coomer, 'Home Health Care: A Dialogue,' audiotape A114 available from The Center for Bioethics and Human Dignity, Bannockburn, Illinois 60015 USA.

15. Larry Richards and Paul Johnson, *Death and the Caring Community* (Portland: Multnomah Press, 1980), pp. 7–8.

16. See for example Hans O. Mauksch, 'The Organizational Context in Dying,' in *The New Meanings of Death* ed. Herman Feifel (New York: McGraw Hill, 1977):16.

17. John Donne, 'Meditations XVII,' *Norton Anthology of English Literature* (New York: Norton & Co., 1968), p. 528.

Index

Biblical References

Printed in the United States
17226LVS00004B/134